or be

The Short Oxford History of Europe

The Seventeenth Century

The Short Oxford History of Europe

General Editor: T. C. W. Blanning

NOW AVAILABLE

The Seventeenth Century
edited by Joseph Bergin

The Eighteenth Century
edited by T. C. W. Blanning

The Nineteenth Century
edited by T. C. W. Blanning

Classical Greece
edited by Robin Osborne

IN PREPARATION, VOLUMES COVERING

The Romans
The Early Middle Ages
The High Middle Ages
The Late Middle Ages
The Sixteenth Century
The Early Twentieth Century
The Late Twentieth Century

The Short Oxford History of Europe

General Editor: T. C. W. Blanning

The Seventeenth Century

Europe 1598–1715

Edited by Joseph Bergin

OXFORD
UNIVERSITY PRESS

OXFORD

UNIVERSITY PRESS

Great Clarendon Street, Oxford OX2 6DP

Oxford University Press is a department of the University of Oxford.
It furthers the University's objective of excellence in research, scholarship,
and education by publishing worldwide in

Oxford New York

Athens Auckland Bangkok Bogotá Buenos Aires Calcutta
Cape Town Chennai Dar es Salaam Delhi Florence Hong Kong Istanbul
Karachi Kuala Lumpur Madrid Melbourne Mexico City Mumbai
Nairobi Paris São Paulo Shanghai Singapore Taipei Tokyo Toronto Warsaw

with associated companies in Berlin Ibadan

Oxford is a registered trade mark of Oxford University Press
in the UK and in certain other countries

Published in the United States
by Oxford University Press Inc., New York

British Library Cataloguing in Publication Data

Data available

Library of Congress Cataloging in Publication Data

Data available

ISBN 0–19–873168–X (hbk)
ISBN 0–19–873167–1 (pbk)

10 9 8 7 6 5 4 3 2 1

Typeset in Minion
by RefineCatch Limited, Bungay, Suffolk
Printed in Great Britain by
T.J. International Ltd., Padstow, Cornwall

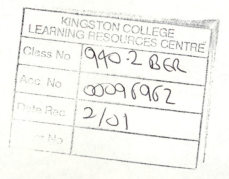

General Editor's Preface

The problems of writing a satisfactory general history of Europe are many, but the most intractable is clearly the reconciliation of depth with breadth. The historian who can write with equal authority about every part of the continent in all its various aspects has not yet been born. Two main solutions have been tried in the past: either a single scholar has attempted to go it alone, presenting an unashamedly personal view of a period, or teams of specialists have been enlisted to write what are in effect anthologies. The first offers a coherent perspective but unequal coverage, the second sacrifices unity for the sake of expertise. This new series is underpinned by the belief that it is this second way that has the fewest disadvantages and that even those can be diminished if not neutralized by close cooperation between the individual contributors under the directing supervision of the volume editor. All the contributors to every volume in this series have read each other's chapters, have met to discuss problems of overlap and omission, and have then redrafted as part of a truly collective exercise. To strengthen coherence further, the editor has written an introduction and conclusion, weaving the separate strands together to form a single cord. In this exercise, the brevity promised by the adjective 'short' in the series' title has been an asset. The need to be concise has concentrated everyone's minds on what really mattered in the period. No attempt has been made to cover every angle of every topic in every country. What this volume does provide is a short but sharp and deep entry into the history of Europe in the period in all its most important aspects.

T. C. W. Blanning

Sidney Sussex College
Cambridge

Contents

List of contributors

JOSEPH BERGIN is Professor of History at the University of Manchester and a Fellow of the British Academy. He has published extensively on sixteenth- and seventeenth-century France, including two studies of Richelieu: *Cardinal Richelieu—power and the pursuit of wealth* (1985), *The Rise of Richelieu* (1991), and a large-scale study of France's bishops, *The Making of the French Episcopate 1589–1661* (1996). He is currently working on the French church in the age of Louis XIV.

LAURENCE BROCKLISS is Reader in Modern History at the University of Oxford, and Fellow of Magdalen College. His most important works include *French Higher Education in the Seventeenth and Eighteenth Centuries* (1987) and, with Colin Jones, *The Medical World of Early Modern France* (1997). He has published extensively on early modern medicine, philosophy and learning generally, and is currently working on a study of the diffusion of enlightenment ideas in southern France.

THOMAS MUNCK is Senior Lecturer in History at the University of Glasgow. He is the author of *The Peasantry and the Early Absolute Monarchy in Denmark* (1979), *Seventeenth-Century Europe 1598–1700* (1990) and most recently *The Enlightenment, a comparative social history* (1999). He has published essays on enlightened reform in late eighteenth-century Denmark and is preparing a study of publishing and public opinion in late eighteenth-century Copenhagen.

R. C. NASH is Lecturer in Economic History at the University of Manchester. He has researched and published on English trade in the later seventeenth and eighteenth centuries. His current work focuses on financial and commercial links between Britain and its colonies, especially the West Indies and the Carolinas, in the eighteenth century.

ANTHONY PAGDEN, formerly Reader in Intellectual History and Fellow of King's College, Cambridge, is now Harry C. Black Professor of History at the Johns Hopkins University, Baltimore. He has researched and published extensively on the cultural and intellectual dimensions of Europe's encounter with other societies since the sixteenth century, notably *The Fall of Natural Man* (1982), *Spanish Imperialism and the Political Imagination* (1989), *European encounters with the New World* (1992), and *Lords of All the World* (1995).

DAVID PARROTT is a Fellow of New College, Oxford. His research has mainly focused on French political and military history, and he is author of a forthcoming book, *Richelieu's Army*. He has published essays on aristocratic politics in seventeenth-century France, and has explored the diplomatic, dynastic and military history of northern Italian states in the same period.

ANTHONY UPTON is Professor Emeritus of Nordic History at the University of St Andrews. He has written on Baltic politics in the twentieth century, but more recently his work has been on early modern Swedish history, especially in the later seventeenth century. He is the author of *Charles IX and Swedish Absolutism* (1998), and of a general history of Europe in the seventeenth and eighteenth centuries (forthcoming).

Introduction: the uncertain prospect

Joseph Bergin

Most people with a smattering of historical knowledge can still read-ily associate certain centuries with a series of events or a process—usually if not always of a vaguely positive kind—which they feel have some underlying historical significance. Equally, other centuries fare much less well in this competition for attention. So the sixteenth century is instinctively yoked to the Protestant Reformation, the eighteenth to the Enlightenment, since both phenomena loom large in most explanations of how the modern world took the shape it did. But what, one may ask, about the century in between, separating or connecting—depending on one's point of view—these two great 'peaks' of early modern history? In the Anglo-Saxon world at least, seventeenth-century Europe's place in historical memory is insecure, doubtless because of the absence of any defining characteristic resembling the Reformation or the Enlightenment. Relatively few his-torical surveys of the century have succeeded in finding a title that encapsulates a widely-shared view of the century's essence. Interest-ingly, this lack of an overarching 'identity' applicable to seventeenth-century Europe as a whole coincides with the use in different parts of the continent of a variety of captions with which to label the century, in whole or in part. Their very proliferation, as much as their diver-sity of meaning, may be one reason why it is so difficult to clearly identify the century for Europe as a whole! A few examples should suffice to make the point. Sweden's 'age of greatness' undoubtedly spanned the entire seventeenth century, with the Dutch 'golden age' not far behind. The Spanish *siglo de oro*, as the tag suggests, also signifies a century of greatness not just in the political and international arena, but in the literary, spiritual and artistic spheres, too, though in this case, the 'century' in question includes the second half of the sixteenth century and ends sometime before 1640, the 'year of catastrophe' in Spanish history. The French *grand siècle* is different again: it may not be shared with another century, but it has mainly been associated, thanks largely to Voltaire's emphasis on cultural leadership and creativity, with the period of Louis XIV's personal rule (1661–1715) and does not really embrace the previous half-century. And, as if to confuse the picture yet further, much shorter time-spans, packed with events that are held to have shaped later history, have remained graven in the historical memory of certain countries, implicitly defining for them the century as a whole. Thus it is with the Polish 'deluge' of the 1650s, which destroyed the country's political independence, and to a lesser extent with the Russian 'time of troubles' (1584–1613), which ended with the accession of the Romanov dynasty and the prospect of political stability.

One result of all this 'confusion of tongues' is that historians of the century have had to think harder than usual and coin their own interpretative terms. The seventeenth century as *the* 'age of absolutism' commanded considerable acceptance for generations, but postwar scholarship has done much to reveal the real limitations of absolute monarchy even in those countries where it was not subject to major challenges, while the expansion of historical research beyond the traditional ken of political history has enriched but also complicated traditional views, even of politics. If there is any broadly familiar label presently attached to the seventeenth century, it is that of a period—and so not necessarily embracing the entire century—of 'crisis'. It is perhaps paradoxical, in the light of what has just been said about a French *grand siècle*, that it was a French historian writing in the 1950s (Roland Mousnier) who characterized the *entire* century as a century of crisis in *every* sphere of activity, and throughout Europe as a whole. But this sweeping analysis attracted little support, then or subsequently, though it has not prevented historians from proposing several possible 'crises' or periods of crisis: along with the alleged 'general' European crisis of the middle decades of the century, shorter, but no less 'general' ones have been constructed for both the 1590s and 1680s. Despite its widespread use, many historians remain sceptical of the explanatory value of the term 'crisis', especially where it seems all-embracing—as in the notion of a 'general' crisis which was either pan-European in scale, or which embraced the social, economic, political, cultural and other spheres of life. What is clear is that the older view of the century as a century of 'greatness', one of high achievement and progress towards modernity, is now a Humpty-Dumpty that cannot be put together again. The reservations which historians may entertain about a century of crisis have certainly not dispelled the widely held view that seventeenth-century Europe was more beset by demographic and economic difficulties, internal social turbulence, and major wars than either the sixteenth or the eighteenth. The chapters that follow will provide ample evidence for that.

Certainly, the century began under what were at best rather mixed, if not unpromising auspices, since the 1590s were a period of distress and turbulence in many parts of Europe. The French wars of religion and the Dutch revolt, conflicts involving several other European powers, both reached their peak of intensity at this point. The resolution of the first conflict by 1598 enabled French society and monarchy to rebuild and recover; but the suspension of the second in 1607–09 was only temporary, and it resumed in 1621. The political crisis of the grand duchy of Muscovy eventually enveloped much of Eastern Europe, and drew in both Sweden and Poland. Even if Muscovy began to regain its stability under the new Romanov dynasty, a three-cornered struggle for hegemony in the region had been triggered, and would endure for another century until Peter the Great's Russia belatedly emerged as the winner in the 1710s. Between 1593 and 1606, Austrian Habsburgs and Ottoman Turks fought a protracted and inconclusive war in the Balkans, but the new century would soon prove that it could do far better as far as 'long wars'—as this one was called at the time—were concerned. Conflicts like these were hardly new in European history and, because they rarely involved more than a few states, they could usually rumble on in relative isolation from other conflicts or from other parts of Europe. The new century would witness the gradual concatenation of many of these initially regional conflicts into larger, virtually 'European' wars, from the Thirty Years War itself to those of the age of Louis XIV.

The 1590s also saw the return of plague and high levels of mortality, even to parts of Europe that were fortunate enough to be spared the effects of political or military conflict. The 1590s exacted a very heavy toll on the Spanish population, from which it would not recover for decades, with plague and poor harvests devastating whole areas of Castile. Parts of Italy, especially the south, experienced similar if less acute problems of plague and high mortality. The exacerbation of the civil wars in France at this point also did serious damage to the rural economy, leading to high rates of mortality but also to revolt by desperate peasants in many places. Henry IV's new government found itself having to remit large arrears of unpaid taxation during the late 1590s, as overburdened and indebted communities struggled with their fiscal obligations. On the other periphery, the conflicts in Russia—or more accurately Muscovy—had the effect of scattering large numbers of peasants, desperate to escape southwards from the exactions to which they were being subjected. On the other hand, as if to confound expectations, the young Dutch Republic, still locked in a massive military confrontation with Spain in the 1590s, found itself moving into a higher economic gear, its merchants aggressively entering new markets, partly as a result of a successful blockade of the ports of the Spanish-controlled southern provinces. The latter suffered correspondingly in the 1580s and 1590s, not least because of a large exodus of merchants and artisans to the north, but here too there were signs by the late 1590s of economic recovery, albeit on a much smaller scale. Here as elsewhere, peace, even in the form of temporary truces in ongoing conflicts, offered the population the hope of resuming its normal round of planting and reaping, making and selling. The first two decades at least of the new century suggested that the misery of recent conflicts and disasters might be over, but this was before the outbreak of Europe's biggest war to date and the beginnings of a no less serious commercial crisis between them set a different course for much of the continent from about 1620 onwards.

Of the many legacies of the sixteenth century to its successor, religious issues were among the most intractable and explosive. The age of religious upheaval giving rise to new confessions and new churches was largely over (save for England and the new sects spawned by the Civil War), but the transition to confessional orthodoxy in the seventeenth century was anything but smooth. As Laurence Brockliss shows in this volume, almost the entire population of Europe shared the same pessimistic, Augustinian world-view which underpinned the Christian faith, the Protestant as much, if not more, than the Catholic variety. If this united 'elites' and the wider population within the same underlying mental set, it did little to prevent confessional hostilities of an often acute kind from growing and festering, ensuring that early modern authorities everywhere found great difficulty in mastering them. Indeed, as sixteenth-century experience had shown, their best bet was to embrace one confessional orthodoxy and try to impose it on their subjects with every means at their disposal. But the continuing instability of the confessional map, especially in the Empire, bred serious political as well as religious and social tensions, to the point of triggering the conflict we know as the Thirty Years War in 1618. But the impact of these as yet incomplete confessional developments in different parts of northern and central Europe, France included, would continue to be felt in many a bitter struggle down to the age of Louis XIV and William of Orange. The confessional affiliations of Europe's states could still weigh heavily in their search for allies in both war and peace, even though the sphere of international relations might be thought of as less susceptible than domestic politics to such influences. Rulers had to exercise considerable caution before they resorted to arguments from *raison d'état* to justify cross-confessional alliances because their reputation, both at home and abroad, could be badly damaged in the process. So expulsions or exiles of religious minorities, from the Moriscos of Spain in 1609 to the French Huguenots after 1685, continued to occur across the century, creating diasporas in several parts of Europe and even in the New World. These measures were a logical outcome of the contemporary meaning and practice of toleration—putting up with an unsatisfactory situation pending the search for a lasting solution. In a continent where authorities at both local and central level worried about the debilitating effects of religious dissent, exiling or evicting dissenters remained a 'thinkable', even attractive solution, in harmony with the widely shared demand for religious uniformity.

For the great mass of the population, religious change in the direction of confessional orthodoxy continued apace throughout most of Europe. Only the authorities in the Dutch Republic seemed reluctant to positively impose a single faith and religious observance on its population, while continuing to insist that it publicly recognized only one (the Calvinist) church. But elsewhere, efforts by established churches to discipline and indoctrinate (in the original sense of educating them in the elements of the faith as defined by their church) their members were still only gathering steam after 1600. Europe's churches, old and new, might have carved up much of the continent between them, and been as omnipresent in town and country as their medieval predecessor, but it is increasingly clear that that did not of itself provide them with the means to achieve their new objectives—congregations which were at least aware of the central tenets of Christian belief, particularly those which differentiated their church from its rivals, and which adhered to a regular set of religious practices. None of the churches was really prepared for the consequences of confessional division and competition, and the instruments at their disposal, beginning with the clergy, were largely inadequate. Educating, forming and disciplining the lower clergy was widely regarded as the indispensable first step towards the broader change the churches aimed at, but that proved to be extremely slow, too, especially in Catholic Europe where the lower clergy remained extremely numerous and heterogeneous in both status and activity. Protestant Europe suffered less acutely from that particular problem and the rash of new universities and academies founded during and after the Reformation helped to produce a tolerably educated clergy. But that did of itself not guarantee the desired results, and Protestant pastors were wont to complain about the indifference, lack of devotion, materialism and so on of their congregations; the failure of 'godly reformation' was not confined to England in the age of Oliver Cromwell. Of course, the real reason for this state of affairs may well have been that a more austere set of religious observances and the more stringent demands made of congregations in the spheres of social and moral behaviour, set the bar dividing 'good' from 'bad' Christians unrealistically high for all but a committed minority. At any rate, the notion of a short and successful 'reformation' in Protestant Europe now seems facile, and the process of 'protestantization' continued well into the seventeenth century.

Catholic Europe went about the business of religious reform in a more conservative vein, and in many parts of Europe relatively little had been attempted, let alone achieved by 1600 or even 1660. Previous generations of historians used to think of the Counter (or Catholic) Reformation as running out of steam by around 1600 or, at a pinch, 1648, but this chronology was tied to a 'political' understanding of the phenomenon, especially the rise and alleged decline of papal leadership. A generation of scholars have exposed the limitations of such a view, and the French historian Jean Delumeau provocatively claimed nearly thirty years ago that the high water mark of Catholic reformation in France (and much of Europe) was not reached until the early to middle decades of the eighteenth century, which most people would think of as the high point of the Enlightenment. The improvement of the lower clergy was slow and often of limited scope, but that did not prevent the parishes of Catholic Europe from being intensively 'visited' by bishops and their officials, who also promoted extensive 'missions' preached by members of religious orders rather than secular priests. New confraternities and devotional groups grew up almost everywhere. They were in many ways the key to the emergence of a new type of 'ordinary' Christian, both male and female who, according to Louis Châtellier, were to be an important legacy to later modern Catholicism. As the century wore on, sometimes surprising forms of the religious life, especially for women, evolved, breaking with the rigid prescriptions of the council of Trent about enclosure and separation. That in turn enabled the members of the new 'congregations' and 'institutes' to live simple lives in close proximity to lay society, to whose charitable and educational needs they ministered.

In all of this, it seems clear that the most successful reforms occurred not just in those parts of Europe where religious and secular authorities were in essential agreement on the objectives of reform, but where secular power was also sufficiently strong to sustain such efforts; elsewhere, the fragmentation of political power, as in parts of the Empire, stymied those efforts for well over a century after the council of Trent.

Attempts at religious change, whether from 'above' or 'below' also needed the support of the broader social and cultural elites, whose Augustinian mindset also enabled them to accept the need for religious reform as a means of disciplining the unruly and disorderly mass of the population. It would be facile to claim that their appreciation of religion's capacity to achieve non-religious objectives was based on cynical calculation, but elites were almost programmed to make the connection since they lived in an age when riot, revolt and popular disturbances of one kind or another were commonplace. Here, too, the scene was set by the later sixteenth century, when there were major peasant rebellions in southern France and Austria, with many more to follow in the early, but especially the middle decades of the following century. The duration and seriousness of these 'popular emotions', as the French called them, varied enormously, and no doubt the vast majority were small in scale and in threat, even if contemporaries were fearful of the suddenness and destructiveness of 'peasant furies' and their urban counterparts. Seventeenth-century authorities were constantly worried by the 'humours' of the populace, and were particularly scandalized when members of the nobility and elite groups openly sided with them in pursuing their grievances. Contemporary commentators warned elites of the folly of joining the lower classes in this way since they were fickle and unreasoning, driven by their passions—something which reasoning members of the social elite should avoid at all costs.

Historians of riot and revolt have shown that they reached a crescendo in many parts of Europe in the wake of economic recession, war damage and escalating fiscal exactions from the 1620s to the 1660s which, precisely because they struck more or less together, placed enormous strains on communities, rural and urban. Moreover, it was because the burdens they bore were communal rather than individual in character that they reacted collectively to defend a status quo which, if not perfect, they at least accepted as 'normal', and therefore as in some sense 'just'. In such circumstances, they naturally looked to their social superiors, the local squires and even the parish clergy, for help and leadership, and in some instances they obtained it. But the social solidarity of most local communities was soon exposed by such crises as being fragile and limited, and increasingly as the century progressed, members of the local elites proved increasingly reluctant to participate in open challenges to authority. A combination of religious and cultural change, reinforced by political pressure from governments, began to wean them away from their social inferiors. No less importantly, in many parts of Europe their interests were in any case moving closer to those of the states of the day, thanks to their involvement in taxation, office-holding, government borrowing and so on. When and wherever this particular shift occurred, lower-class revolts posed far less of a threat and could mostly be contained at source by local authorities who still remained lukewarm about the intervention of external authorities. But until then, lower class revolt could merge with the discontents of political and social elites, as in the great revolts of the middle decades of the century, to threaten the political stability of the governments of the day.

More than its riots and revolts, the seventeenth century is remembered for its wars, though perhaps less for the military set-pieces than for the social devastation caused by the wars, which was possibly greater than for any similar period before the wars of our own century. Many of these wars were the consequence of unresolved conflicts from the previous century, as we have already noted. Seventeenth-century Europe was one of the least 'peaceful' centuries of modern history, with only four years of complete peace across the continent. One historian has calculated that five million soldiers died in the wars between 1618 and 1713, but that figure, which is no more than a crude estimate, hardly begins to convey the impact of war on Europe during the period. The tendency of conflicts to expand geographically and suck in other powers as allies of the main protagonists was another significant development. The net effect was to ratchet up the scale of military campaigns and the size of armies, unleashing something which in many cases the states engaged in war could not finance or manage effectively and, consequently, were unable to bring to a decisive conclusion. Not many parts of Europe escaped the encounter with war and, as David Parrott shows in this volume, the states involved were usually determined to fight on enemy soil so that war could be at least partly self-financing. Scandinavia, central and southern Italy as well as the Iberian peninsula were the most successful in keeping warfare at arm's length. It was only after 1704 that Spain, for so long Europe's greatest military power, directly experienced warfare within its own borders (though Catalonia had been partly occupied by French troops in the 1640s).

But there was something else about the impact of war in this century which makes it stand out against those of the previous or following century. The soldier as a 'universal' type came into his own for the first time, a symptom of the dyspepsia of the age. As early as 1641, an Italian poet declared that this was 'the century of the soldier'. Twenty years later, a former participant in the German wars, Jakob von Grimmelshausen, wrote one of the first modern novels in which the theme of war dominated, *The Adventures of Simplicius Simplicissimus*, in which he unforgettably excoriated the conduct of war in

Germany in the 1630s and 1640s as a gigantic racket perpetrated by those under arms against the rest of society. And the engravings of Jacques Callot, a Lorrainer whose native land experienced the full horrors of the same war and military occupation, depict the gruesome human dimension of seventeenth-century war, with summary executions and hangings of men and women whose offences ranged from refusing to pay protection money or to provide food, to simply defending themselves against marauding soldiers. Even if we should guard against facile generalization from such texts and images to the effect that seventeenth-century wars were ones of escalating brutality at every level, the widening geographical scale of the conflicts, beginning with the Thirty Years War itself, clearly brought the horrors of war closer to the population across much of the continent, from Burgundy, Lorraine and the Netherlands to Poland and Russia, not forgetting the Empire and north Italy, traditionally the military cockpits of Europe. In fact, with so much of the fighting still done by military enterprisers and volunteer, mercenary soldiers, whose discipline was vastly superior to that of unwilling press-ganged recruits, the brutality of war may have been rather more contained than we think, and instances of wholesale massacre of soldiers and civilians were probably not everyday occurrences. Yet Callot's depictions of the miseries of war for soldiers and civilians alike will surely remain at least as emblematic of the century as the untroubled landscapes of his fellow Lorrainer, Claude Gellée, *alias* Le Lorrain, or the historical allegories of their more famous contemporary, the Norman Nicolas Poussin.

1

The economy

R. C. Nash[1]

Since the 1950s, historians have seen the seventeenth century as a period of economic stagnation, decline and even of 'general crisis', one that contrasts with the rapid economic growth characteristic of the centuries on either side. Originally, such decline was explained by the tailing off of silver imports from Spanish America after 1610, monetary-fuelled growth thus giving way to deflation and recession. The key problem with this explanation is that it now seems that the fall in silver imports was restricted to the years from the 1630s to the 1650s and that, in fact, imports after 1660 exceeded levels set at the start of the century. Then, in the 1960s and 1970s, under the influence of Malthusian demographic theory, historians explained the crisis of the seventeenth century as the outcome of the population growth of the previous century. Population growth eventually outstripped the supply of food which, given the failure to innovate in agriculture, led to subsistence crises which, in turn, destabilized the wider economy. A Marxist inflection of this theory stresses that this failure to innovate was itself the product of the social limits on growth imposed by a society of peasant farmers and urban craftsmen, petty producers of village and town who were hostile to economic change.

The major problem with the idea of a 'general crisis' is that it is impossible to identify a period in which all or most of the European economy was simultaneously gripped by a depression. In Spain, for example, economic and population decline was at its worst from 1590 to 1630, a period in which, however, the Dutch 'economic miracle' reached its height. Likewise, when Spain embarked on a fragile economic recovery after 1670, the Low Countries, southern France and

[1] I wish to thank Dr S. H. Rigby for his excellent comments on an earlier draft of this chapter.

much of eastern Europe tumbled into deep and protracted economic recessions. This diversity makes it impossible to reduce to a simple formula a series of regional economic crises which, while exhibiting certain similarities, varied widely in their timing and intensity.

Despite an understandable scepticism about the existence of a general crisis, historians nevertheless agree that the European economy experienced profound problems in the seventeenth century and they continue to use the concept of crisis as a major organizing theme of the economic history of the period. However, the defining feature of the crisis is now seen as the divergence rather than convergence in the economic performance of Europe's major economic regions. First, there was the diverse character of the regional cycles of growth and depression spread over the period 1590–1720. Second, the divergence between the economic development of western Europe, whose economy was based on free labour, and eastern Europe, where serfdom was greatly extended in the seventeenth century. Third, in western Europe, economic recession in the Mediterranean contrasted with economic expansion in north-west Europe, although even in the north-west there was a divergence between France, where cycles of growth alternated with deep agrarian recessions, and England, where the crisis was conspicuous by its absence.

These divergent regional developments are central to the approaches adopted by historians since the 1970s to explain economic developments in population, agriculture, and in trade and industry. First, research on population has identified that demographic trends in north-west Europe, where population grew quite rapidly from 1600 to 1650 and then stagnated, contrasted with the rest of Europe, where population fell sharply to 1650 and then regained its former levels by 1700. Historians have vigorously debated the relative weight which should be given, in accounting for these contrasting regional trends, to Malthusian positive checks, that is mortality crises, and to Malthusian preventive checks, in which population was controlled by late marriage and low fertility rather than by upsurges in mortality (see: Population and the economy, page 13). Second, historians have explained divergences in regional economic development in terms of the differing outcomes of rural class struggles between landlords and peasants. Thus, in eastern Europe, landlords imposed the economically-crippling system of serfdom whereas in much of western Europe the state protected peasant communities against predatory landlords. Even in the West, however, peasant agriculture could not escape the cyclical crises inherent in the system's static technology and lack of investment. Economic progress was thus fastest in England, where landlords expropriated the peasants and created a dynamic agrarian capitalism. Other historians argue, however, that the crisis of peasant farming was the result of forces external to agriculture, principally the crushing increase in state taxation on the rural sector; taxation peaked at different times in different countries, providing the best explanation of the diffused pattern of economic crises (see: Agriculture and agrarian society, p. 18). Third, the collapse of Europe's great urban industries in the period has been explained, within the proto-industrialization model, in terms of the advantages enjoyed by expanding rural industry, such as access to cheap peasant labour. The competition between urban and rural industry occurred at the international level, that is between rather than within regional economies, which explains the shift of industrial power from the declining urban industries of central and Mediterranean Europe to the rising rural industries of the north-west. The thesis that industrial development was dominated by the dynamic properties of rural industry has been vigorously challenged on the grounds that urban and state institutions continued to curb the growth of manufacturing in both town and countryside (see: Industry and trade, p. 36).

Population and the economy

Given that there was little improvement in the productivity and per capita output of the pre-industrial workforce, aggregate production in the European economy was closely linked to total population size. The demographic trend was the key determinant of the economic trend: rising population meant an increase in aggregate output; a stagnant or falling population brought about the opposite. In the seventeenth century, Europe's population grew by less than 5 per cent compared with 30 per cent in the sixteenth century and 50 per cent in the eighteenth [Table 1]. Moreover, such growth as did occur was concentrated in north-west Europe before 1650. Elsewhere, population fell from 1600 to 1650, with very sharp falls of 15–20 per cent

Table 1 Population of Europe by territory and region, 1600–1700 (in millions).

	1600	1650	1700
North and west			
Scandinavia	2.0	2.6	2.8
England & Wales	4.4	5.6	5.4
Scotland	1.0	1.0	1.0
Ireland	1.4	1.8	2.8
The Netherlands	1.5	1.9	1.9
Belgium	1.6	2.0	2.0
Central			
Germany	16.2	10.0	14.1
France	21.0	21.0	21.4
Switzerland	1.0	1.0	1.2
Mediterranean			
Northern Italy	5.4	4.3	5.7
Central Italy	2.9	2.7	2.8
Southern Italy	4.8	4.3	4.8
Spain	8.1	7.1	7.5
Portugal	1.4	1.5	2.0
Eastern			
Austria-Bohemia	4.3	4.1	4.6
Poland	3.4	3.0	2.8
Region			
North and west	11.9	14.9	15.9
Central	38.2	32.0	36.7
Mediterranean	22.6	19.9	22.8
Eastern	7.7	7.1	7.4
Total	80.4	73.9	82.8

Note: The figures given are approximate ones, especially those for Scandinavia, Germany, Portugal, and Eastern Europe.

Source: Jan De Vries, *European Urbanization, 1500–1800* (Cambridge, Mass., 1984), p. 36. Additional data for Scandinavia, Germany, France, and Portugal from, Jean-Pierre Bardet and Jacques Dupaquier, *Histoire des Populations de l'Europe* (Paris, 1997).

registered in Germany and Mediterranean Europe, and then merely regained its preceding levels by 1700. Consequently, historians regard the sixteenth and eighteenth centuries as eras of economic expansion while the seventeenth century is seen as one of economic stagnation and crisis. Why, then, did population stagnate in the seventeenth century, compared with the startling growth in the centuries on either side?

The modern discussion of this issue has taken place in a neo-

Malthusian framework. Malthus argued that populations had an inherent tendency to grow faster than the means of subsistence, resulting eventually in falling incomes and even in catastrophic famines and epidemics. Malthus assumed that rising population would not be offset by increasing agricultural productivity; indeed, he argued that average productivity would fall, as population pressure led to diminishing returns to labour on the existing stock of land and promoted the extension of cultivation into marginal, less fertile lands. The *positive* check of mortality crises could only be avoided if populations were regulated by the *preventive* check. This restraint came into operation if falling living standards induced people to marry at a later age, or not to marry at all, which had the largely unintended effect of reducing the birth rate and hence the rate of population growth. Demographers used to argue that the positive check, caused by starvation and by epidemics induced by famines, was the main cause of population stagnation in the seventeenth century. However, recent research emphasizes that mortality crises were caused by autonomous epidemics rather than by famines and has concluded that, in any case, it was the preventive not the positive check which mainly repressed seventeenth-century population growth. The key question is clear—which did most to curb population growth in seventeenth century Europe, the positive or the preventive check or some combination of the two?

The prediction that rising population would lead to falling per capita incomes was certainly borne out by events in the sixteenth and early seventeenth centuries, when the standard of living of the mass of Europe's population fell to historically low levels. This impoverishment was associated with mortality crises, years in which 'normal' death rates doubled or worse, crises which wiped out the population increases achieved in the inter-crisis years. Such crises were more frequent in the seventeenth century than in the sixteenth or eighteenth, and they did much to prevent long-term demographic growth in western and Mediterranean Europe, although their impact in England and the Netherlands was much more muted than in the major Continental societies. Mortality crises were at their worst from the 1590s to the 1660s, largely because bubonic plague broke out in the most virulent cycle of epidemics seen since the Black Death. Such epidemics caused enormous mortalities in France, Germany and the Mediterranean countries, where they were invariably preceded by major harvest failures. The worst crises occurred when plague was combined with famine and warfare, as in Germany in the 1630s, when many districts suffered population losses in excess of 30 per cent, or in Catalonia in 1647–51, when 20 per cent of the population died. The frequency and severity of mortality crises was much reduced from the 1660s to the early 1690s, which allowed a strong recovery of population, for three reasons. First, plague disappeared from western Europe, mainly because central and municipal governments adopted stringent steps to prevent the spread of the disease. Second, an improvement in the level of harvests which, because of better weather conditions, were adequate or abundant across western Europe in these years. Finally, the reduction of warfare and troop movements, which before 1650 did so much to spread disease and disrupt agricultural output. However, generalized warfare, famine and mortality crises, although not bubonic plague, returned from c.1690. France, for example, experienced three major crises, in 1693–94, 1709–11, and 1718–19, all of which followed on harvest failures; crises which caused mass mortality through epidemics of typhus, smallpox and dysentery, and which prevented any population growth in France from 1690 to 1720.

Mortality trends in the Netherlands and England, where population increased by 25 per cent from 1600 to 1650 and then stagnated, followed a different path from that found in the major Continental societies. The Netherlands, which modernized its agriculture in the sixteenth century, experienced no subsistence crises, but as Europe's most urbanized society it suffered inevitably from high rates of endemic plague and later smallpox mortality, as infectious diseases in this period struck much harder in towns than in the countryside. In England, periodic food shortages were associated with higher death rates before 1650, but such mortality crises were small-scale and localized compared with those which afflicted continental Europe and they did not prevent vigorous national population growth to mid-century. From 1650, as agricultural improvement in England gathered pace, mortality crises disappeared altogether, although normal mortality rates rose, the result of England's rapid urbanization which, as in the Netherlands, increased the proportion of the population most at risk from endemic diseases like smallpox.

Mortality crises in most countries then, as Malthus argued, combined famine and disease, although the relationship between the two was an intricate one. Indeed, recent research has minimized the role of famines in seventeenth-century mortality crises. Famines did not cause mortality through mass starvation and neither did they prepare the ground for epidemics by lowering the population's resistance to disease. Indeed, it is currently argued that the population's susceptibility to the major diseases of pre-industrial Europe, smallpox, typhus and above all plague, was not increased by poor nutrition. Demographers now highlight the *autonomous* role of disease, demonstrating that epidemics often occurred in years when food supplies were abundant and, conversely, that famines not followed by epidemics had little impact on mortality levels. However, while there was no systematic correlation between famine and disease, it remains true that the *major* mortality catastrophes of the seventeenth century followed a clear pattern—famine followed by epidemics. But if the malnourishment of the population did not prepare the ground for disease, why did the most devastating crises combine famine and epidemics? The primary role of famines in mortality crises was a powerful, albeit an indirect one: they provoked the mass movement of the poor in search of food and work, a geographic mobility which knitted together isolated pools of endemic diseases into major epidemics. For example, although deaths from disease were rising slowly in some areas of northern France from the late 1680s, these outbreaks of mortality remained localized until they were drawn together into mass epidemics by the frantic population mobility engendered by the famines of 1693–94.

Finally, current demographic research is shifting the focus more and more from the positive to the preventive check, arguing that restraints on marriage and fertility, rather than mortality crises, were mainly responsible for halting Europe's population growth in the seventeenth century. The picture is clearest for England and the Netherlands, where population growth ceased from c.1650. In England, fertility was checked by the late seventeenth-century increase in the age at which women married and, more importantly, in the proportion of both sexes who never married, which rose from 6–8 per cent of the population in 1600 to the historically high level of 20–25 per cent in 1700. In the Netherlands, where there was an huge out-migration of young men for service in Dutch East Indies and elsewhere, urban rates of female non-marriage reached similar levels by c.1700 and the country's population would have shrunk if it had not been bolstered by a heavy, mainly female in-migration from neighbouring countries.

Demographers also argue that preventive checks were strengthened greatly in France, Spain, and Italy in the seventeenth century and that here, too, such checks provided a more effective brake on population growth than mortality crises. However, the demographic data, when viewed from a comparative perspective, and extended into the eighteenth century, suggest that preventive checks functioned at a relatively weak level in these countries before 1700. In France, for example, from 1660 to 1700, marriage ages were lower and fertility rates much higher than in England and the Netherlands in the same period, while rates of female non-marriage, seen by demographers as the *key* preventive mechanism, oscillated around 5 per cent of the population, rates so low as to indicate that marriage was a near-universal experience for French women. In contrast, preventive checks on population were much intensified in the eighteenth century in France, Spain and Italy; in France, for example, marriage ages and female celibacy rates rose steadily from the late seventeenth to the late eighteenth century. Despite this strengthening of the preventive checks, population from *c.*1720 grew rapidly all across western Europe. On the other hand death rates fell in western Europe in the eighteenth compared with the seventeenth century, reflecting reductions in infant mortality and in the incidence and severity of mortality crises. Taken together the evidence on mortality and fertility suggests that, outside England and the Netherlands, fluctuations in mortality had a more critical influence than variations in marriage and fertility rates in determining population growth in western and Mediterranean Europe over the period 1600 to 1800.

Agriculture and agrarian society

The agrarian sector was by far the largest in the European economy and in most countries it employed 70–80 per cent of the labour force. In western and Mediterranean Europe the land was worked by free peasants, whose taxes, rents and tithes provided the bulk of the revenues drawn by the state, the landowning nobility and the Church. These transfer payments, paid in kind rather than in money, supplied the urban and rural markets for food while the peasants retained most of what was left over for their subsistence needs. There were also more substantial farmers who used hired labour to produce for the market and who were most numerous in the Low Countries, England and northern France. In eastern Europe, the majority of peasants were serfs who paid rents for the land they cultivated not in cash or in kind but in the forced labour services they rendered to the lords' demesnes; a system revived in east-Elbian Germany and Poland in the sixteenth century and which swept across most of the rest of central and eastern Europe in the seventeenth century. The agrarian systems of western and eastern Europe thus followed radically different paths of development and hence it is helpful to treat them separately.

Western and Mediterranean Europe

The achievements of the agricultural sector in the seventeenth century were not impressive; total output in nearly every country in 1700 was the same or lower than a hundred years or so earlier, a dismal performance which reflected the general failure to raise farming productivity through better techniques and management and higher investment. Two economies, England throughout the century and the Netherlands before 1650, did improve their agriculture, the basis of their fast rates of economic growth and their freedom from subsistence crises. Robert Brenner explains such divergences in agricultural performances in terms of the intricate social interaction between the state, noble landlords and peasants. In those countries ruled by absolutist regimes, like France, the peasants paid the bulk of taxation and hence their property was protected by the state, which guaranteed their hereditary tenures and common rights against expropriation at the hands of noble landlords. This persistence of peasant farming, explained by socio-political not economic causes, perpetuated the cycle of stagnation and subsistence crises, since peasant farms were too small, undercapitalized and conservatively-managed to act as the vehicles for agrarian innovation. In England, where the propertied classes' alliance with the state facilitated the expropriation of the peasants' property rights, agrarian capitalism emerged, a system in which scattered peasant plots were amalgamated into large farms run by capitalist and improving tenants who paid market rents to landlords, and who revolutionized agricultural methods and organization. Three key issues thus need to be addressed. Why did so many western European regions experience prolonged agricultural slumps in the seventeenth century? Are these crises best explained by the persistence of peasant farming? Why was agricultural improvement in this period limited to England and the Low Countries?

Agricultural stagnation and crisis

In nearly every western European country the expansion of population and agriculture which had begun c.1500 eventually gave way to a sequence of agrarian crises, encompassing dramatic falls in agricultural output and profits. However, these crises varied greatly in timing, duration and causes. The first and most important cluster of crises occurred from 1590 to 1650, in a context of rising markets and inflated agricultural prices [Figure 1]. In central Spain, the crisis began with the harvest failures and plague epidemics of the 1590s. But

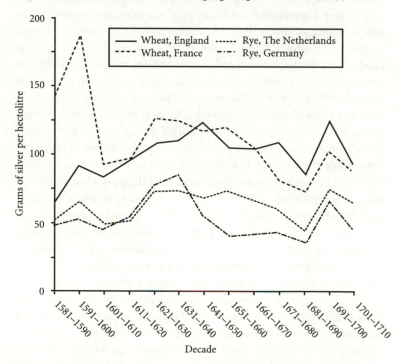

Figure 1 Graph showing agrarian crises in grams of silver per hectolitre in Europe, 1581–1710.

these merely initiated an enormous and protracted slump in agrarian production, when cereal production fell by between 30 per cent and 50 per cent, depending on the locality, for periods of forty years or more. In northern Italy, the subsistence crisis and plagues of 1630–31 inaugurated a collapse in output which rivalled that of Spain in severity and which persisted until the 1660s or later. In France, the crisis was centered in the north and east where, from the 1630s to the early 1660s, cereal production fell by 20–40 per cent. Germany experienced enormous losses of population and agricultural production from the 1620s to the 1650s, in the Thirty Years War and its aftermath. The second cycle of crises came after 1660, in a climate not of rising but of falling markets and prices, and had its greatest impact in western and southern France and the Netherlands [Figure 2].

The economic model commonly used by historians to explain agricultural crises assumes that rising population caused a steep rise in the relative prices of cereals, for which demand was inelastic. This induced farmers to expand grain output, not by improving their methods but by converting pasture and hitherto uncultivated waste and woodland to cereal production. This led to declining agricultural productivity as the contraction of pastoral farming starved the old grain lands of manure, the only source of fertilizer, while the new grain lands, assuming that the best lands were used first, were of an intrinsically lower fertility. Many historians have argued that this model provides an explanation of the first cycle of agricultural crises in western and Mediterranean Europe. In Spain, for example, the sixteenth-century increase in rural and urban demand for bread led to the ploughing up of marginal lands and the widespread conversion of pasture to arable to feed humans and mules, which replaced oxen as draught animals and which fed on oats rather than natural pasture. The difficulties of Spanish agriculture were worsened from c.1550 by the mass sale and conversion into arable of community pasture lands which made up 30–40 per cent of land in most districts.

However, while rising food prices indicate a growing pressure of population on land, there is in fact little evidence of a progressive Malthusian crisis of productivity in European agriculture from the late sixteenth century. Rising prices, and falling wages, suggest that *labour* productivity was declining, but data on agricultural yields, though arising from well-capitalized tenant farms and directly-managed ecclesiastical domains rather than peasant farms, do not show a decline in the productivity of *land* in the decades which preceded agricultural crises. In Spain, there was a rough stability in agricultural yields in the years from 1550 to 1590, indicating that there was no general crisis in productivity before the general slump of the 1590s. In northern France, the years 1600 to 1630, which preceded the mid-century crises, were ones of rapid recovery from the devastation caused by the French Religious Wars in the 1580s and 1590s; in the Paris basin this was a period of farming prosperity, increasing investment and rising arable output. For Italy, there is evidence of a decline in land productivity on large estates in the central provinces, but across the north of the country, where many regions supported an advanced agriculture, yields were stable.

There was also no decline in average yields in European agriculture during the protracted slumps in production, although of course yields fell in years of poor harvests. For example, in the Ile-de-France, average cereal yields were as high in the crisis period from 1630 to 1660 as in the period of prosperity from 1600 to 1630. Indeed, the clearest evidence of declining yields in western European agriculture occurs in the final decades of the century, in a context of falling demand and plummeting prices, when low profits discouraged farmers from devoting enough labour and cash to thoroughly manure and plough the land. But if arable yields did not fall either before or during the agrarian crises, then what explains the prolonged slumps in total output? There are two possible explanations. First, the fall in population triggered a classic Malthusian response in the form of the widespread abandonment of marginal land and the conversion of land from cereals to other forms of production. Second, a general decline in output on the smaller units owned or leased by peasants, which provided the bulk of production, but about which we possess no information. There is some evidence that production ceased on marginal lands in regions which suffered severe falls in population, as in Lombardy in the 1630s, where the Milan government took the extreme step of offering full ownership rights to anyone prepared to resume cultivation on abandoned farms. It is impossible to assess the general extent of deserted farms in Europe as a whole, although the fact that average yields did not rise in periods of crisis suggests that there was no general move to concentrate cereal production on more fertile lands. We have better evidence about land converted from cereals to livestock and other products but this suggests that these alternative forms of production did not compensate for the decline in cereal output. In northern Italy, the fall in cereal output from 1630–60 was in fact accompanied by a decline in wine and olive oil production. In Spain, in the Tierra de Campos region north of Valladolid, where cereal production fell by 30–40 per cent from the 1590s to the 1630s, there was a simultaneous decline in wine production and a massive fall in the size of sheep flocks. The main disincentive to reallocating land use in Spain and Italy was the depressed prices for livestock and other products, caused by the extraordinary collapse in the city economies, which reduced demand for meat, oil and wine (see: Industry and trade, p. 36). The main agricultural response to depression in these regions was therefore a switch from wheat to inferior cereals such as rye and barley, and later maize, which required less labour and which did better on poorly-prepared land.

Logically, then, it seems that the general slump in agricultural production in seventeenth-century Europe must reflect the second explanation given above; that is, a decline in the output and productivity of peasant farming. This crisis in peasant agriculture was invariably triggered by clusters of subsistence and mortality crises which had multiple effects. First, epidemics killed productive workers in large numbers, population losses which reduced the supply of labour to peasant farms. The shortage of labour is shown by the way in which wages rocketed in post-crises years, as in Spain from 1600 to 20 and in northern Italy in the 1630s and 1640s. Second, crises also impoverished the peasantry, reducing their stocks of money and livestock, as resources were liquidated to pay for food and seed-corn. Even worse, crises led to an extensive dispossession of the peasant's land and its transfer to other, privileged owners, rent-extracting rather than investing classes. The small-to-middling peasant proprietors were the chief victims of the peasant expropriation which followed crises; they now paid high rents on land which they had formerly owned or even sank into the ranks of the day labourers (see: Peasant farming and agrarian social changing, p. 25).

The greatest burden on the peasants, however, was caused not by crises but by the increase in their tax obligations, and there is a remarkable coincidence between the emergence of centralized governments with strong-tax raising powers and the difficulties of peasant agriculture. In Castile, the real burden of taxation fell from

1530 to 1570, when the economy was growing, but then increased three-fold from 1570 to 1600, precisely when population and agriculture stagnated and then collapsed. Gross taxation, although not the per capita burden, fell slightly from 1600 to 1630, and then increased to a new peak in 1630–80, preventing any sustained recovery of Castile's agriculture. In France, too, there was a close fit between tax increases and the rise and fall of the agrarian economy. Taxes were low from 1600 to 1630, when the French peasant economy prospered, and then increased threefold in real terms under Richelieu and Mazarin from 1630 to 1660, when northern France was gripped by agrarian crises. In Germany, there were rising levels of tax from 1600 to 1620, and enormous increases in the 'contributions' levied by the civil authorities and by occupying armies from 1618 to 1648, a period which coincided with the collapse of German agricultural production. Taxation increased even further after 1648, as stronger governments built up standing armies and this thwarted the recovery of the agrarian economy.

Rising taxation was also instrumental in the second major cycle of European agrarian crises which had their greatest impact from the 1670s in two very different economies, the Netherlands and southern France. The agrarian problems of these regions were not linked to subsistence crises which were absent from the Netherlands and muted in southern France, a region not of corn-monoculture but of a diversified and hence less crisis-prone 'Mediterranean' agriculture of cereals, wine, olives and maize. Rather, the context of these 'late' crises was the European-wide depression in agricultural prices from 1650 coupled with a recession in the Netherlands' urban manufacturing and trading economy from the 1660s and a slump in the Languedoc woollen industry from 1650; depressions exacerbated by tax increases. In the Netherlands, agricultural profits disappeared from the 1670s to 1720, as rural taxes increased sixfold to finance the Republic's wars of national survival against France, which caused a sharp fall in urban investment in agriculture. In southern France, taxation peaked in the middle decades of the seventeenth century as landlords in this region, who were not usually exempt from taxes, shifted their burdens on to tenant farmers. In Languedoc, there was a collapse in wine and above all in cereal production, which in some areas fell by 50 per cent from the 1670s to c.1720 [Figure 2]; the crisis bankrupted many Languedoc farmers, precipitating a spiral of decline in agricultural productivity, which resulted from the 'poverty of the farmers not of the land'.

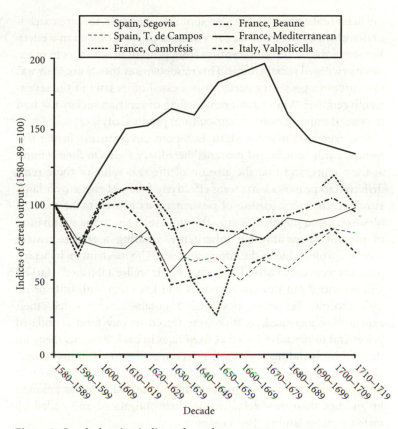

Figure 2 Graph showing indices of cereal output, 1580–1719.

Taxation provides the best explanation for the timing and duration of agrarian crises in the seventeenth century. Negative evidence for this proposition is provided by England, where we see an absence of serious agrarian crises, the most consistent rates of agricultural improvement, and levels of rural taxation which, except in the Civil War years of the 1640s, were extremely light by continental standards.

Peasant farming and agrarian social change

The identification of the problems of peasant farming as the root cause of seventeenth-century agrarian crises may seem to support Brenner's view that the tenacity of peasant ownership of land acted as the main brake on economic development. However, this approach is undermined by the evidence for a massive transfer of land in western Europe in the seventeenth century from peasant proprietors to other, more privileged social groups. This raises two key questions. Why was the European peasantry partly dispossessed of its land in the seventeenth century? Why did this remodelling of agrarian society not lead to general improvements in agricultural productivity?

It is true that many western European governments in the sixteenth century confirmed peasants' hereditary rights to their tenures at fixed rents, and that the erosion of the real value of these rents delivered to peasants what were effectively freehold rights over land. However, the confirmation of peasant rights proved to be a mixed blessing. Rapid population growth before 1600 led to the subdivision of peasant farms through inheritance, creating a fragile peasant economy vulnerable to the effects of crises. The mechanism by which peasants were dispossessed in such crises is well-established. Harvest failures wiped out peasant surpluses and left them with little or no cash income. Yet while peasants' disposable incomes fell, their expenditure increased, as they were forced to buy food at inflated prices and to pay taxes levied at fixed rates in cash. Peasants made up the gap by spending their cash reserves, selling their animals, and, above all, by borrowing on the security of their land. In this way peasants over-extended themselves, and if one bad year was followed by another, then they defaulted on their obligations and ended up forfeiting their land to their creditors.

Although Philip Hoffman has described the view that economic and demographic cycles explain the loss of peasant land in France as 'vacuous', clear national and local evidence shows that the rhythm of the expropriation of the peasantry echoed that of subsistence crises. Indeed, as Hoffman himself shows, losses of peasant land in France were concentrated in the years 1580–1720, when subsistence crises were at their peak; whereas peasant proprietorship was stable in the years 1500–80 and from 1720 to 1780, when subsistence crises were many fewer in number and less severe in their effects. For example, the urban elites of Amiens acquired much peasant land around the city in the years of crisis (1630–63, 1694–1711), while in years of abundance (1660s–90s), the land market was moribund. In the Beauvaisis, north of Paris, five successive poor harvests in the years 1647–51 led to a profound remodelling of rural society: 'crushed by debt the small

peasants had to give up a large part of their land to their creditors.'
Likewise, in Castile, peasants lost a formidable amount of land to the
Church and bourgeois landlords from the 1590s to 1720, transfers
which were almost entirely condensed into years of crisis.

So, while western governments confirmed peasant tenures, they
lacked the means to regulate the private land and credit markets, and
hence could do little to prevent peasant indebtedness and its consequences. However, the state had more scope with communally
rather than privately-owned land. In France, villages had a collective
responsibility for paying taxes; when taxes rose from 1630 to 1660,
many villages became indebted and sold off their common lands.
From the 1660s, Louis XIV's government put village finances in the
hands of the *intendants*, who prevented further sales of common
land, although in practice little could be done to reverse earlier sales.
This stabilized the ownership of communal property, which in the
late eighteenth century made up about 10 per cent of all land in
northern France. But the state's manipulation of community lands
for fiscal purposes could have adverse as well as positive effects for
agriculture. In Spain, virtually all peasant communities had access to
vast common lands, the *baldias*, lands reserved to the crown under
settlements made during the *Reconquista*, but invariably leased to
peasants at nominal rents. However, from c.1550, the crown, under
acute financial pressures, sold these lands, usually to the municipal-
ities in whose hinterlands they were located, which financed the
purchases by loans from urban capitalists. In the economic crisis
from the 1590s, when civic revenues fell away, the communities
invariably defaulted on debt repayments and were forced to cede
nearly all these lands to their creditors.

It was in western Germany, as Brenner argued, that the state had
the greatest success in protecting the peasantry. This seems an
unlikely outcome, given the Thirty Years War's unparalleled destructive impact on agrarian society. However, in west Germany the basic
elements of the pre-war agrarian system were reconstructed after the
war, creating the most resilient peasant society in Europe, one which
controlled 90 per cent of land. So, recent studies of west-German
rural communities desolated by war have shown that the proportion
of middling and larger peasants remained fairly stable from 1600 to
1700, while the numbers of near-landless peasants fell, the opposite of
what happened elsewhere in western Europe. In all these communities

the vast proportion of land transfers occurred not through the land market but by inheritance and intra-family agreements.

Stability in German landed society, as Shelagh Ogilvie has shown, reflected the steps taken by both the larger bureaucratic and the many smaller patrimonial states to protect the peasantry as a tax base. In the post-war scramble between peasants and lords to establish ownership rights to land abandoned during the Thirty Years War, state governments confirmed hereditary peasant tenures at fixed customary rents. They also wrote off wartime arrears of tax and waived fiscal demands during the period of reconstruction. States in western German also intervened in land and credit markets in ways which were unthinkable elsewhere; for example, forbidding peasants to sell land to or borrow money from residents of nearby towns. The victory of the states over landlords reflected the weakening of the territorial nobilities in the war, when they had failed to protect rural communities against intruding armies, and when the overwhelming necessity for states to raise money meant that they disregarded the nobility's customary rights to assent or object to increased taxation. The German peasantry, of course, paid a high price for its survival, namely, the burden of some of the heaviest rates of state taxation in Europe.

The dispossession of the peasantry was not the work of the traditional landed nobility but of successful members of the urban commercial and professional classes, who bought land to enhance their social prestige and to underwrite their aspirations to noble status. Land came to form the heart of 'old' bourgeois fortunes; for example, it provided more than half of the wealth and annual incomes of the *grands bourgeois* of Beauvais and Amiens by the later seventeenth century. Indeed, urban elites became so divorced from their commercial origins that they frequently constituted themselves as self-perpetuating oligarchies, which excluded new members from the still-active commercial classes. This practice of social closure on the part of urban elites was most common in the small states of northern Italy and Germany, but it also spread throughout Spain, France and even in the Netherlands' larger cities.

Agricultural improvement

The crises in agricultural production and major shifts in the distribution of land in the seventeenth century thus reflected the destabilizing of peasant agriculture by *exogenous* forces, that is by influences external to the peasant economy, principally mortality crises and taxation increases. However, even stable peasant societies had little capacity to improve productivity. Thus, the most durable peasant economy, west Germany, had the most stagnant techniques and the lowest productivity levels found in any west European agriculture. The limitations of peasant agriculture reflected the intense concern with growing cereals. Peasant land usually followed perpetual rotations, in which cereal crops were produced for two years, followed by a fallow year to restore the soil's fertility; although in many Mediterranean regions the land was fallowed every other year. Under these systems, one third to one half of the land was uncultivated each year, while the cultivated land yielded only four or five units of harvested grain for each unit sown. Agricultural improvement required the elimination of the fallow and the raising of yields, but such innovation required more animals: manure-machines for the arable. However, rearing more animals was difficult to achieve given the lack of pasture and the inflexible allocation of land to growing corn. The low productivity of the classic agricultural system could be improved by two basic means. First, the adoption of new rotations, incorporating fodder crops which nitrogenized the soil and supported larger animal herds. Second, by convertible husbandry, in which land was converted flexibly from arable to pasture and back again.

Both systems eradicated fallows and raised cereal yields but in the first instance they were geared to rearing more animals. They were therefore introduced when market prices favoured livestock products over cereals. This happened in two circumstances. First, when agriculture was dominated by urban markets, as in sixteenth-century northern Italy and the Low Countries, which generated an immense human, equine and manufacturing demand for animal products, fodder crops and raw materials such as wool. From the 1580s to the 1670s, however, first the Flemish, then the Italian and finally the Dutch urban economies entered periods of deep recession, at which points agricultural development geared to urban demand ceased.

The second circumstance which encouraged agricultural improvement was the European-wide shift in relative prices after *c.*1650, as cereal prices collapsed and livestock prices rose. This price shift had little impact upon peasant farmers, who commercialized only a small part of their output and hence were unresponsive to market stimuli; for example, in the Tierra de Campos during the prosperous years from 1550 to 1580, the mass of peasants sold almost no cereals, while even the largest peasant farmers sold only 15–20 per cent of their output. In theory, the dispossession of the peasantry gave landlords a golden opportunity to amalgamate small plots into large farms, creating a production system more geared to market forces. In practice this opportunity was rarely taken up. In Spain, ecclesiastical institutions were amongst the greatest gainers of land, but they leased out land in small plots, fearing that the collapse of urban markets had removed the economic rationale for large farms and that a high degree of land concentration would drive away labour from the depopulated countryside. In northern Italy and in France, south of the Loire, the main tenurial development of the seventeenth century was a massive extension of share-cropping, whereby land-lords received rents as a fixed percentage of their tenants' crops. This reflected the poverty of the farmers, who looked to the landlords to supply them not just with land but with equipment, stock, even seed-corn. Many share-croppers were in effect glorified subsistence farm-ers or labourers; in Tuscany, for example, increasingly indebted share-croppers worked off their debts by labouring on the landlords' farms, giving them more the appearance of serfs or debt peons than of free peasant farmers.

In only two regions did the loss of peasant land lead to creation of a large-farm sector which dominated market-agriculture, central and southern England and northern France. In these regions, the general growth of markets for livestock products was reinforced by increased demand from the massive urban growth of London and Paris. Eng-lish agriculture raised its productivity by investing in improved methods and by fashioning major interregional changes in land usage. New rotations boosted cereal output in regions like East Anglia and the southern downlands, as they improved arable-land quality in these light-soiled areas, formerly dominated by sheep rearing. On the heavy clay soils of the Midlands, cereal farmers adopted convertible husbandry in response to higher livestock prices and to the superior productivity of the new cornlands. As a result, agricultural output grew faster than population and after 1700 England replaced eastern Europe as the major exporter of cereals to international markets. Much recent work on France has argued that French agriculture also made major strides in productivity and that the traditional view of

French agriculture as incapable of improvement is a myth. But even Hoffman's comprehensive study concludes that although French agriculture expanded in the sixteenth and seventeenth centuries, the best estimate is that its output *failed to keep pace* with population growth and was subject to frequent underproduction crises.

What explains these divergences in agricultural output, which were particularly marked from *c*.1650 and which account for a good part of the differing overall economic progress of England and France in the seventeenth century? Brenner argues that large farms were the main vehicles of agricultural innovation and that there were, relatively, far fewer such farms in France than in England. This view disregards the lengthy process by which bourgeois and clerical landowners in northern France patiently acquired peasant plots and fashioned them into large consolidated farms which came to dominate agriculture in many regions. For example, in the Hurepoix, south of Paris, in the 1550s, 33 per cent of land was owned by peasants, the overwhelming majority of whom possessed tiny holdings under 2.5 acres in size. The remaining land was owned by elite landowners: but their holdings were units of *ownership*, not of production; that is they too were dispersed over numerous small plots rather than amalgamated into large farms. By *c*.1670, the peasants' share of the land had fallen to about 20 per cent. The gainers were Parisian office-holders, who both fore-closed indebted peasant land and created large, consolidated farms of 125 acres or more, which now covered about 40 per cent of the cultivated surface.

However, these large farms were less innovative than their English counterparts. In the Paris basin, the most advanced region, attempts to introduce fodder crops were limited and most of the modest gains made in the period 1600–40 were reversed in the mid-century crises. This had two linked consequences. First, northern French farms supported far fewer animals than English ones. Second, while in the late seventeenth century large farmers achieved cereal yields as high as those found in England, the lack of animals meant they only did so by fertilizing the arable with off-farm manure obtained from Paris and by keeping one third of their land in fallow. Large French farms were 'corn factories', which supported few animals and which withdrew one third of land from production every year.

But why did these farms not innovate? Brenner's view is that innovation was unnecessary because large farms in France could draw cheap labour from the sea of peasant farms which surrounded them. His view that the process of expropriation was carried less far in France than in England is surely correct. Despite the French peasantry's loss of land, there was a difference between the villages of northern France, where the *manouvriers* (labourers) who owned a few acres formed the majority of households and those in southern England, where only a quarter of the village labour force possessed an acre or two and a few animals. But why then was there a larger labour surplus in France than in England, given that the transformation of the English peasantry into a landless proletariat was so much more thorough-going? Brenner suggests that surplus English labour was absorbed into rural industry, but this invokes England's rapid industrial development as a *cause* of agrarian advance, when generally his thesis construes it as an *effect* of agricultural improvement. Moreover, the economic rationale of large farms in France, given their lack of innovation, was the efficiency with which they used labour, labour productivity being much higher on large than on small farms. It seems unlikely then that the crucial difference between English and French agriculture lay in the relative availability of peasant labour.

Two things mattered more. First, the comparative freedom of English agriculture from taxation and mortality crises underpinned the prosperity of the tenant farmers and richer peasants, the farmers who actually implemented the improved methods of agriculture. Second, the differing economic behaviour of the English and French landlords in the agricultural depression after 1660, when England made its irreversible breakthrough in agricultural productivity, while France failed to build on the modest innovations of the early seventeenth century. The reaction of the English landlords to the depression was to abate rents and to write off arrears, to assume some responsibility for taxes and to increase investment in agriculture. In the public sphere, English landlords compelled a reluctant government to put a floor under agricultural prices by, for example, granting substantial bounties on corn exports. French landlords had no comparable influence on state policy, while as private landowners they strove to keep rents up until the end of the century. French commercial farmers were trapped between low prices and high rents, but the reaction of landlords was to bankrupt the farmers, even their largest tenants, rather than get them out of their predicament. How can we account for these differences?

A key element was that French landlords had to cope with a succession of agrarian reconstructions, which in the end destroyed any hope of co-operative relations with their tenants. The first reconstruction followed the devastation of the French Religious Wars of the 1580s and 1590s, when landlords remained faithful to their commercial tenants, the *laboureurs*, and did everything they could to restore agriculture. The second followed the mid-century crises, when landlords bankrupted those *laboureurs* who ceased to make profits and concentrated their lands in giant tenancies leased to *fermiers*. Finally, in the depression from the 1660s, landlords evicted numerous *fermiers* and seized their assets. From the 1640s, then, French landlords, pressed hard by successive crises, ruined the only rural classes capable of improving agriculture. English landlords dealt with only one shortlived crisis, that of the 1640s, when the Civil War and heavy taxation disrupted commercial farming; the agricultural economy, however, recovered by 1660, and the mid-century crisis left no long-term imprint on English agrarian society.

The co-operative nature of the relations between English landlords and their tenants in the agrarian depression also reflected a nexus of interests which bound landlords to the rural areas and their tenants. English landownership was dominated by the gentry, whose families had, or believed they had, a centuries-long connection with rural society. Gentry landlords were resident in the countryside, had close social and political as well as economic links to their tenant farmers, and also took a lively interest in farming practices, judging by the voluminous literature on farming published for a gentry readership. In France, by contrast, the clerical and bourgeois landlords who dominated landownership were resident in the towns, had few social links to the countryside and were indifferent to rural political opinion; the meagre French agronomic literature before 1700 also suggests that landlords were uninterested in their tenants' economic problems. Brenner sees these differences in landlord strategies as part of a structural contrast between an English capitalist and a French peasant or pre-capitalist economy. However, in the Netherlands, where agriculture was clearly organized on a capitalist basis, landlords in the agrarian depression followed the French not the English pattern. When agriculture ceased to be profitable after 1660, Dutch landlords, again an urban bourgeois not a rural gentry class, fled the countryside, sold their land at rock-bottom prices and switched their capital to urban property and government bonds. This strategy worsened the depression in agriculture, but the behaviour of Dutch landlords was perfectly rational given that they viewed land purely in economic, one could call it capitalist terms, rather than, as in England, as the essential foundation of elite social and political power. The divergences in agrarian performances and strategies in north-west Europe before 1700 reflected broad differences in economic and socio-political structures rather than a stark contrast between capitalist and peasant economies.

Eastern-central Europe

In the sixteenth century, the agrarian economies and societies of eastern Europe diverged from those in the West. Western landlords increased their incomes by raising the rents received from their tenants; eastern landlords could not follow this path since the region's low density of population meant that land generated low-rental values. Eastern landlords, notably in Poland and eastern Germany, therefore became direct producers for the home and foreign market, working their demesnes with serf labour; in other words, higher rents were extracted from the peasantry in the form of forced labour services rather than in cash or in kind. Until the late sixteenth century, however, the burdens of serfdom were not so excessive as to undermine the peasant economy; thus, while serfs did not supply the export market, the much bigger domestic market was chiefly provisioned by a core of large and reasonably prosperous peasant farms.

In the seventeenth century, serf agriculture in eastern Europe was transformed by two factors. First, the Thirty Years War and later conflicts caused widespread depopulation and agrarian crises in the vast east-Elbian region and, second, warfare and declining demand in the west caused a sharp contraction in eastern exports of grainstuffs and livestock. Eastern landlords therefore confronted the twin problems of reconstructing agriculture in conditions of massive shortages of manpower and of maintaining their incomes in the face of falling demand for their staple products. The economic logic of the landlords position forced them to increase the demesnes' share of shrinking markets either by intensifying serfdom, where it existed, or by imposing serfdom from scratch where it did not.

Labour services were thus intensified in the first half of the seventeenth century in Poland and in the Baltic provinces, such as Livonia and Pomerania, which were annexed by Sweden in the Polish-Swedish Wars of 1600–30. Labour services were also imposed on a significant scale for the first time in Hungary from c.1600 and in Bohemia, Moravia and, to a lesser extent, in Austria in the aftermath of the Thirty Years War. The precondition for this escalation of serfdom was either that states endorsed increased landlord powers over peasants or that they were too weak to oppose them. In Poland, the state's fiscal powers were limited from 1569 and the penurious monarchy depended on the magnates to finance and organize the defensive wars of the period 1600 to 1721, a political dependency which permitted the landlord-propelled extension of labour services. In Austro-Hungary, the defeat of the Bohemian Protestant nobility's insurgency against the Emperor, the immediate cause of the Thirty Years War, led to a transfer of their land to indigenous and immigrant Catholic nobles whose imposition of a thorough-going serfdom on the peasantry, who had supported the rebellion, was tacitly underwritten by the Imperial government. In Hungary, the Habsburgs depended on the aristocracy and their private armies in ceaseless frontier wars against the Turks and could hardly do otherwise, despite noble rebellions, than yield them increasing powers over their serfs. For Brandenburg, however, Hagen has recently shown that the intensification of serfdom was not the inevitable result of the crisis of east-European agriculture. Here in the Thirty Years War, the seigneurial system collapsed and serfs refused to perform labour services. After the War, the emerging absolutist state gave the peasants more protection than they received in other eastern states and Brandenburg landlords found that in reconstructing their demesne economy they were required to negotiate with peasants whose scarcity increased their bargaining power, rather than simply coerce them. Indeed, as late as 1700 Brandenburg peasants were paying lower labour rents than they had a hundred years earlier. But the Prussian state stepped in to skim off the surpluses which the landlords failed to collect and, by 1700, Brandenburg peasants paid as much or more in taxes to the state than they did in rents, showing that the *total* financial burdens imposed upon them increased substantially in the seventeenth century.

The productivity of the eastern system of agriculture declined in the seventeenth century. Yields were lower on the demesne than on the peasants' land because coerced work was performed reluctantly and badly and because peasants ensured that their animals' haulage power and manure was used to benefit their own lands more than the landlords' demesnes. The increasing use of forced peasant labour and resources on demesnes rather than on their own farms thus led to a progressive deterioration in the productivity of eastern agriculture. This can be illustrated from Poland's experience, where agricultural output stagnated from 1570 to 1650, collapsed in the wars of the 1650s, and then recovered to only 70 per cent of former levels by the end of the century. Labour services imposed on Polish serfs were doubled from 1570 to 1650 and were ratcheted upwards further following the Cossack and Swedish wars of 1648–60. The excessive demand of the demesnes for labour prevented the reconstruction of the peasant system after the mid-century wars: only two-thirds of peasant plots resumed full production and the number of substantial peasants, the serf system's chief productive force, fell even more drastically. Demesne farms were reconstructed and indeed extended, but there was a 20–25 per cent decline in their productivity as the labour upon them was increasingly performed by gangs of manual labourers who lacked the animals and equipment needed to work the lords' land adequately. Landlords did not replace more than a fraction of this lost capital as they remained resolutely opposed to productive investment.

Industry and trade

Although agriculture was the dominant activity in the European economy *c.*1600, Europe also had the manufacturing capacity to process agricultural commodities and to supply basic producer goods and a wide range of consumer products. Manufacturing was carried on in a variety of settings. The core of the manufacturing system was made up of artisans in towns and villages who produced textiles and many other goods and services for local markets. In most rural areas peasant households processed food and drink and made coarse textiles for their own consumption. In a few regions, these households were employed by urban merchant-organizers to make goods, usually textiles, for sale in non-local markets, a form of production called the putting-out system or proto-industry. The largest concentrations of manufacturing, however, were found in the craft and workshop industries of large towns and cities, which produced high-quality textiles and other goods for well-to-do consumers in national and international markets.

Industry and trade, 1600–50

The years 1600–20 were the Indian summer of the commercial and industrial system established in the sixteenth century, when many industries and trades reached peak levels of activity. But the boom ended in the trade crisis of 1619–22, a watershed in the development of the European economy, when many indices of trade and of industrial production took a downward turn and remained depressed until 1650 or beyond [Figure 3]. This international economic crisis had its greatest impact in France, Germany, and in central and Mediterranean Europe. In England and the Low Countries, commercial and industrial expansion was much less interrupted, leading therefore to a decisive shift of the core areas of trade and manufacturing to north-western Europe. The crisis was precipitated by the

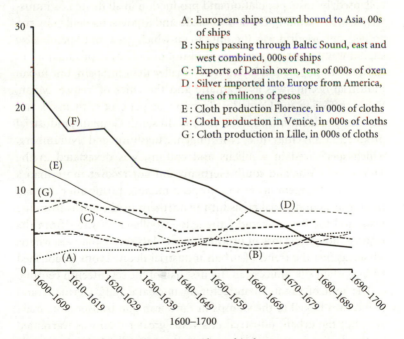

A : European ships outward bound to Asia, 00s of ships
B : Ships passing through Baltic Sound, east and west combined, 000s of ships
C : Exports of Danish oxen, tens of 000s of oxen
D : Silver imported into Europe from America, tens of millions of pesos
E : Cloth production Florence, in 000s of cloths
F : Cloth production in Venice, in 000s of cloths
G : Cloth production in Lille, in 000s of cloths

1600–1700

Figure 3 Graph showing European trade and industry, 1600–1700.

Thirty Years War, which caused massive currency devaluations and market disruptions in Germany and central Europe, destabilizing foreign trade and industry in a region containing about one-third of Europe's population. More generally, consumer demand in Europe for manufactures was depressed from 1630 to 1660 by the three mutually-reinforcing economic trends established above: the fall in population caused by mortality crises; the crises in agricultural production and incomes; and the huge increases in taxation required to finance the Thirty Years and Franco-Spanish Wars (1618–60). The slump in European trade was reinforced by a contraction in the world economy. Silver imports from Spanish America fell from the 1630s to the 1650s, reducing Spanish-American demand for European goods. Europe's commerce with Asia stagnated from 1620 to 1650, a period when trade was disrupted by the English and Dutch attack on Portugal's Asian-trading monopoly.

The core of the early seventeenth-century crisis in trade and industry was the spectacular and irreversible decline in urban manufacturing. In Spain, urban industrial output stagnated to 1620 and then collapsed; by 1650, population and production in all the major industrial towns, including Cordoba, Toledo and Segovia, had fallen by 50–70 per cent. Madrid was the only town which grew, but Spain's new capital was a centre of consumption not of industrial production. In Italy, urban population losses were smaller than in Spain, but urban industrial decline was as dramatic and the cities of Venice, Milan, Florence, Genoa and Como lost from 60–80 per cent of their silk and woollen production from 1620 to 1660. In south Germany, industrial production in cities like Nördlingen, Augsburg and Nuremberg, which specialized in woollens and cottons, was devastated in the Thirty Years War and south Germany did not recover more than a fraction of its preeminence in European manufacturing after the war. In France, an industrial crisis hit the northern textile towns from the 1630s and the Britanny and Languedoc woollen industries from the 1650s, although the loss of production was less severe than elsewhere, while, against the trend of urban industrial decay, Lyons established an important silk industry in the first half of the seventeenth century.

The rout of urban manufacturing in Spain, Italy, Germany and France was linked to the slumps in European and transoceanic markets; but the urban industrial crisis was greater than was warranted by the decline in trade. The problem was not solely or even mainly one of shrinking markets, but of intensified international competition. Industry diversified in England and expanded in the Low Countries from 1600 to 1650 and it was the superior competitiveness of these economies which undermined the older centres of urban manufacturing. So, both the Spanish and later the French textile industries were overpowered by imports of light, cheap woollen goods from England and the Low Countries which supplanted indigenous products in the huge Franco-Spanish domestic markets and in the export trade to Spanish America.

The 'proto-industrialization' model developed by historians since the 1970s has provided the most comprehensive explanation of the changing balance of international competitiveness amongst Europe's industrial regions in the seventeenth century. This argues that Europe's urban industries collapsed in the seventeenth century because industrial production was relocated to the countryside, where peasants combined manufacturing with agriculture, integrating the tradition of rural handicrafts into market production. Rural industry had two key advantages. First, wages, which made up the larger part of manufacturing costs, were lower in the countryside than in the towns. Second, rural industry was free from urban guild regulations which increased costs and prevented urban industry from responding to changes in consumer tastes. Urban capitalists organized proto-industry, 'putting out' raw materials and semi-finished goods to rural workers and marketing the finished products in national and international markets. How successfully does this model explain the reorganization of European industry in the seventeenth century?

The model is correct in seeing that the key to industrial competitiveness was product innovation and the lowering of wage costs. Given the general lack of cost-reducing technical innovations, diversification and lower costs could only be achieved by driving down wages and by reducing standards of quality. The classic 'innovation' of the seventeenth century was the replacement of expensive and durable woollens, the 'old draperies', by the 'new draperies', which used the same technology but adapted to the production of flimsy, gaudily-finished textiles, made from cheap, coarse wool, often mixed with fibres such as cotton. This was part of a fundamental shift in European consumer tastes from expensive, durable consumer goods, to semi-durable and cheaper substitutes. The problem of the declining urban industries was that city-guildsmen did not alter the basic design of their products, even when faced with overwhelming evidence of changes in market tastes. Recent research suggests, however, that craft workers, for example in Italy, did in fact wish to innovate but were held back by the opposition of merchants and city-governments who feared that change would undermine a city's greatest asset, its reputation for quality production. In either case, urban manufacturing was inherently inflexible in an international economy which demanded a continuous revolution in product types.

However, major innovations in industrial products and methods were achieved in north-west Europe, although until 1650 this reorganization took place much more in an urban than a rural setting. This emergence of the north-west as Europe's major industrial region cannot therefore be squared with the proto-industrial model's emphasis on the growth of rural production. In the Netherlands, Europe's industrial leader, woollen production was concentrated in Leiden, by 1650 the most important textile centre in Europe and the second Dutch city after Amsterdam. This outcome hardly seemed likely in the sixteenth century when Leiden's 'old drapery' woollen industry was unable to compete with the English textiles which flooded the Netherlands' market: by 1580, the traditional industry was virtually extinct. From 1580, however, Leiden received thousands of Protestant refugees from Flanders who had pioneered the manufacturing of 'New Draperies' in the southern Low Countries. In Leiden, these textiles were produced not by guild craftsmen, as in the old, defunct industry, but by Flemish and later indigenous merchant-capitalists, who 'put-out' work to dependent labourers on wage rates, in non-guild manufactories which frequently changed their product-types. Similarly, the recovery of Flanders' industrial economy in the early seventeenth century was based on flexible urban, not rural, production, where linen merchants put-out work to guild-trained craftsmen working for wages in large, unregulated city workshops. In England, rural as opposed to urban industry dominated textile production by the end of the sixteenth century, long before this happened elsewhere. But even the English textile industries combined rural and urban elements. In the East Anglian 'new drapery' industry, the major English exporter to south European markets, spinning was done in the countryside; but weaving and finishing, which made up by far the largest proportion of total costs, were concentrated in Colchester and Norwich and other towns which, like Leiden, were failing, over-regulated textile centres, revitalized by the introduction of new products by Flemish refugee-migrants, activities in which strict guild controls never took hold.

Industry and trade, 1650–1700

After 1650, there was, in nearly every European region, an increase in the importance of rural industry at the expense of urban production, an industrial reorganization which fits much better with the proto-industrial model than developments before 1650. First, Dutch urban industry, which had swept all before it from 1580 to 1650, experienced absolute decline. At Leiden, by 1700 textile production had fallen by a third to a half from the peak years of the mid-century. Haarlem, in 1650, had 3000–4000 linen weavers; by 1700 linen weaving had almost disappeared from the town. The decline of Dutch urban industry was, to a modest degree, compensated for by the relocation of production to rural areas in the eastern Netherlands, and across the border into Westphalia and Brabant. In Flanders, the stagnation of the urban linen industry, and the sustained expansion of the rural, has been dated precisely from the middle of the seventeenth century. In England, woollen exports trebled from c.1650 to 1700, increased output flowed from the rural industries of the West Country, and above all Devon, Lancashire and Yorkshire, while the more urbanized East Anglian industry turned to the domestic market. From c.1650, urban merchants in Italy, France and Germany also reacted to the earlier collapse of urban industry by establishing rural industrial networks. In France, new drapery production spread across the Picardy and Champagne countryside, while Brittany and Normandy became major rural producers of linens and later cottons. There was also, from c.1680, a modest revival of woollen production in certain northern textile towns, such as Amiens, while Lyons replaced northern Italy as Europe's premier producer of the finest silk fabrics, an industry organized by *marchands-fabricants* who 'put-out' work to an army of dependent urban silk-weavers. In Italy, it was once assumed that the collapse of urban industry led to the country becoming wholly deindustrialized. In fact, north Italy generated numerous major rural industrial sectors in the period, including iron, paper manufacture, linens and woollens. Most important was silk production in Piedmont, Lombardy and the Venetian State, where rural producers replaced the towns as the manufacturers of plain silk fabrics and the chief source of supply of raw and spun silk to international markets, especially Lyons. A number of Italian towns, including Venice, Florence and Lucca, also revived their luxury industries, notably of fabrics woven from silk and gold thread. Finally, from the end of the Thirty Years War, rural production, mainly of iron and above all linens, expanded in central and eastern Europe: in Germany—in the Rhineland, Westphalia, Saxony and the south-west—and in Switzerland, Silesia, Bohemia and Moravia.

The proto-industrial model argues that an industry's degree of competitiveness was determined by its capacity to adapt production to market demands and also by its ability to drive down wage levels. In general, wages in Europe fell from the mid-sixteenth to the mid-seventeenth century, but they declined much more in the countryside than in the towns. Low rural wages were caused by population growth combined with the peasantry's loss of land, which created a near-landless, 'cottager' population, an ideal labour force for rural industry. The sharper fall in rural wages opened up a large gap between rural and urban manufacturing costs. Wages in Italy's urban industries, for example, were pushed up from the 1590s by labour scarcities caused by plague epidemics. In England, on the other hand, Italy's chief competitor in the Mediterranean and Turkish markets for woollens, wages fell steadily to 1650, by which time rural wages were much lower than those in Italian cities. One might expect that the collapse of Italian urban industry would have forced a reduction in manufacturing wages, but wage levels were set by the demand for labour in general rather than by the fate of particular industries. Employment and wages were kept up in Italian cities not by guilds but by the fact that declining revenues from industry and trade were offset by an increasing flow of tax and rents from the countryside; thus, labour was shifted from export-orientated to service and luxury industries, patronized by the urban, rent and tax-receiving elites. Urban industries in Italy and elsewhere failed to cope before 1650 with competition from English *rural* industry but they crumbled even before Dutch *urban* industry. The Netherlands was a high-wage economy where real wages rose steadily in the late sixteenth and seventeenth centuries. However, before 1650 the increase in wages was matched by an increase in investment and labour productivity. At Leiden, for example, the Protestant refugees from the south brought in ample capital and more advanced manufacturing techniques and established a large enough scale of production to create economies through the division, specialization and deskilling of labour. In time, this led to the employment of cheap female and even orphan labour.

From c.1650, the stagnation or fall in population began, very slowly, to push up wage rates in every European country. Rising wages contrasted with declining textile prices, which fell remorselessly in every textile industry for which we have data. Manufacturers were ground between falling prices and rising costs, a scissors movement which proved fatal to those urban industries which had flourished before 1650, and which gave the vital impetus to the growth of rural manufacturing. In the Netherlands, wages rose by a third to a half from 1650 to 1700, outpacing gains made in other regions. However, higher wages were no longer offset by innovation and rising productivity, measured at least by statistics of new industrial patents, the number of which peaked in 1620–50 and then fell off sharply. Rising real labour costs, coupled with escalating taxes, undermined the hitherto dynamic Dutch urban economy. At Leiden, textile output fell by more than a third from 1650 to 1700, but by two-thirds in the production of new drapery textiles, in which labour made up the highest proportion of total costs. At Haarlem, the labour-intensive activity of linen-weaving died away, while the capital-intensive, linen-bleaching industry survived. Rural industry expanded in the Netherlands, but agricultural and craft workers in most regions were well-paid specialists and not much attracted to rural industry; it was only in the agriculturally-backward eastern provinces that one found pools of underemployed 'cottagers', the staple labour force for rural industry. Wages and taxes also rose fast in the southern Low Countries after 1650, inducing a shift of linen weaving from the towns to the countryside, where labour was much more plentiful than in the northern Netherlands, reflecting the extreme fragmentation of farm size.

Elsewhere in Europe wages rose less quickly after 1650 than in the Low Countries, with the slowest rates of growth occurring in the countryside. In Germany, the repopulation of the rural areas after the Thirty Years War, and the huge drop in food prices, dampened down rural manufacturing wages which hardly rose above wartime levels. In northern France, there was a widening gap between urban and rural wage rates and by the 1690s weavers in the expanding rural sector near Amiens were paid about a third of the rates received by guild workers in the city. In England, relatively buoyant rural wages after 1650 were offset by the decisive shift of textile production to Devon and to northern England, exploiting the fact that average rural wages in these remote regions were lower than in the south and east.

Low wages were probably the major cause of the expansion of proto-industry, but the advocates of proto-industrial theory, as we have seen, have placed as much emphasis on rural industry's freedom from urban and guild restrictions. Critics of proto-industrial theory, notably Ogilvie, have argued, however, that the idea that rural industry escaped the net of corporate controls is a myth. The revisionists argue that in every region, with the exceptions of England and the Low Countries, rural industrial expansion was checked, sometimes smothered, by non-market institutions. So, urban merchants who organized rural production were often members of guilds, as were the rural industrial workers whom they employed. These corporate organizations hampered the free entry of capital and labour into rural industry. Similarly, towns defended their own industries, and raised revenue, by imposing restrictions and taxes on the sale of rural industry's raw materials and finished products.

It can certainly be agreed that rural industry in eastern Europe and most of Germany was hampered by controls imposed by governments, landlords, and guilds. In the larger German territories this reflected the post-1648 growth of state power while in the smaller states, including the imperial cities, it was relatively easy for small groups of manufacturers to organize cartels to lobby the authorities for protection. Consequently, textile cities like Cologne and Aachen stagnated in the late seventeenth century as guilds outdid each other 'in devising schemes meant to suppress anything that suggested change.' In east Germany and central Europe, the shift of industry from towns to the countryside delivered it into the hands of feudal lords who levied hefty taxes on serf-weavers and on yarn and raw material sales and who often compelled rural workers to join guilds.

However, in parts of Germany, and generally in western and Mediterranean Europe, corporate controls had far less effect on rural industrial development. In Germany itself, industrial development was rapid where state and guild regulations were largely absent, notably in the rural Rhineland, Germany's most successful industrial region. Even where guilds existed in the Rhineland, their edicts were laxly enforced. For example, in the Wupper Valley, merchant-organizers of the linen and ribbon industries belonged to a guild organization, the *Garnnahrung*, one replete with regulations: however, Kisch argues that infringements of the regulations were 'the rule rather than the exception' and that they did little to restrict the region's industrial boom after the Thirty Years War. In France, guilds multiplied in the seventeenth century, as governments from Richelieu to Colbert and beyond attempted to extend corporate controls over industry. Yet these guilds, and their regulative codes, were aimed at urban not rural industry; the state left the latter in an unregulated limbo, against which municipal authorities made futile protests. For example, from the late seventeenth century the cotton industry spread very rapidly in the countryside near Rouen; the city's magistrates and manufacturers 'protested and denounced this rural competition in vain.' French towns had more success in regulating urban markets for proto-industrial goods, although this policy did more harm to urban than rural interests. At Lille, for example, it was not until 1696 that the town permitted 'the importing and finishing of a few types of cloth woven in the countryside'. In Italy, it was mainly in central regions, notably Bologna and Tuscany, where the power of city governments and of landlords was used to cramp the development of rural industry. In most northern regions, the state and the city authorities did more to encourage than to suppress rural manufacturing. In Milan and Genoa, for example, protests from urban silk guilds against unregulated rural industries were ignored by city rulers. In Milan, as elsewhere, the ruling patriciate's connections with urban commerce and industry had been severed, and it now benefitted from strong rural manufacturing which, from *c.*1650, was generally given a higher priority by the city's rulers than urban industry. In Catalonia, the collapse of Barcelona's woollen industry in *c.*1650 led to its vigorous reappearance in small towns and villages where manufacturing was less stringently regulated. In central Spain, urban guilds remained strong, but their capacity to fend off rural industry was not tested, as merchants interested in organizing rural proto-industry hardly emerged after the industrial crisis of the early seventeenth century.

The impact of local institutions on rural industrial development varied enormously, but for most regions the view expressed recently that such institutions seriously hampered the growth of proto-industry is debatable. Rural industry grew fast in Europe in the seventeenth century, both in relation to urban industry and to economic activity as a whole, suggesting that we should emphasise its dynamic qualities rather than those institutional forces which in some regions impeded the development of rural manufacturing. Besides, an emphasis on local institutions leads to the neglect of central-state policies of an economic nationalist or mercantilist character, whose impact on commercial and industrial development was far reaching.

The state and trade and industry

The seventeenth-century crisis in the international economy bolstered the contemporary belief that world markets were fixed in size and prompted states to defend their market share by protecting industry and trade against foreign competitors, of whom the most feared were the Dutch. Protectionist ideas were fully evolved in the sixteenth century but governments did not systematically act upon them until *c.*1650. In the industrial sphere, the most widely-used tactic was to reduce imports of manufactures through tariffs: a policy designed to strengthen indigenous industry and employment by eliminating foreign competition; to create a favourable balance of trade and a net inflow of bullion; and to increase state revenues by maximizing the number of taxable market transactions. France took the lead in tariff policy, reacting to the mid-century collapse of its urban industries by raising import duties on English and Dutch textiles, most decisively under Colbert in the 1660s. Having protected the huge French market, the government, which prioritized industry over other economic sectors, made strenuous efforts to revive the old textile centres and to establish new luxury industries by importing foreign artisans and techniques and by the granting of subsidies, tax concessions, and market monopolies.

Protectionism was applied to foreign trade and shipping as well as to industry. England and France both founded empires in the Caribbean and North America in the early seventeenth century and from *c.*1650 these became major sources of sugar and other tropical staples and major customers, not so much for manufactured goods, as for mercantile services and for shipping. English, although not French, trade with Asia also grew very fast from 1650: this, again, was an import-driven trade, where exports of silver were exchanged for spices and above all Indian cotton manufactures. The transoceanic trades and shipping industries were arguably the most dynamic sectors in the English and French economies from 1660 to 1690; in France, for example, the Caribbean trade stimulated a strong commercial and industrial response in the Atlantic ports and in northern and western regions of rural manufacturing. However, both England and France faced stiff competition in their colonial and carrying trades from the Dutch. England, in fact, was much harder-pressed by Dutch competition in trade and shipping than in industry. Hence the centre-piece of English mercantilism was not the tariff protection of home industries, which was hardly applied in the seventeenth century, but the Navigation Acts of 1650–63, designed to exclude Dutch shipping and capital from England's transoceanic and shipping trades. France, after 1670, adopted similar policies to protect its colonial interests from Dutch competition.

Most historians, however, doubt that mercantilist policies brought real benefits for trade and industry. Colbert, for example, is said to have lavished attention on France's urban and centralized industries, creating a corporatist and state-dependent industrial culture, at a time when industry's future lay with dispersed and unregulated rural manufacturing. This scepticism has been moderated in recent years. Protectionism distorted the pattern of European production and trade but it did so mainly to the benefit of those countries which followed mercantilist policies. Without protection and state assistance, the ailing French textile industries would have shifted much more slowly to producing the English and Dutch-style textiles for which there was an overwhelming consumer preference. Without the English and French navigation systems, the Dutch, whose mercantile capital and proficiency dwarfed their competitors, would have engrossed a much higher proportion of world trade than they did, thus curbing the development of England and France's buoyant Atlantic economies.

Those countries which failed to protect their trade and industry from foreign competition undoubtedly experienced the slowest rates of commercial development. Spain's imports of silver from its American colonies increased substantially from 1660, part of the wider growth of the Atlantic economy in this period, which, in turn, financed a growing volume of manufactured exports to America. However, virtually all this silver was re-exported from Spain to northern Europe, which also provided the vast bulk of Spain's manufactured exports to America. Consequently, while Spanish-American demand acted as a major stimulus to European manufacturing after 1650, this benefitted not Spain but the rural textile industries of northern France, Flanders and the Rhineland. Spain had plenty of laws to prevent this happening, for example those prohibiting the export of bullion, the problem was that it did not enforce them. Indeed, Spain did almost nothing to protect its native industry, trade and shipping. Historians have been dubious about the benefits of mercantilism, but they have also been unanimous in attributing much of Spain's industrial and commercial underdevelopment to the absence of such policies.

Conclusion

Recent research on the seventeenth-century European economy has sought to explain the three central features which distinguished it from the economically expansive sixteenth and eighteenth centuries: the stagnation of population; the slump in agricultural production, associated with frequent subsistence crises; the decline of urban manufacturing and the rise of rural industry.

Demographic research has dismissed the role of famines as a major factor in the seventeenth-century stagnation of Europe's population, emphasizing instead that it was epidemics which had exogenous or non-economic causes and preventive checks on marriage and fertility which restrained population growth in the period. The model works well for the Netherlands and England, where subsistence crises were unimportant, and where marriage ages and rates of non-marriage shifted dramatically upwards from 1650. The recent attempt, however, to extend the model to France, Spain, Italy and elsewhere is less convincing. First, famines triggered all the major mortality crises which beset these societies, albeit that the links between famine and mortality took an indirect rather than a direct form. Second, the idea that the weak preventive checks which operated in these countries in the seventeenth century were sufficient to stop population growth is undermined by comparisons with the eighteenth century, when such checks were intensified greatly and yet proved quite incapable of holding back the massive population growth which swept across western Europe from c.1720.

Agrarian crises in western Europe, this chapter has argued, cannot be conceptualized as Malthusian crises caused by internal developments within a closed economic system, in which population pressure led inexorably to the collapse of agricultural production. Agriculture was undermined by a slump in the output and productivity of peasant farmers, but this decline was caused by three factors exogenous to agriculture: mortality crises, which dislocated rural labour markets; the post-crisis transfers of land from peasants to other social classes; and, above all, by the rise of crushing fiscal exactions. If the crises did not have Malthusian causes then neither did they give rise to classic Malthusian adjustments in the post-crisis period: rising cereal yields, as production was concentrated on better land; a shift of resources into non-cereal output; or an increase in per capita landholdings and incomes; outcomes prevented by the same exogenous forces which had precipitated the crises in the first place. In eastern Europe, population never pressed hard on resources and here agricultural crises clearly had socio-political rather than Malthusian causes.

Finally, the collapse of urban industry in the Mediterranean, much of France and central Europe after 1620, and its contraction in the Low Countries after 1650, meant that overall the seventeenth century saw a substantial decline in urban manufacturing. In the long-run, urban production was engulfed by rural competition in the production of low or medium-quality manufactured goods, in which the main production cost was cheap, semi-skilled labour. Urban industry retained a clear advantage in capital-intensive processes, as in textile dyeing and finishing; it was also dominant in the production of luxury goods, such as fine silks, which embodied the costliest raw materials worked up by skilled labour, and where, moreover, the market could bear the high costs of urban quality-regulation. However, the demand for rural industrial goods, such as cheap woollens, proved to be much more elastic than that for urban, luxury goods and such demand also set the pace for the expansion of urban industries like dyeing and finishing, which were tied to a rural industrial base. The proto-industrial model has attracted more criticism than any other theory put forward in early modern history, but its major theme has not been discredited: namely, that, in the long-run, low-cost and unregulated rural, rather than urban, manufacturing set the pattern of industrial growth in the seventeenth century.

2

Society

Thomas Munck

In 1690, a group of peasants from the village of Borre on Møn in Denmark found themselves in open conflict with the bailiff in charge of the estate. At issue was a sum of money allegedly due from the peasants in lieu of labour services. The bailiff, claiming the payment was overdue, seized some cattle as security, but without due process of law. When the peasants initiated legal proceedings he had all but one of them arrested. The one who escaped submitted a statement to the local court: the sheriff declared the arrest illegal, fined the bailiff, and insisted that the original dispute over labour payments could be heard only when the men were freed. The bailiff now secured the dismissal of the sheriff himself. The peasants did not recover their freedom until six months later, and then only on condition that they sign a statement (not read out to them) which was subsequently used against them as evidence of insubordination. The bailiff now threatened them with eviction and loss of tenure unless they paid up the original disputed sum and formally apologized for their 'unnecessary' litigation. He also persuaded the district governor to have the original court judgment annulled. The whole tale of abuse of power did not come into the open until seven years later, when the accumulation of more than 200 individual and collective complaints finally forced the crown to institute a formal enquiry. That enquiry uncovered systematic falsification of records by the bailiff, misappropriation of funds totalling at least 13 000 thalers, abuse of power by the governor, and (with specific reference to the case just cited) perversion of the course of justice. Eventually the bailiff was charged and his property sequestrated, the governor was removed and later arrested, and—fifteen years after the original dispute—compensation payment made by the estate to some of the peasants.

There are several aspects of this case which deserve our attention. The most important, perhaps, is that we only know about it because the estate was under crown ownership: unlike on private estates, significant problems were likely to be reported to the exchequer, and if necessary a formal enquiry could be mounted. If this had been a private estate, judicial proceedings could have dragged on forever, or simply been circumvented—a point reinforced by the fact that even here the annulment of the 1690 court hearing resulted in the case being formally crossed out in the court protocol (though not enough to make it illegible). Yet we might also note that the various forms of pressurization used by the bailiff and his superior—including illegal arrest, forcing individuals to sign a statement under duress, and threatening with reprisals—were recognized as unjust both by the victims and by the crown. Two other fundamental points can be made: first, that the peasants, though at least partially illiterate, were not easily cowed; and second, that it took a great deal of what we would now call 'whistle-blowing' before the bailiff and the governor were brought to task by their superiors. Differences in social status and rank mattered enormously: there was no assumption of a 'level playing-field', and no guarantee that the exercise of power would be either orderly or accountable. For those with little status or influence, stability and security must often have seemed like an illusion, to be sought at great personal cost.

Historians of the seventeenth century encounter significant difficulties in documenting and analysing social relations in this period, because so much source material is one-sided. On the whole, contemporaries did not think in quantitative terms, so the basic fabric of society (such as household structure and occupations), which might provide clues regarding the distribution of wealth, rank and power, cannot easily be unravelled. This chapter will discuss society not as the neat, divinely-ordained and static pyramid idealized by those at the top, but rather in terms of a complex organism liable not only to long-term evolution but also to sudden (if often only temporary) disaggregation under stress. Change is particularly apparent in the composition and function of the elite itself, in the uneven pace of urbanization, and above all in the volcanic eruptions of popular revolt and the recurrent disasters of economic failure which feature so prominently in this period.

Social rank and social mobility

The structural elements of seventeenth-century society can be portrayed in several different ways. In theory, horizontal divisions marked out a clear hierarchy of estates, of which the first consisted of servants of the church, the second of the nobility, the third of commoners, and (in Sweden and a few other parts of Europe) a fourth estate was constituted by the peasantry. Except in the few republics, everyone agreed that ultimate authority was best vested in a personal (and usually hereditary) form of monarchy, whose incumbent represented God on earth. His (occasionally her) authority was not unlimited, in that it was bound by law and convention; but such restrictions were on the whole neither clear nor sustainable. In practice, the authority of an able and adult prince was reflected downwards through society, via a closely controlled and religiously observed hierarchy built both on real power and on visible prestige. Just as the authority of the prince embodied the unity of the whole, so, at the other extreme, the authority of the (usually male) head of the household guaranteed the maintenance of order at the individual level. King and paterfamilias were the poles around which stability and authority were maintained, each sacred, each virtually unchallengeable.

In reality, however, society was rather more complex. The evolution of economic and administrative structures during the seventeenth century brought out far more (and potentially overlapping) layers than the simple schema of three or four estates might imply. Around the king were the princes of royal blood, the great magnates and the lesser landowning nobility, supported by (and often closely linked by family ties to) the most prominent functionaries of the church. Below them were officeholders and other servants of the crown, the entrepreneurs of the military state (including the commanding officers themselves, their agents, ship-builders, arms suppliers and financiers), and the judiciary—some of whom might well exercise more real political influence than members of the traditional nobility. What we might call 'the middling sorts', namely merchants, ordinary manufacturers, shopkeepers, craftsmen and artisans, were mostly confined to urban communities, whose prosperity was contingent both on special status (in terms of taxation, security and some measure of self-government) and on the preservation of peace. The proportion of the total population that lived in towns of more than 5000 inhabitants remained small, and the growth patterns of most cities was unsteady at least until after mid-century. Outside the usually clearly defined urban perimeters, or beyond the slum peripheries of larger cities, lay what was still the normal environment for most Europeans: a mosaic of small-scale peasant holdings, controlled by more or less dominant landowning interests whose power was visibly embodied in the substantial manor buildings that were scattered through the richer rural areas of Europe. Formally, the distinction between town and country was clear, but in practice there was some fluidity both amongst the semi-skilled and poorly paid workers of the growing domestic industries (particularly textiles) and, at the lowest level of society, amongst the unskilled labourers who moved between rural and urban work, the elusive dependents often described as 'servants', and the begging or vagrant underclass that contemporaries tried their best to ignore.

Trying to make all this fit into a 'class' structure is not very helpful. Contemporaries were accustomed to use the word more when referring to classes of knowledge (within a tree of knowledge) or classes of tax-payers (on a scale of twelve or twenty steps). They rarely observed anything that we might identify as 'class consciousness', except perhaps amongst the nobility. For those who belonged to the third estate, all kinds of labels were available, ranging from 'bourgeois' (as in 'bourgeois de Paris', often meaning someone living off unearned income, or someone with specific civic rights) and 'middling sorts' down through 'mean' or 'industrious' people and 'mechanics'. The genuinely poor (either in town or in countryside) had neither rights nor entitlements, and were not normally counted as part of any estate.

It may be more fruitful to see society in terms intelligible to contemporaries. They recognized the local community, often the parish or village to which they belonged, with its specific allocations of rank and power (both secular and ecclesiastical), as well as its obligations of loyalty. They recognized the deference owed to individuals who owned land, held office, or had other less obvious attributes of status. If they lived in a town, they would be well aware of the corporations and guilds that protected and preserved each occupational sector, and often minutely regulated aspects of their daily lives. And above all, even if they could not see all its ramifications, they might be aware of the pervasiveness of privilege, not just for the elite, but also sanctioning the rights and entitlements of the middle ranks of society in carefully measured steps.

Even at the top, however, there were demarcation problems. Already in 1613, the French lawyer Charles Loyseau had clearly identified what was to become a growing problem: namely that the most successful and influential members of the third estate, although commoners, might as crown officeholders not only acquire noble status, but were liable to become a new elite with greater power than that of the traditional nobility. Ranking those with traditional heredity-based status against those who had acquired it through actual service to the king was bound to become a growing problem as the apparatus of government—and the professionalism of its most important servants—rapidly increased in the course of the seventeenth century. Everywhere, from Samuel Pepys's London to the court of Versailles, from Venice to Copenhagen, this conflict between old and new elite was liable to cause bitter and increasing resentment, especially amongst the traditionalists who saw their position in society threatened. Up to a point they were right, because, as some contemporaries noted, commoners promoted on their merits could become more useful to a centralizing monarch than the traditional elite with their own autonomous patronage network and hereditary interests. To retain a semblance of order amongst these rival groups, some rulers had recourse to formalized tables of ranks: the Swedish order of nobility of 1626 can be regarded as an early attempt at such regulation, but more comprehensive schemes, incorporating the service elite, were imposed by Leopold I in the Austrian lands in 1671 and by Christian V in Denmark the very same year.

Promotion on merit did happen, but usually only within a narrow social spectrum. A far more significant vehicle for upwards social mobility was money. Especially in western and central Europe, money could provide access to all the trappings of elite status, including noble titles, landed estates, fiscal privileges, coats of arms, seigneurial rights (such as hunting rights, powers of justice and punishment, entitlement to labour services from tenants) and, given time, even honorific entitlements. Inversely, lack of assets and failure to 'live nobly' could in certain circumstances lead to derogation or loss of nobility. In practice, the acquisition of elite status usually involved a mixture of personal and financial services to the crown— as in Sweden, where military or financial service to the crown during the long period of heavy war commitments (1617–48) was increasingly rewarded by direct grants of noble titles and land. A similar trend was apparent in the Habsburg lands during the same period, and became more clearly apparent in Denmark after 1660, in Brandenburg-Prussia over the next century, and, less openly, in other parts of Europe.

Some governments, however, allowed simple sale of offices and titles (venality) to become an accepted means of social mobility. This had been established practice in the Papacy for some time, and also spread within the government of Castile in the later years of Philip II at the end of the sixteenth century. In 1611 James VI/I created a new order, the baronetcy, specifically in order to raise much-needed revenue, and he also allowed other titles to proliferate in ways that some contemporary critics regarded as corrupt. By the time of the assassination of one of the main profiteers, Buckingham, in 1628, venal titles had become so devalued that the practice had to be officially abandoned for a time—though private deals between individual state office-holders of course continued.

However, it was France that provided the most spectacular example of the impact of venality of offices both on the nature of government itself and on contemporary notions of social differentiation. Sale of offices and titles by the crown can be traced back at least to the fourteenth century, and had become a major part of the patronage and clientage system in France during the civil wars of the later sixteenth century. It was formalized in 1604 with the creation of the *paulette*, an annual payment to the crown which guaranteed the hereditary right of each office-holder to pass his office (like any other property) to his nominated heir without restriction. The *paulette* became one of those indispensable sources of regular income for the crown, which, like other tax farms, became too lucrative and convenient to be reformable. By the 1630s, revenue from the sale of titles and offices made up approximately one quarter of total state revenues, and although the market was as unstable as other parts of the French fiscal system, the long-term trend was one of expansion. By the 1690s, when renewed warfare had ensured that French state finances were as heavily over-committed as they had been during the 1630s, Louis XIV even had recourse to the sale of blank patents of nobility at 6000 *livres* each. A wide range of other offices came with a varied range of conditional or substantive noble entitlements, some taking gradual effect over a period of decades, others with specific privileges that could be accumulated selectively as part of a family strategy for preferment. Given the European-wide fascination with status and the minutiae of privilege, it is not difficult to see why this system was far too convenient to be terminated both for the state and for upwardly mobile wealthy members of society. Offices were attractive not necessarily for the power or duties they conferred (many offices were sinecures), but rather as a way of promoting long-term family strategies of upward social mobility, whereby offices, like land, became a form of hereditary property with significant cumulative effect on status. It is not surprising, therefore, that efforts to reform venality in 1618 and again in 1648 on both occasions precipitated significant political instability, and by the time Colbert took over financial management of the kingdom in the early years of Louis XIV's personal reign, all he could do was to try to limit the inevitable impact that venality of offices had on the crown's own freedom of manoeuvre. The system as such remained an integral, almost defining, feature of French high society until 1789.

Although France is the most striking, and best studied, example of the impact of sale of offices and titles in seventeenth-century Europe, we should resist the temptation to regard it as exceptional. In other parts of Europe social mobility into and within the elite may have been less obviously state-sponsored, but probably nearly as common, and certainly just as susceptible to the power of wealth. If we look at the rise and fall of factions at court and in local government, at the turn-over in landed estates over time, at the composition of all kinds of corporate bodies from the military to the law courts, at shifting networks within municipal politics and amongst the upper financial sectors, we almost always in western and central Europe find striking evidence of measured social mobility lubricated by wealth, of changing attitudes to privilege, and of extensive reliance on personal connections—with comparably complicated channels for the exercise of power. In short, social demarcation lines, at least in those parts of Europe with more complex political and corporate structures, were infinitely variable and subjective, and no longer determined solely (or even primarily) by birth.

To what extent these observations hold true of east central and eastern Europe is more questionable. In those regions of central Europe severely affected by the Thirty Years War (1618–48), notably Bohemia, patterns of landownership changed drastically in the 1620s and 1630s, as did seigneurial relationships both with peasants and with urban and manufacturing sectors. There, as in parts of Poland and East Prussia, economic dislocation tended to exacerbate rather than soften social distinctions, by weakening those mechanisms on which social mobility depended. Poland was unusual in that its monarchy was elective, and so there were recurrent opportunities for nobles (the *szlachta*, who constituted the electors) to make further demands to confirm their rights and privileges and even (from 1601) to gain sole control of the process of ennoblement itself. Nobles acquired not only the exclusive right to landed estates, local offices and higher ecclesiastical positions, but also considerable economic powers over both town and country. Market conditions encouraged large-scale grain farming, which in turn led to increased labour demands (resolved through increased serfdom) and reduced economic diversity.

Even so, social polarization here still fell far short of that in Muscovy, where both the law (formally codified in 1649) and the close alliance between the state and the orthodox church (fundamental until the reign of Peter the Great) confirmed an unusually rigid social hierarchy based partly on heredity, partly on service to the state. Precise rank was determined by the *mestnichestvo*, a detailed code of placement and precedence based on detailed genealogical claims and historic precedent. Its abolition in 1682 did not end obsessive status-consciousness within the Russian elite. The Petrine reforms of central government service, which ensured some degree of social mobility amongst non-nobles and for those foreigners who joined Russian service, may have tightened autocratic control of the central administration, but did not bridge deep social divides. For the vast mass of the Russian peasantry, the escalating demands of forced labour and military services for the state, compounding an already well-established system of serfdom and a lack of urban escape routes, guaranteed further deterioration. Travellers from the west who ventured this far may well have been right in seeing Russia as a fundamentally different society, based on levels of violence and social inequality exceptional even by their unsentimental standards.

Peasants, serfs and subservience

Dealing, as we are, with an age which had not yet begun to collect national statistics routinely—and which, despite significant quantitative work in astronomy, fiscal surveying and accounting, was only beginning to grasp the potential of political economy—we cannot hope to find much reliable data with which to summarize the broad conclusions of the previous section. But, depending on definition and locality, we might suggest that nobles made up around 1–3 per cent of the total population in England and France, slightly more in the German lands, and, because of widespread usurpation of noble rights, perhaps as much as 5 per cent in Spain and 8 per cent in Poland. Equally, most historians agree that those of peasant status and below constituted the vast bulk of the European population, probably 70–90 per cent depending on region. However, as with the elite, the term 'peasantry' describes not a cohesive and readily definable social category, but rather a broad spectrum of layers from wealthy landowning cultivators (notably in the regions of agricultural innovation in the Netherlands, parts of England and a few other pockets of development), through lesser tenant-occupiers and small-holders, to cottagers, foresters, landless rural labourers and migrant labour. Large-scale enclosed farming was gaining acceptance in parts of England, and in the very different circumstances of the serfdom-dominated grain belt of eastern Prussia and Poland. But even comparing Norfolk with Friesland reminds us that profitability was not necessarily contingent on large-scale production: given stability, the right market conditions, and well-judged use of local resources, modest holdings could provide significant prosperity and peasant autonomy.

For most of the seventeenth century, however, conditions were anything but ideal. The economy, marked by recurrent and disastrous harvest failures with far-reaching consequences (see p. 20), was markedly more unstable than during either the previous or the subsequent centuries. The worst crises, in the late 1640s and late 1650s, and again in the 1690s, were so protracted and devastating over large parts of the continent that recovery was a lengthy and costly process for peasants and landowners alike. To that cyclical instability most of the European governments added a rapidly escalating fiscal burden which necessarily hit the peasantry worst, and which left massive arrears during the relatively brief interludes of peace before 1618, in the 1660s and in part of the 1680s. Both economic instability and fiscal overloading had enormous repercussions on rural social relations.

Traditionally, rural society in early modern Europe has been described in terms of two opposing poles: an exploitative and repressive serf-based rural economy in eastern and east-central Europe on the one hand, and a supposedly 'free' peasant economy in the west. As a generalization, such a model may have some use, but it should not be swallowed uncritically. In parts of central Europe where serf and non-serf tenures co-existed, some of the most sought-after holdings could be those operating under serfdom. Equally, some of the tenure systems of the west, such as share-cropping in Brittany, resulted in conditions of unparalleled social oppression and unprofitability. The legal rights of 'free' peasants in the west were of little value when eroded by chronic debt—especially if such rights could not be tested in courts other than those staffed by appointees of the landowner. Even where peasants owned a significant proportion of their own land outright, as appears to have been the case in many parts of France, debts and market instability could make legal or contractual independence seem largely illusory. In Scandinavia, freehold status was comparatively easy to undermine in law, given the uneven power-distribution in the countryside and the near-universal lack of effective mediating powers by central government, even where fiscal interests were at stake. What really mattered, therefore, was not so much the theoretical framework based on law, but more the social-political context, and above all perhaps the economic reality.

We should not, however, assume that the interests of peasants and landowners were always incompatible. In the huge anti-fiscal revolts that became endemic in France in the 1620s and 1630s, landowners and sometimes even the church sided with their peasants against the arguments of 'necessity of state' proffered by the intrusive fiscal agents of the crown—most spectacularly so in the Croquant revolt of 1636–37 (at one stage engulfing most of the south-western quarter of the kingdom), and in the Nu-Pieds revolt in Normandy in 1639. Occasionally, as in Catalonia during the winter of 1639–40, a whole province united to throw off what was perceived as the unreasonable demands of a militarily hard-pressed central government. But once the power of central government recovered after the mid-century crises, peasant revolts not only became more sporadic, but also more likely to revert to their traditional local targets, the landowner and his agents.

As the incident recounted at the start of this chapter indicated, social relations were contingent on a number of different factors, not all of which are as visible as those that precipitated the major revolts of the seventeenth century. Friction between landowner and peasant, as between state and tax-payer, might have been minimized if expectations and obligations on both sides had been relatively clear-cut, but that is precisely what they were not. In eastern Europe, serfdom came about through a gradual process of erosion, the chronology and emphasis of which varied, depending on local circumstances. In Muscovy, for example, political pressures had brought about the elimination in the 1590s of the right of peasants to terminate their tenancy at a specific time of year. The law code of 1649 marked another clear stage in the consolidation of unrestricted seigneurial power, a process which ultimately left the Russian peasantry with nowhere to turn. This may have been the most extreme case of a mutual alliance between state and elite, but there are signs of a similar trend further west. At stake above all else were worries amongst landowners that they would be short of labour—worries that in many parts of Europe led to mounting restrictions on the freedom of movement of the peasantry. This could be achieved in part by controlling the legal machinery which would mediate over disputed tenancy contracts, thus potentially depriving the peasantry of impartiality in hearings. Equally, seigneurial control could be strengthened by raising individual demands on tenants in such ways as to make fulfilment of a contract more difficult. All over Europe, actual tenancy contracts, if they existed in writing at all, were couched in general terms. They usually included an obligation of obedience and subservience to the landowner, a succession fee related to the value of the holding being taken on, and a range of annual rental payments in kind and in money 'according to traditional custom', or some similarly imprecise phraseology. We know that, as the demands of the state on all levels of society increased, and as the economic environment remained unstable, landowners naturally tried to maximize profits. The most common way of doing that was to increase compulsory labour services on the demesne (manorial) land itself. The worst increases came in the eighteenth-century, but where we have usable data it is visible earlier as well, notably in Bohemia after the military defeat of 1620, and in Denmark after the end of war-time disruption in 1660. Labour demands triggered one of the largest peasant revolts in the later seventeenth century, affecting 129 estates in Bohemia in 1680. The Habsburg government tried to control the situation by introducing restrictions on maximum labour services, but here as elsewhere central government legislation proved unenforceable in the face of concerted landowner resistance to any attempts at interference in what they regarded as their property rights. Quite aptly, peasants in the Habsburg lands were commonly referred to as *Erbuntertanen*, hereditary subjects.

The early modern state was ill equipped to regulate or resolve tensions in rural society. Most of the churches, and especially the Lutheran one, encouraged deference and subservience, whilst offering little help when tensions flared up. Everywhere in Europe the crown itself was a landowner, and therefore unlikely to want to restrict seigneurial power even if it had had the means of doing so. Nevertheless, it is characteristic of the period that faith in the justice and fairness of the ruler seems to have been a universal belief across most of Europe—perhaps inevitably so, given the lack of alternatives. It is striking that even in Sweden, where after all the peasantry had their own representation as a fourth estate in the Riksdag (parliament), trust in the good intentions of the crown was maintained even when (as in the later years of Christina's reign up to 1654) such trust seemed misplaced. Elsewhere, rural communities with grievances often had no alternative but to try to appeal directly to the crown, but that carried risks of reprisals. Some peasant petitioners under pressure would claim they were illiterate and had not known what had been written on their behalf; to pre-empt reactions, others would adopt the more innovative strategy of attaching their signatures (or marks) in a neat circle at the bottom of the petition, so that it would be difficult for the authorities to pick out the ringleaders. To many, no doubt, the stability allegedly achieved with the consolidation of the military state must have seemed illusory.

Urbanization and social change

The seventeenth-century town was smelly, noisy, and, especially where old or where rebuilt military ring defences survived, over-crowded. Its crucial and arguably defining function as a market centre had led to an array of special economic regulations on trade and customs. Yet it probably deserved its contemporary reputation, relative to the countryside, as a place of opportunity and freedom. In central and western Europe most towns of any significance had acquired a measure of self-government and corporate autonomy which liberated them both from the feudal obligations and jurisdictions of the countryside and, at least to some extent, from the encroaching fiscal control of central government. The cyclical growth of urban economies and institutions through the late medieval and early modern period is beyond the scope of this chapter, as are some of the distinctive urban demographic patterns (see p. 13). But we would be missing a key aspect of social change if we did not recognize that, both during the Thirty Years War itself and during the period of consolidated absolutism after 1660, many cities acted not only as economic engines but also as structural innovators. The potential for this is most dramatically illustrated in the legendary vitality and social diversity of the towns and cities of the United Provinces. Of course they were heirs to a tradition stretching from the north Italian Renaissance cities to Antwerp and Bruges; but they also broke new ground in trade, finance, outward investment, economic specialization, and integration with the agrarian economy. It was not all a story of success: inland cities did not experience the same growth, and centres of textile production like Leiden and Haarlem became increasingly prone to pauperization and the social unrest often associated with proto-industrialization. Nevertheless, by the time the 'Dutch economic miracle' slowed down around 1675, urbanization embraced over 40 per cent of the population of the whole of the United Provinces, and perhaps as much as 60 per cent of the population of the province of Holland itself—several centuries in advance of any other part of Europe, and probably three times higher than, for example, England. Even if we allow for some imprecision both in the figures themselves (based on a variety of disparate information such as tax rolls and parish records), and in the somewhat artificial distinction of what constituted an urban settlement as opposed to a large village, these figures suggest that there were parts of Europe which had evolved well beyond the bounds of traditional social structures.

If the misleading term 'bourgeois republic' has any value for the seventeenth century, it might well be used to describe the great maritime city-states that retained a large measure of autonomy, notably Venice and Hamburg, but by extension perhaps also Amsterdam. Like all towns, these depended for survival on the careful control of supply networks for food, labour and raw materials: they can be said to have played a role in relation to their hinterland not unlike that of great landlords over their estates, and were certainly never open partners in their region. Nor, in terms of their internal government, were they remotely egalitarian communities. All three were run by fairly exclusive oligarchies of patrician families—those of Venice even claimed noble status—whose main concern was to protect the narrowly hierarchical structures of power in municipal government, in law and in the church, and down through the guilds and artisanal community.

What these three cities had in common, however, was an ability to exploit both the advantages of maritime trade and the confusion of contemporary politics to secure an exceptional level of stability and prosperity. Venice had the longest history of the three, and despite its demographic stagnation at around 140 000 people and its difficult adaptation to changing economic circumstances during the Thirty Years War, retained a legendary reputation for administrative efficiency, effective social policies and hence long-term internal stability. Amsterdam underwent much more rapid growth in the period after 1585, reaching a population of 175 000 by 1650. As the largest city in a loose confederation of provinces catapulted into a pivotal role in European politics, Amsterdam was never truly independent; yet for much of the time it either dominated the politics of the whole, or, as illustrated in the political crises of 1618, 1650 and 1672, defended its own interests with vigour. A surprising degree of consensus was nevertheless maintained within the city, partly because political awareness was widespread and relatively sophisticated, partly because the ruling elite seemed to remain reasonably open and accountable at least until 1672. That, initially, could hardly be said of Hamburg, but its survival as an independent city was even more remarkable. Its ability to ward off the political pretensions of Christian IV of Denmark, without falling under the control of any other belligerent in the Thirty Years War, ensured that it became virtually an island of prosperity in a sea of destruction, attracting craftsmen, musicians and shipping entrepreneurs from all over the German lands. Like Amsterdam, Hamburg also became a safe haven for a variety of religious refugees, including Jews from the Iberian peninsula and (especially after 1685) Huguenots from France.

The opposite end of the spectrum of urban change in this period is represented by the administrative centres of the main nation states. Capital cities as such were a recent invention, with Madrid perhaps one of the strangest examples of rapid urban growth based solely on the needs of a royal court, with little economic logic. Much the same could be said of Versailles, created nearly from scratch on marshy ground, and from 1682 the official setting of a highly theatrical court, utterly obsessed with social rank and patronage, and serviced by an impressive array of liveried attendants and ill-paid domestic workers. Usually, however, economic logic, social diversity and administrative importance went hand-in-hand, both for capital cities (London, Paris, Copenhagen) and for major regional centres (Leipzig, Naples, Lyons, Seville). Such composite growth created considerable potential friction between the needs and interests of families employed in administrative or military capacities on the one hand, and on the other, those of families primarily engaged in finance, trade and manufacture. In times of crises, such differences could have significant political repercussions, as in Copenhagen in 1660, when the city patricians and burghers allied with the king to displace the old military and administrative elite in favour of newer social groups more directly under royal control. That, however, did not diminish the overall numerical significance of administrative, military and court-related staff and their families in the city—estimated at 40 per cent of the total population a few years later.

London is perhaps the most striking example of a centre with critical economic as well as political functions. Like Paris, London doubled in size between 1600 and 1650, and passed the half-million mark in the second half of the century. It encompassed the whole social spectrum, from high nobility in attendance at court, senior lawyers and churchmen, through financial and merchant sectors with wide-flung interests, to broad manufacturing and service groups supported by a large labour market. It had a thriving cultural life, which not surprisingly was prone to open rivalry between court and city patronage networks—as seen in the periodic brawls between the city waits and the more specialized musicians in the pay of the highly artistic Charles I. It also had endless opportunity for individuals who felt driven to make their mark—whether as religious reformers, female artists, gentry politicians elected to parliament, aspiring writers, or (especially with the Restoration of 1660) purveyors of fancy new consumer goods like hot chocolate or oranges. Equally, as contemporaries were wont to complain, it provided the perfect hunting ground for pick-pockets, or the ideal camouflage for anyone who wanted to 'disappear'.

It may seem a statement of the obvious, but each town was a reflection of the society of which it was part. The importance of this may be more obvious if we turn briefly to the east. Towns in Muscovy and in Ottoman Europe lacked many of the characteristics of their western counterparts, serving primarily military and administrative needs rather than commercial ones. Townsmen in Muscovy, like other subjects of that state, lacked clear corporate autonomy and rights, and were closely bound by universal service requirements. Even when situated on potentially lucrative trade routes, they rarely acquired sufficient prosperity to attempt the limited autonomy of, for example, Königsberg in East Prussia (which in 1634 openly defied seigneurial demands not to shelter runaway serfs). In Poland-Lithuania, as in Hungary and other parts of east-central Europe, urban development had deeper historical roots, but was retarded during the seventeenth century by recurrent warfare and the tightening noble control which political instability frequently entailed. Not even great cities like Danzig and Cracow could rival the prosperity and diversity of their counterparts in the west.

Political domination of towns by the state, however, was not an exclusively eastern European phenomenon. Historians have noted persistent attempts by Louis XIV to reduce the independence of French towns, not only by making the most of the state's responsibility for barracks and local defences, but also by using his intendants to manipulate municipal government through appointments and the sale of offices, interfering in their fiscal self-government, and after 1673 even regulating guild structures. The Electors of Brandenburg-Prussia did much the same with their great cities, including Königsberg itself in 1662, or Magdeburg in 1680. Even the wealthy city of Frankfurt had to submit to external intervention in 1612 and 1614 as a result of on-going internal tension between a narrow ruling oligarchy and the broader merchant community demanding limited reform. In all, it is no coincidence that the most successful cities in Europe were either political capitals, benefiting from the side-effects of the growth of the state, or maritime ports whose prosperity enabled them to protect their political autonomy.

Poverty, vagrancy and crime

Shortly after the 1688 Revolution in England, Gregory King compiled a summary estimate of the total population of England and Wales, divided into 25 different social categories, each with indications of average family size and income. Based on carefully selected samples, his summary was intended to represent the social pyramid in 1688. Although some of his methods and calculations have been criticized, and his representation of social inequality may for various reasons be understated, King's estimate nonetheless represents a unique attempt at social quantification. Significantly, King included only one clear-cut horizontal division in his scheme, at the lowest end of the social scale: he divided the whole population between those whom he deemed to be 'increasing the wealth of the kingdom' and those 'decreasing' it—meaning, it seems, essentially those who were well enough to accumulate some savings, and those who were too poor. Amongst the latter were common seamen and soldiers, labourers, servants, cottagers, paupers and vagrants, all of whom had a yearly income of £20 or less—a figure which matches contemporary evidence from the overseers of the poor. What is striking is that these poor made up just over half his total population, and that the category which he describes as 'cottagers and paupers', with the lowest annual income of less that £7, alone made up nearly a quarter of the total population. Such a tally seems very pessimistic; but it is not out of line with other findings. King's contemporary, the military expert Vauban, who travelled throughout France on official duties, estimated that 10 per cent of the French population were beggars, another 50 per cent near-beggars, and another 30 per cent 'fort malaisés' (very badly off)—though admittedly this was in the 1690s, when severe economic dislocation had set in. Other types of evidence suggest that these estimates are not an exaggeration.

We should approach with considerable caution all apparently tidy quantitative summaries of the scale of poverty in early modern Europe. Not only are there serious problems of definition and quantification; more important still, the actual number of poor fluctuated wildly with changing economic circumstances. Given the results reached by any form of reckoning, however, no discussion of seventeenth-century society would be complete without recognizing the enormity of the task of effective relief. We may also be in a better position to understand why so much early modern legislation on vagrancy, begging and relief of the poor seems repetitive and unsympathetic—often representing no more than a routine reaction when a problem could no longer be ignored, and usually aiming to repress the symptoms of poverty rather than to address its causes. Every European country legislated against vagrancy, often insisting that vagabonds should be returned to their parish of origin, and if necessary whipped or branded to deter them from trying again. The traditional 'worthy' poor—those whose duly-registered illness, incapacity or misfortune made them suitable objects of charity—might be given assistance from collective relief-funds, but even they were not normally to beg except if they had a licence to do so. In Protestant Europe, all casual alms-giving was increasingly discouraged or even banned, the assumption being that community-organized voluntary relief would provide a more effective and fair assistance for those deemed to be in genuine need. Children would be apprenticed as soon as they were old enough, to help them secure gainful employment. Work was to be created for those who were sufficiently fit to be able to contribute towards their own keep.

This kind of legislative framework, repeated throughout most of Europe by the end of the sixteenth century, remained essentially unchanged until the eighteenth, but there were some significant variations. In England, for example, the Elizabethan poor law (an accumulation of separate acts) envisaged a compulsory poor rate levied locally on those who could afford it, to help finance relief within that parish whenever required. Although it took time for such a rate to win general acceptance, it was probably becoming effective in around half the parishes of England by mid-century, creating a sufficiently reliable funding structure for more complex relief organizations (like the Corporation of the Poor in London from 1649, which survived the Restoration). By 1696, according to the Board of Trade, the poor rate in England and Wales raised altogether £400 000 for a total population of 5.5 million. Alongside this official framework there were substantial private charitable initiatives, but how the two compared, either in terms of funding or in terms of priorities, is difficult to say because of the lack of reliable information on the private sector.

In Catholic Europe, the private charitable sector remained predominant, partly because there was a long-standing tradition of outdoor relief and of helping special groups of 'deserving' poor, partly because government intervention was generally ineffectual. In France, for example, the crown from 1662 required every city to establish a so-called general hospital (poor-house). This stemmed directly from efforts in 1656 in Paris to co-ordinate its institutional provision, itself an update of earlier efforts ranging from various sixteenth-century foundations to the Lyons poor-house of 1614. Despite the absence of any clear guidelines on funding, quite a number of new institutions were created in France. But although the decree of 1662 had aimed primarily at the deserving poor, these new institutions soon became dumping-grounds for all kinds of vagrants, and acquired reputations more like prisons than places of relief. The main targets were invariably individuals who were regarded as undesirable (beggars, vagrants, criminals, prostitutes); admission was rarely voluntary; the internal disciplinary regime was brutal, with some inmates deported; and in practice few of the institutions succeeded in providing any real care for the unfit, let alone training or work for the able-bodied. The creation of a new Police Council in Paris in 1666, one of whose tasks was to raid the criminal slums of the city, serves to illustrate the priorities of the government.

Contemporary understanding of the problems of poverty, it seems, continued to hinge on a distinction between the humanitarian and charitable needs of the worthy or deserving poor on the one hand, and on the other the importance of suppressing parasitic begging and idleness by allegedly 'unworthy' poor. There is little evidence at the time of any recognition of the importance of what we might call conjunctural poverty—impoverishment caused by the widely fluctuating unemployment or underemployment which was the inevitable result of the extreme instability of the economy. Although many governments were becoming aware of the frightening volatility of the price of basic foods like grain, there is little indication that anyone understood the enormous repercussions of unsteady grain prices on the rest of the economy (especially the vital proto-industrial textile sector). It was easier to blame begging and vagrancy on a supposedly criminal and idle underworld.

Government and local authority responses during the seventeenth century seem to amount to little more than a criminalization of conjunctural poverty. Nowhere do we see this more clearly than in the ubiquitous and eternally optimistic proposals for workhouses. The London Bridewell of 1555, the Amsterdam workhouse of 1596, and numerous similar institutions created in many European cities over the next decade, were all houses of correction designed to remove fit beggars and vagrants from the streets. Unlike the original intention behind the almshouses and general hospitals in France, they were never meant to provide care for the poor; rather, they were supposed to use the productive work of the inmates to achieve financial self-sufficiency. We do not have detailed records from the earliest of these workhouses, but better evidence exists for the period of economic crisis in the 1690s when various European cities had to review institutional provision. In Copenhagen, for example, we know that the workhouse had already in 1670 been given a priority right to supply the militia and the navy with cloth and finished uniforms, and in the late 1690s an entrepreneur of Flemish descent was given a ten-year lease of part of the workhouse building in order to modernize the cloth production there, with a view to employing up to 1000 inmates. He did at one stage manage to employ one quarter of that number, but even with the monopoly on army supplies he never broke even. A commission of enquiry in 1703 heard a well-known litany of woes, ranging from the untrainability and idleness of the inmates to the unpredictability of market forces. The experiment ended in protracted litigation, followed by another commission of enquiry into the whole system of poor relief. The implementation of its recommendations was interrupted by the outbreak of war in 1709.

Criminal records for the early modern period probably tell us more about the attitude of the authorities, the law-courts and the establishment than about the actual nature and types of criminality. Certainly, not all crime was related to poverty, and not all criminality was a form of social protest. Nevertheless, research completed so far suggests that petty theft in particular—though also influenced by a variety of other factors including army demobilization, certain forms of civil unrest, and the characteristics of particular communities— may have fluctuated in part in relation to short-term conjunctural economic instability. Theft and other property-related offences (such as trespass) remained by far the most common prosecutions in local law-courts, but most cases were opportunistic, non-violent and lacked any signs of planning or criminal organization. This may help explain why, despite the severe penalties in law for such offences, petty thieves who were known locally and demonstrated suitable deference when caught had a good chance of being let off lightly. Much of the recurrent legislation against vagrancy may in fact have been a routine reaction to the supposed criminality of the more mobile poor, whose lack of local connection made them easy targets of ostracism or prosecution, and afforded them little or no protection against being rounded up for forced labour or even deportation. In the larger urban communities petty crime may have tended to involve more violence, but the evidence is too incomplete to allow convincing conclusions to be drawn at this stage.

Riots and social control

In July 1647, the huge city and port of Naples was shaken by the first of several major popular revolts brought about by a shortage of food and the continued imposition of an unpopular tax on fruit. Charac- teristically, trouble broke out on 7 July, at the start of two consecutive religious festivals in honour of the Virgin Mary. As groups of youths prepared for a carnivalesque mock battle that was to have been the popular centre-piece for one of these festivals, the celebrations turned into a riot. After a ritual assault on the tax office, a young fisherman, Masaniello, emerged as leader, redirecting the rioters to a food store and then on to the viceroy's palace (which was sacked when he abandoned it to the rioters). Over the next few days, the violence escalated. Senior religious leaders tried to restore calm by initiating religious processions and displaying crucifixes and other images, but Masaniello won the support of part of the respectable city militia.

The joint force regrouped to sack the houses of a number of prominent individuals associated with the Spanish government. When an attempt was made against Masaniello's life the crowd turned more violent, carrying out the first of several ritualized executions. Masaniello was proclaimed Captain-General of the People, but when he was assassinated on 16 July his head, like those who had been lynched a few days before, was carried round the city on a pike. Only when the local authorities reduced the size of the regulatory loaf of bread was Masaniello transformed back into a popular hero and given an honourable funeral. Other groups of rioters now became involved, notably impoverished silk-workers and labourers from the surrounding countryside. As a result, the revolt became more overtly political, and when the Spanish authorities finally lost control late in October a republic was declared. Only in April of the following year was Spanish control of the city restored.

Despite inconsistencies and misrepresentations in the accounts of the first stage of this revolt, a number of significant features stand out, many of them characteristic of seventeenth-century rioting. The unrest in Naples was almost certainly inspired by the immediately prior riots in Palermo, which had involved attacks on government buildings, the opening of prisons and the temporary seizure of control by one of the rioters, an escaped convict. As in Palermo, unrest in Naples started with the ceremonial burning of the physical records in the tax office, seen as a way of notionally destroying all outstanding claims. The alleged participation of symbolically armed women (possibly disguised men) alongside the militia in the second phase of rioting was meant to emphasise the 'legitimacy' of the grievances, and perhaps to downplay its potential violence. Loaves of bread carried on sticks made an important grievance plain for all to see, as did the selective use of fruit. During the sacking of the houses of the local aristocracy, pillaging was sufficiently controlled for some of the furnishings to be given to the poor, to deflect accusations of theft. But we should also note some more striking elements. At one stage of the riots, portraits of the reigning monarch, Philip IV of Spain, were displayed alongside that of his 'good' ancestor, Charles V, to underline that the rioters respected 'good' government as such, and were attributing the current problems to particular abuses that had crept in. Equally, both sides tried to appeal to divine justice—the senior church leaders by hurriedly organizing processions with religious images, the rioters by seizing some of these symbols as their own, and in the subsequent weeks in fact winning the support of a significant part of the church. The rioters also had the active assistance not only of the city militia (mostly recruited from more comfortable elements in society) but also of various advisors with significant political experience. In other words, what started as a fairly common riot over specific grievances turned into a wider and more complex revolt supported by groups with significantly different concerns: the crisis became generalized.

The revolt in Naples has become famous amongst historians partly because of the richness of contemporary descriptions, allowing us a better insight into how a confrontation took shape. We have necessarily had to pass over much detail, but even in a summary account like this it is clear that neither Neapolitan social ideals nor apparent reality is easily reduced to tidy generalizations. As elsewhere in Europe, social stability was at best only skin-deep, and frustrations quick to boil over. That perhaps explains why so much effort was made everywhere to inculcate notions of deference, legitimacy and order. All over Europe, the churches invariably played a key role, even though their outward forms and activity varied greatly. Patronage of the arts and architecture was also part of the communication system, creating images—sometimes illusions—of power, wealth and grandeur. We see this in public buildings (including town halls, cathedrals, public squares and monuments), processions (like those sponsored in many Lutheran states to commemorate the Reformation of 1517), music (as in the public concerts organized by Buxtehude in Lübeck in the 1670s and 80s to mark the wealth and grandeur of that city), as well as official prints, court diaries and histories. Similar ideas lay behind the personal building projects of magnates and princes—the most famous of which was the building of Versailles, its dramatic approach roads, grand courtyards, formal gardens, statues and interior fittings all designed to impress. All princes, city patricians and local magnates adopted techniques of this kind, with varying intent and variable results. Not surprisingly, individuals followed suit on a level commensurate with their social standing, from the Duke of Buckingham down to Samuel Pepys, from the Amsterdam patrician to the parish priest. The daily importance to everyone of outward symbolism is perhaps most tellingly demonstrated in the detailed and frequently repeated sumptuary legislation, designed to restrict and finely gradate precisely what could be spent on weddings, funerals and personal attire in accordance with rank, status, wealth and accepted social convention—an attempt at social control which positively invited infringement and rivalry.

In accordance with the prevalent interpretation of Christian scriptures, what held civilized society together was a pervasive respect for authority. Western tradition dictated that that authority should be paternal. The prince would control and discipline his people in their own best interest, just as the head of a family would regulate and chastise his household—not as a tyrant bent on maintaining power, but as a benevolent yet firm father-figure. Paternal authority was always right in principle, and ultimately unchallengeable: everyone owed obedience to the head, not just as a practical means of preserving stability, but as a religious duty based on fundamental Christian precepts valid for all time. The legitimation of authority was fundamental to the ritual of anointment of a new prince, just as it figured in the investiture of lesser religious and secular offices. The first and most important prerogative of a reigning monarch was the power of judgment and pardon, from which stemmed legislative powers and the legitimacy of the whole legal system. Similar hierarchical notions of authority validated the priesthood and Catholic religious orders, and sustained the fundamental structures of nearly all the variant Christian churches until mid-century. By extension, secular and religious authority alike sanctioned the right of chastisement of the seigneur over his tenants, the master craftsman over his apprentices, the head over his wife, children and any other individuals who made up the commonly composite household groups of early modern Europe.

The use of 'reasonable force' in order to maintain such a patriarchal system must be one of the aspects of seventeenth-century society most out of alignment with modern liberal norms. The law, however, was quite clear in this respect. For example, the major Danish law code completed in 1683 made clear that 'a head of household may discipline his children and servants with a stick or strap, though not with a weapon; but if he wounds them with a sharp implement, breaks a limb or damages their health, then he is to be punished as if the damage had been inflicted by a stranger'. The very next clause stated that a wife had precisely the same rights over her children and servants. But elsewhere it was made clear that a wife who beat her husband, and harmed him, would be treated as if she had assaulted a stranger; whilst a husband who behaved 'in a tyrannical and unchristian fashion' towards his wife, and whose deeds were proven in law, was to be punished with forced labour 'or other severe punishment in accordance with his status and condition'. In practice, enforcement of such restrictions undoubtedly hinged on the tolerance or otherwise of the local community. There is evidence that husbands were sometimes brought to law for excessively violent behaviour towards their wives; lords and their bailiffs are also known to have been forced to account for gross violence towards their peasants. But we may be entitled to suspect that such rare cases have come to light only because they were so gross as to be impossible to cover up. And we should almost certainly remain equally unimpressed by the apparent absence of cases where parents were prosecuted for any violence against their own children that fell short of actual infanticide.

A high degree of violence was tolerated, condoned and even encouraged at all levels of society. It may have been most visible in the institutionalized violence of the mercenary armies and navies of the age, but corporal punishment could be equally brutal and degrading in civilian life. Nowhere were the demands imposed by social superiors subject to any significant restrictions or checks. The apparent cheapness of human life itself may perhaps in part be attributable to high mortality rates from disease, starvation and other factors. But seen in the context of contemporary intolerance of non-conformity of any kind (whether religious, behavioural, intellectual or any other), it also suggests that the interests of the individual were habitually subordinated to those of the community or neighbourhood as a whole. In the absence of any publicly accountable authority to maintain law and order, enforcement was commonly the prerogative of each community, or of the vigilante volunteers within it—often bands of youths who inflicted humourous or humiliating *charivaris* on their targets, harassed individuals who transgressed local customs or unspoken norms, and enforced the pervasive gender and age stereotyping of the age.

Alternative ideologies: the world turned upside down?

So far, the emphasis has been on the predominant balances that tended to restore society to normality even after serious upheavals. Most people, if they had a concept of overall social and economic change at all, would have seen it in terms of generational shifts—or at best would have sought the return of some past ideal, or perhaps scriptural precept, rather than welcoming change for its own sake. Those few religious radicals who dared to think the unthinkable were often rejected by contemporaries—as had happened to Michael Servetus as well as Giordano Bruno, both burnt at the stake, one in 1553 in Calvin's Geneva and the other in 1600 in Counter-Reformation Rome. These two thinkers influenced the undercurrent of intellectual scepticism which continued into the early seventeenth century, though neither could have foreseen the extraordinary outburst of radical and iconoclastic ideas which transformed England (and to a much lesser extent France and some other parts of Europe) in the 1640s and 50s.

The English civil war, revolution and commonwealth was by far the most substantial social and political upheaval anywhere in seventeenth-century Europe. It will be apparent (p. 22) that its impact was magnified by the economic instability that rocked so many parts of Europe in the later 1640s. Its consequences in terms of the structures of state are examined elsewhere (p. 90): here it will suffice to note that some of the most radical ideas came to light precisely because civil war itself raised significant questions about the nature and quality of government, especially once parliament had entered uncharted territory in its open confrontation with Charles I. Already in 1641, the poet John Milton (1608–71) had attacked the established church for its narrowness. He continued with a tract in favour of divorce as the only humane answer to the irrecoverable breakdown of marriage (1643), a tract advocating freedom of the press (1644), another in 1649 justifying revolution by the people, and two expositions (1651 and 1656) of the principles of government by contractual consent between state and people. He also exercised considerable influence on a group of younger writers, including Dryden,

Marvell and James Harrington. Milton's contemporary, Thomas Hobbes (1588–1679), adopted a less partisan approach in his massive work *Leviathan* (1651), a careful exploration of the nature of sovereignty which he wrote while he was in exile from war-torn England. More conservative writers, by contrast, exploited the trial and execution of Charles I to proclaim the king's 'martyrdom', whilst warning contemporaries against the threat of real social revolution and anarchy.

Historians have argued at length about the impact of such new ideas, and the extent to which either conservatives or radicals made much impression against mounting war-weariness and disillusionment in civil war England. We are unlikely ever to reach definitive conclusions on this, but if we restrict our assessment solely to those movements that appear to be of long-term significance, we shall miss the point. The Leveller movement, for example, had a recognizable identity for only three years (1646–49). During that time, they demonstrated the potential for agitation both in the rank and file of the parliamentarian armies, and amongst London artisans, journeymen and tradesmen concerned about the lack of effective political leadership in a period of acute economic instability. Leveller leaders such as John Lilburne, Richard Overton and William Walwyn sought to create something genuinely new from the unprecedented uncertainty of the time. Not without justification, they criticized the parliamentary tyranny that had replaced royal government. Their religious egalitarianism provided the basis for ideas of freedom and self-government based on universal general principles of natural rights for men and women alike. In the three Agreements of the People (published between November 1647 and May 1649) they laid out the principles for an accountable republican government based on an explicit contract, to be endorsed by all citizens in frequent parliamentary elections. They sought to restrict the powers of parliament itself, so as to ensure that some reserved rights (including religious toleration and equality before the law) could never be undermined. They also advocated what appears to be near-universal manhood suffrage—though there is some ambiguity in their language which no doubt reflects significant disagreement within the movement itself. Perhaps most important in the present context, however, is the fact that the Levellers made good use of political meetings and of the press to secure as wide an appeal as possible, recognizing that different types of audiences needed different emphases and levels of explanation. It is not difficult to understand why, when mutinies occurred in the armed forces in May 1649 over arrears of pay, the political leadership around Cromwell used the occasion to crush the Leveller movement.

Post-revolutionary England was a military state, but radical ferment did not disappear overnight. Oliver Cromwell does not deserve all the criticisms made against him, and he was certainly not the most intolerant politician of his time. During the 1650s, Leveller ideals were taken up by various other groups. Some, like the Ranters and Muggletonians, may never have existed as an identifiable and proselytizing movement as such: perhaps they served primarily as scarecrows, and as targets for legislation such as the Blasphemy Act of 1650. Others, like Gerrard Winstanley's Diggers, triggered immediate reprisals when they tried to create an egalitarian communal settlement. The Fifth Monarchists seem to have concentrated mostly on their apocalyptic visions of what might be. One group, however, will serve better than most to illustrate the potentially revolutionary social ideas of this period: the Quakers. They had a much broader base, bringing in northern England, and may have reached a total membership of 50 000 by 1659. Their profound disregard for social convention and customary deference seemed to threaten the whole fabric of hierarchical society. They did not need churches or ministers for worship, they recognized no external authority, and they recognized no social rank. In their religious services women were as free to speak spontaneously as men, and the Quakers even rejected that women were naturally subject to male authority. Their deep religious faith in the 'inner light' seemed, to their critics, a supremely irresponsible invitation to religious and social anarchy.

How far the Quakers were a major factor contributing to the reversion to monarchy in 1660 is still open to debate, but the movement survived as a reminder of what might have been. Whilst Restoration England seemed to brush much of the overt activism of the interregnum under the carpet, some of the fundamental questions remained unanswered. One of the influential soldiers who took part in the crucial Putney debates in October 1647, Colonel Thomas Rainsborough, had highlighted the need for English electoral reform with the ringing phrase that:

The poorest he that is in England hath a life to live as the greatest he; and therefore truly, sir, I think it's clear, that every man that is to live under a government ought first by his own consent to put himself under that government; and I do not think that the poorest man in England is not at all bound in a strict sense to that government that he hath not had a voice to put himself under.

Neither the social nor the political implications of such a contract between state and subject were worked out for more than a century—and we can understand why, after the Restoration of 1660, John Locke and the Dissenters were more careful about what they said, and how they said it. But the very fact that such words were spoken at all, in the 1640s, gives us a brief glimpse of what lay beneath what others would have preferred to see as a calm surface.

Conclusion

Social change is nearly always slow, and the seventeenth century is in this respect no exception. Because of the political and economic instability especially of the period up to 1660, we may be tempted to look for a crisis of the aristocracy, the emergence of a 'second serfdom' in east-central Europe, or the emergence of a new capitalist society in the north-west. We may point to the growing bureaucracy of the military state to explain the blurring of social barriers between nobles and wealthy non-nobles, or we may attribute the vitality and fluidity of urban growth to governmental non-interference and political autonomy. Each of these ideas has generated lively discussion amongst historians in recent years, and has added something to our understanding of the period; but each has also succumbed to a host of qualifications that illustrate how difficult it is to generalize convincingly on such a vast scale. In reality neither the basic assumptions of hierarchical social inequality, nor the deep and pervasive polarity between rich and poor changed significantly between the Reformation and the late Enlightenment. What did change was the economic balance within Europe—against east-central Europe and the Mediterranean, towards the north-west—and, with it, the pattern of social expectations and relationships within each community. When such changes coincided with major political upheavals, as was the case in much of Europe in the 1640s and 1650s, the outcome could be dramatically revealing.

As the Neapolitan revolt of 1647 shows, riots and civil unrest were often inspired by fairly traditional expectations. But the truly extra-ordinary social demands brought out by the extreme conditions of the English civil war remind us that a few contemporaries were capable of thinking the unthinkable. Equally, the reaction in 1660 indicates that change on such a scale was premature, and far beyond the limits of what those in power could countenance—the urgency of political restoration and reconstruction a clear sign of a closing of ranks amongst those with something to lose.

The return to order was almost certainly broadly welcomed by the vast majority of the European population, for whom stability was the best hope. The traditional order depended on a large pool of cheap labour, and resigned itself to recurrent crises of acute poverty and unemployment which seemed impervious either to charity or to remedial administrative action. It also depended on the recognition of mutual self-interest at the top, and effective exercise of control further down. Traditional religious beliefs continued to provide plenty of material with which to reinforce social deference and sub-servience, all the more so in a society accustomed to conformity, intolerance and the overt use of force. Where necessary, the ties of family and kinship, the orderly functioning of a neighbourhood or parish, and respect for traditionally defined vertical and horizontal loyalties could help defuse conflicts. The absolutist tax state emerging as the norm in Europe during the second half of the century, in so far as it had much impact at all on society as a whole, seems to have had enough fiscal, military and institutional strength to offer reasonably plausible incentives to those elements in society whose co-operation and consensus ultimately mattered.

3

Politics

Anthony Upton

The political structure of Europe in 1600

The outstanding characteristic of the European political system in 1600 was diversity. Politically it was a collection of independent political entities in a state of permanent competition. This was driven by the dominant military culture, which had made Europe's history one of incessant warfare. The acquisition of additional lands by making war had always been the main preoccupation of Europe's rulers. Europe was also an old and mature society built round a common religious culture, and still commonly defined by contemporaries as Christendom. The world was perceived as God's creation, following an historical course mapped out from the beginning in the mind of the Creator. The original Garden of Eden had been lost by the sin of Adam, which tainted all his descendants, so that all men and women were sinners and deserved damnation. The sacrifice of Christ for the sins of mankind gave a hope of salvation, which would be resolved at Judgement Day. God had ordained civil society, and provided that it be ruled by kings, priests and magistrates, so that the natural wickedness of mankind should be restrained and the work of salvation proceed. All lawful authority derived from God and was exercised by divine right. God's order was hierarchical, a favourite metaphor was 'the Great Chain of Being', and patriarchal, the model of authority was that of absolute power of a father over those entrusted to his care. The concept made sense because it corresponded with the reality of most men's lives (see chapter 5). The patriarchal values were learned in daily life, preached in the churches, emphasized by public ceremonial, built into the educational processes. No alternative world view was presented publicly. The society was indoctrinated into a divinely ordained culture of deference which made it, in normal circumstances, comparatively easy to govern.

In Europe, power was widely diffused. At the top of the chain of authority, literally hundreds of spiritual and secular lords claimed sovereign authority, that is they acknowledged no earthly superior but God, and were therefore possessed of absolute authority over all their subjects by divine right. A ruler was usually advised and assisted by a council, and in addition, employed two specialized groups of administrators, one judicial and one financial. It was the duty of every lord to dispense justice to his subjects, and there was a wide variety of systems. Most lords also had a financial institution, a Chamber or Treasury, to collect and account for their revenues. Looking at administrative machinery as a whole, what is striking is how small the number of professional officials was, and how amateurish the administration tended to be. This was possible because of the very high level of devolution of authority. In a world where rulers could not afford to finance professional administrations for their realms, they had no choice but to let groups of their subjects come together in collective institutions, which were largely self-administering, self-financing, and highly competitive with one another. Wherever feudal jurisdictions survived, which they did over most of Europe, they meant that large groups of subjects were to a greater or lesser extent excluded from the central authority. A feudal magnate could exercise more power over his tenants than the king who was his overlord. Devolution extended right down through society, the church had extensive governmental responsibilities, towns were usually self-governing corporations, and guilds and merchant corporations, authorized by the rulers, controlled much of the community's economic life. On the lowest level the village commune, through meetings of heads of households and its elected officers, ordered daily life in the countryside. By 1600 these self-governing institutions were being modified by a general trend towards an oligarchic concentration of power. Decision making was passing from general assemblies to select groups, usually of the wealthiest members, who directed internal policy and appointments to office. Europe was increasingly concentrating power into the hands of elite groups, who constituted a very small proportion of the total population. These privileged elites had a fundamental common interest in preserving the social order, and mutually supporting each other's claims to authority. They were creating the basis for the development of a self-conscious ruling class with a distinct culture that divided them from the common people.

It is a feature of devolved systems that the groups to whom power is delegated tend to engage in fierce mutual competition among themselves to improve their relative power and influence. This was a universal feature of European societies and could obstruct orderly administration. It was a function of the ruler to prevent this. From his duty to dispense justice to subjects, he developed the role of arbiter over their disputes. Rulers had a powerful tool in the patronage they dispensed. They could make appointments to local positions of influence, they could often grant titles and confer privileges, which would raise the local status of a corporation or individual. Hence the exercise of the ruler's authority could be decisive in determining the outcome of local rivalries. Normal politics in these societies was usually not about policy, for on that there was consensus, but about patronage, access to property, office, privilege, that could give the group or individual a competitive edge over rivals.

Much the most effective way of securing the intervention of the ruler was by direct personal contact, and this was achieved through his household or court. That made rulers' courts market-places of patronage and influence. The system led naturally to politics by faction, succesful courtiers attracted followings of clients, through whom they could develop local power bases, that would in turn enhance their usefulness to the ruler. The result was that early-modern governments worked through negotiated consensus between the ruler and his elites. Power and influence were traded up and down the hierarchy at all levels, government and administration proceded by the multiple exchange of favours between the power-holders. For the great majority of subjects who had no power of any consequence, it meant exclusion. In theory the ruler could exercise an absolute power conferred by God, in practice it could not be done.

The problem of the Reformation

The Reformation had left European societies facing the challenge of religious pluralism, which existed almost everywhere north of the Mediterranean zone of Italy and the Iberian kingdoms and south of the Baltic. It was an unacceptable state of affairs for it challenged the existing power structures. A subject who differed in religion from his superior broke the Chain of Being by asserting a right to disobey, and claim his resistance was legitimate. Governments all over Europe equated religious dissidence with political opposition and sought to eliminate it, strengthened by the obvious fact that it was their religious duty. The dissident was not just defying his lawful superior, he was defying God. God would certainly visit His wrath on societies that tolerated schism and heresy. So the Spanish Habsburgs successfully cleansed the southern Netherlands of Protestants, who converted or emigrated. Richelieu founded his political career by waging war on the Huguenots and after the siege of La Rochelle in 1629 disarmed and neutralized them. In England Charles I in the 1630s used the authority of government to drive puritan dissidents out of the Church of England. Above all the great war that ravaged central Europe from 1618 to 1648 arose from this same potent connection of the religious to the political. No rulers were more harassed by the problems of religious pluralism than the Vienna Habsburgs. As territorial princes, their patrimony was deeply penetrated by Protestantism among nobles and burghers, as emperors their authority was paralysed by the confrontations of the confessional groupings, institutionalized in the hostile military alliances of the Evangelical Union and the Catholic League. It happened that the trigger for the conflict came from Bohemia, a broadly Protestant society, where the elites had struggled to limit the authority of their Catholic king, while the Habsburg rulers had tried to use the Catholic minority in order to extend their power over the kingdom. When the Bohemians were faced in 1618 with the imminent accession of the next Habsburg heir, Archduke Ferdinand of Styria, a notoriously militant, counter-reformation Catholic, the Estates renounced their allegiance and invited the Calvinist Elector Palatine to assume the crown of Bohemia. Ferdinand who had already been elected king of Bohemia had little choice but to take up the challenge.

There is no better illustration than the Thirty Years War of how war is the great driving force of history, or how once started it acquires its own momentum, far beyond the control of the combatants. The system of waging war through private contractors, like Wallenstein, unleashed forces that governments could not fully control (see chapter 4). The initial success of the Catholic Imperialist forces, starting from the battle of the White Mountain in 1620 which crushed the Bohemian rebellion, fed the belief, expressed in the Emperor's issue of the Edict of Restitution in 1629, that confessional unity could be restored in the Empire by force. Now the interconnection of religion and politics brought its own nemesis. The power that such a triumph would vest in the Habsburgs stimulated the fears of Protestant rulers generally, and also of the Catholic princes in the Empire, whose autonomy was endangered, and the Catholic king of France and his minister, Richelieu. This facilitated the dramatic intervention of the Swedish king, Gustavus Adolphus, which turned the tide of military success—though only to create a destructive military stalemate. The Peace of Westphalia, as the product of the first pan-European peace congress, confirmed that the Reformation could not be reversed. Religious pluralism was to be a fact of European life, and rulers would have to learn to take account of this when pursuing the struggle for status and power.

The pressures of war: Richelieu and Olivares

The Thirty Years War demonstrated that the existing political systems could not cope adequately with the demands put on them by advances in the practice of war. The debate over the European 'military revolution' belongs in another chapter (chapter 4), and is still in progress, but all agree that it significantly increased the costs of war. Rulers found it difficult to raise additional revenue and services from their subjects, since the devolved power systems required any adjustments to be negotiated. There was awareness of the problem, which generated a reform agenda. In Spain it inspired public discussion among the *arbitristas*, members of the ruling elites who advanced projects for increasing the public revenues, and rationalizing the structures of government. Similar suggestions were raised in France in the last Estates General of 1614, and the Assembly of Notables in 1627. It was also realized in both kingdoms that for changes to be implemented, there needed to be a period of peace. That was the argument of the Catholic *dévot* faction led by the Keeper of the Seals, Marillac, against Richelieu's programme and of those in Madrid who argued for renewing the Truce in the Netherlands in 1621. Attempts to implement reform by negotiation among the elites were uniformly fruitless. They foundered on the profound conservatism of societies whose members believed the traditional order was divinely sanctioned, and more importantly the force of localism. Most people lived out their lives within the framework of their local community—village, town, province. Their prime allegiance was to the local community. Proposals involving sacrifice of local interests and immunities, in order to strengthen central authority evoked negative responses. This was apparent in France in 1614, and again in 1627: Estates were eloquent in identifying things that needed changing, but sectional interests among the elites prevented agreement about how to achieve this, since any proposal involved some sacrifice and redistribution between the elites. A reform of the system by mutual consent was outside the realm of practical politics.

Change would have to be imposed, and experiences of the chief ministers of the two main protagonists in the European power struggle, Cardinal Richelieu in France and the Count-Duke of Olivares in Spain can illustrate the process. In his *Mémoires*, Richelieu described his project as a politics based on rational, informed analysis, pursued by a strong central government with power to call on the full resources of the whole society. Sectional privileges of feudal nobles, provincial *parlements* and Estates which stood in the way, must be sacrificed for the common welfare. Richelieu can easily be seen as a modern politician, because he thought realistically in terms of power. But he knew that in his world, power was personal. His power was derived from his personal relationship to Louis XIII, who came to accept that Richelieu was the necessary man to handle his kingdom's affairs. But the king could have destroyed his minister at any time. Richelieu needed a personal power base, and it is an historical irony that a statesmen who claimed to have abolished the power of over-mighty subjects, became one himself. At his death, Richelieu was far the wealthiest man in the kingdom, he had built up significant territorial power bases in the provinces, through an accumulation of lands and offices and client networks. He pushed his family and supporters into the key administrative positions. Through marriage alliances, he constructed a family connection with some of the greatest noble families in the land. These policies had nothing modern about them, and contributed little to creating a reformed state, whatever his propaganda suggested. The family and client networks gave him the essential leverage for getting things done. There was some rationalization of the central royal secretariat, some increase in departmental specialization, some introduction of regular bureaucratic routines. His best known initiative, the appointment of royal commissioners, *intendants*, with plenipotentiary powers to inspect and enforce the royal will in the provinces, seems to have emerged as an unplanned pragmatic development. Above all, Richelieu deliberately refused to involve himself in public finance. The core of the modern state is the establishment of orderly budgeting: Richelieu's government survived on unplanned fiscal expedients, permanently on the edge of bankruptcy. No modern state emerged in France, what was achieved was a triumphant demonstration of the power of the will by a gifted and ruthless political operator. Richelieu committed Louis XIII to a dynastic power struggle against the Habsburgs, and held him to it, while using every kind of coercion and persuasion to extract from French society the resources this demanded. The old structure of powerful magnates, a venal bureaucracy, sovereign *parlements* and provincial diversity and privilege survived intact.

The Count Duke of Olivares, *privado* to Philip IV, making him the official guardian of access to the sovereign, had comparable ambitions and even less success. He seemed to start from a better position. The Iberian kingdoms enjoyed religious unity, the politics of aristocratic magnates challenging the royal government belonged to the past. The lead kingdom, Castile, already had central bureaucratic councils, staffed by noble, university trained administrators. There was also a tradition of open political debate, carried on by the *arbitristas*, which discussed the perceived structural weaknesses in the monarchy, and suggested reforms. Olivares shared their concerns, and on taking office had launched a range of measures designed to improve the effectiveness of government and the welfare of the community. In this programme, moral reform, of manners, personal conduct, excess expenditure, came first. The priority was to keep the kingdom right with God, for that was what mattered in the end. Everything came back to Providence, without divine approval no worldly policies would succeed—Olivares and his king had a traditionalist mentality. It was even more significant that the programme came to nothing, the machinery for giving effect to it did not exist. The central bureaucracy was intensely conservative and unenthusiastic for change, while the extent of devolution of local administration in the kingdoms left central government without the agencies needed to enforce it. Olivares was consistently driven to seek to bypass existing machinery by setting up ad hoc commissions, *juntas*, to secure compliance. Finally Olivares himself conceded that internal reform took second place to the resumption of the war, when the truce in the Netherlands expired in 1621. The honour of the dynasty demanded that the United Provinces be compelled to return to their allegiance. Olivares and Richelieu were agreed that the honour, reputation, and status of the ruler must be maintained and enhanced at all costs, and took precedence over all other considerations. In a world built on hierarchy and status, that was obvious.

There was no kingdom of Spain, there were only the three kingdoms of Castile, Aragon and Portugal who shared the same Habsburg ruler. They were completely sovereign, with their own governments, laws, currencies. Olivares could see how this prevented the king from generating the full power of his kingdoms, and envisaged working towards union with the eventual aim of, 'one faith, one law, one king'. Unlike Richelieu, Olivares was very conscious of the importance of orderly budgeting. They would begin by pooling resources to sustain the current round of warfare and he proposed a programme of contributions of men and money for the common war effort, the burdens of which fell disproportionately on Castile. In return for common contributions, the subjects of all the kingdoms should have equal access to offices and patronage. From this intermingling he expected that in time the fuller union would develop. The scheme was entitled the Union of Arms, and extended beyond Iberia to the American colonies, the Italian possessions and the Netherlands. The plan was put to the prospective participants and aroused no enthusiasm at all. The Castilians had no desire to admit foreigners to share in their public offices, particularly the lucrative posts and commercial rights in the empire. The others, who under existing arrangements carried lighter burdens than Castile, were naturally opposed. The underlying concept of an eventual full union got a negative response, it was a novelty that all feared would be the destruction of their age-old liberties and privileges, and they saw no merit in its proposed objective. Catalonia, a dependency of the kingdom of Aragon, actually refused outright to consider the plan. The others agreed to consider it, and negotiated face-saving compromises which fell far short of Olivares' proposals. Still he could claim in 1626 that in principle the idea had been accepted.

The war had gone well for the Habsburgs at first, concealing how seriously their resources were over-extended. This was dramatically exposed in 1628 when the Dutch captured or destroyed the year's treasure fleet, which had carried the security for the bankers advances that paid the Spanish armies. From that point the situation for Olivares steadily deteriorated. He was trapped, there was no way the commitments could be reduced without humiliating admissions of defeat. In the late 1630s he sought to revive the Union of Arms and make a reality of it. This time he was prepared to use force to drive it through and failed. The outcome was the twin revolts of 1640, when first Catalonia and then Portugal renounced their allegiance to the Habsburgs, and added internal warfare within Iberia to all the other existing war fronts. The attempt to force modernizing reforms on the communities from above had failed.

Protest, rebellion, revolution: a mid-century crisis?

Occasional popular protests, accompanied by some degree of violence, were endemic in European societies. These were generally directed at specific local problems, and did not challenge the legitimacy of the established order. They could be settled by concessions, which were commonly reneged on later, with some symbolic executions of selected ringleaders if they could be found. In the 1630s and 1640s, when the pressures of war drove rulers to make new demands on their subjects, popular protests rose to unusual levels, as in the provincial revolts in France which dogged the ministries of Richelieu and Mazarin.

Historians have attempted to see in the wave of unrest a 'general crisis', and the debate on this continues. The main factors arguing against linkage are the reality that the disorders remained specific to local circumstances, even where they coincided in time: they did not coalesce into broader movements. Above all, the demands of the rebels did not challenge the legitimacy of rulers, but sought restoration of customary norms, which was true even of the Portuguese rebellion, aimed at replacing the Habsburg ruler by a member of the Braganza family that had ruled before 1580. Most recent studies of these events show repeatedly that their seriousness depended on the response of the elites. If local elites, town corporations or landlords, saw the measures of the rulers as a threat to their interests, for instance upsetting traditional local power structures, they might refuse to assist in restoring order, even covertly encourage the protests, and then unrest could develop into a serious challenge to government. Catalonia and Portugal were spectacular examples of this, with major political consequences. But in most cases the local elites knew where their interests lay, and would negotiate settlements with the ruler, bargaining for concessions, after which, if the unrest continued, the elites would assist in a restoration of order. All the revolts failed to change the existing power structures because conceptually, the rebels recognized the legitimacy of their rulers, as sanctioned by God. Because the rebels had no political alternative to propose, early modern societies, while they retained credible divine approval, were proof against revolutionary overthrow.

An example of this was found in the Fronde that seemed to threaten the French monarchy in 1648–53. At the end of five years of savage civil wars and general mayhem, the Bourbon monarchy emerged stronger than ever. The context was exceptional, for royal authority was weakened by the minority of Louis XIV. A government run by a foreign queen mother and an Italian adventurer lacked the authority of an adult sovereign. The trouble began when government tax measures seriously threatened the interests of the officers who staffed the central sovereign courts, led by the *parlement* of Paris, which were the main agency by which royal authority was enforced over the kingdom. The settlement of 1649 between the officers of the courts and the crown, did promise abandonment of obnoxious policies pursued under Richelieu and Mazarin, and some general promises for the future of a stricter adherence to traditional legal norms by the monarchy and its agents: for example the use of *intendants* to subvert normal channels of government was to cease. With these paper gains, the magistrates were ready to resume their role as upholders of royal authority. They were fearful that their populist allies, who had held Paris for them, might get out of hand. The other phase of the Fronde was an assertion by aristocratic magnates, like Orléans and Condé, of a right to share in the control of government and patronage. It was not in the interest of these men to destroy royal authority. They wanted a strong monarchy with themselves in control of it. So relations with their commoner and elite allies were always strained, and in the end they could be bought off individually. It is noteworthy how the rebellious magistrates and magnates resisted calls from the petty-backwoods nobility to recall an Estates General. They had no interest in power sharing, except within their own exclusive circle. The Frondes changed nothing—the word, meaning a popular children's game was an appropriate label. During the Fronde there was free political discussion, and hundreds of polemical tracts and pamphlets were published, but these offered no plausible alternative system of government. The revolutionary events in Britain, culminating in regicide, were regarded with horror by nearly all the participants in the Fronde.

The English revolution, 1640–60

The dramatic events in the British Isles in this period were clearly different. There were exceptional circumstances: the English parliament, with its elected House of Commons, and legislative sovereignty, gave the local communities an institutional voice in policy making. The maintenance of a broad political consensus was necessary to the working of the system. Further the English monarchy was seriously underfunded and dependant on supplementary supply, that could be voted only through parliament. But most historians are now agreed that there was no inevitability about the political crisis of the 1640s. The prevailing consensus was put under strain by the accession of a foreign ruler, James VI and I, unfamiliar with the working of the system. But James was an experienced politician, and by nature a conciliator, and in the last parliament of the reign in 1624, came to terms with his critics in a renewed consensus. The political system in England clearly had problems, but these were negotiable until the accession of Charles I in 1625. He was an unusually inept political manager, with a personal agenda at odds with the views of important groups within the elites. This did cause an acute confrontation between a broad opposition faction, led by a section of the peerage and their clients among the gentry, merchants and clergy, which used parliament to attempt to force their political agenda on the king. They failed in this, and in attempts to put effective legal restraints on royal powers through the Petition of Right in 1628. Instead, in 1629, the king openly decided to dispense with parliaments and demonstrated that, by exploiting the full executive powers of the crown, a working government could be sustained. There was no revolution in sight in 1639.

But there were dangerous religious disagreements within English society. The deliberately ambivalent Elizabethan settlement of religion had left a church that was doctrinally Protestant, but retained the institutional framework of the pre-Reformation church. From its inception there had been a committed Protestant minority who aspired to complete a full Protestant reformation—the Puritans. They often coalesced with a broader anti-clerical strain of criticism, that wanted to increase lay control over ecclesiastical affairs, and perhaps proceed to further secularization of church property. What made dissent dangerous was another ingredient, English anti-popery. This grew from a belief that Rome was endlessly scheming to subvert England, God's elect Protestant nation, and bring it back to Rome. This mythology of the popish plot lay deep in the English psyche by 1600. It proved fatal for the king that his foreign and ecclesiastical policies could be plausibly linked to the plot scenario.

The revolutionary crisis was, beyond question, the result of miscalculation. Charles provoked it by extending his church reforms to Scotland, to establish religious convergence between his two kingdoms. The attempt caused the Scottish Covenanter rebellion of 1638. Since the English parliament refused him assistance in repressing the Covenanters, the king was defeated and the English Long Parliament met in November 1640 under the protection of the victorious Scottish army, and quickly dismantled the machinery of the king's authoritarian rule. This secured his English subjects from revival of the regime of the 1630s, but created deadlock over the future of the government. For the king conceived he had been deprived of his sovereign rights by illegal violence, and he had a religious duty to recover his lost authority whenever opportunity offered. This made all compromise with the king worthless and restoration of a consensus impossible.

The programme of the parliamentary leaders, set out in the Grand Remonstrance of November 1641 and the Nineteen Propositions of

June 1642, proposed subjecting the royal powers to control by the two Houses of Parliament, leaving the king a merely titular role. Since the king openly refused to contemplate such a solution, the ensuing deadlock could only be resolved by force. The trigger was the Irish catholic rebellion of 1641, which compelled the raising of an army, which by law would be under royal command. The parliamentary leaders could not permit that, and in the Militia Ordinance of 1642, asserted the right to override the constitution, and as representatives of the whole community, to take their own measures of defence. When the king rightly asserted the illegality of this and appealed to the subjects to assist him to put down open rebellion, civil war followed.

The British civil wars had no revolutionary political programme. Both sides were committed to restoring traditional government by king, lords and commons. Their radical content developed from the necessity of war itself, the need to avoid defeat at any price and from religious forces. In Scotland and Ireland this was obvious, the Scots' interventions were geared to safeguarding their Presbyterian kirk, the Irish from realization in the majority Catholic community that the British conflicts were an opportunity for overthrowing Protestant settler rule. In England, both sides presented their war as religious, the Royalists claiming to defend the Church of England against the threats of sectarian anarchy, the Parliamentarians depicted their opponents as a clique of crypto-papists, part of the universal popish plot. Religion offered the only idiom through which popular support could be mobilized. One radical side-effect of war was that normal controls on free discussion lapsed and political and religious issues could be freely debated. Among the Protestant zealots demands were presented for a degree of congregational autonomy in any national church settlement, to accommodate 'tender consciences', and beyond them a spectrum of more radical sects demanded full religious liberty for every individual. Once the fighting ended in 1646, fear of religious radicalism drove the parliamentary leadership to seek a quick restoration of normality by reaching agreement with the king, clearly stated by the resolution of the two Houses in 1648 to restore the ancient government by king, lords and commons.

This outcome was delayed for a decade by the intervention in politics of the New Model Army, raised by parliament in 1645, which had secured the final victory. Circumstances had given control within the army to religious fundamentalists, like their leading figure, Oliver

Cromwell. Cromwell and his colleagues came to believe, that the army they led had been commissioned by God to make England the instrument for realizing His providential scheme. For this to be realised, the 'people of God' must be assured of full religious liberty to pursue their mission.

It was this conviction that armed them in 1648, having failed to strike a bargain with the king, to purge the parliament, execute the king, and establish a Commonwealth, 'without a king and House of Lords'. The Commons, as representative of the people, held all sovereign power. The failure of the republic is easily accounted for by the underlying reality that it was solely sustained by the force of the army. All the indicators are that any free consultation of the community would have revealed an overwhelming consensus for a restoration of the Stuart monarchy. Responsibility for government weakened Cromwell's religious enthusiasms, and after his installation as Lord Protector at the end of 1653, he spent his remaining years seeking political consensus, each new proposal moving closer to restoring the traditional government, except that Cromwell's beliefs required the retention of religious liberty for the people of God, and his government maintained almost complete religious toleration. This stood in the way of settlement, and could only be imposed by military force. In view of Cromwell's political agenda it seems mistaken to speak of the failure of the English revolution—the men in power were political reformists, not revolutionaries. Their revolutionary aspirations were religious.

In the period of political turmoil a number of radical movements did emerge, all of them from religious roots. The Levellers developed from a demand for individual freedom of conscience, to demand a comparable political liberty for the individual. Their Agreements of the People were blueprints for a democratic government. The Levellers are probably the first democratic movement in world history, and as such seem enormously significant to posterity. To the contemporary elites they were an alarming aberration, for conventional wisdom was agreed that any democratic system must result in anarchy and the destruction of property. The common people they professed to speak for mostly found the Leveller message beyond their mental horizons. The Levellers remained 'democrats without an electorate'. In the 1650s radicalism turned back to its religious roots, fracturing into generally chiliastic sects of insignificant strength. Only the early Quakers developed a national following, and their aggressive egalitarianism appalled all conventional folk, and became a factor strengthening the call for the restoration of the monarchy, and religious discipline. The English revolution, for all the striking political and religious happenings that it triggered, proved as empty as the Fronde, in terms of permanent changes in society. Alternative scenarios had been articulated and discussed, but all attempts to translate them into political action simply reinforced the determination of the ruling elites to defend and consolidate their power.

The search for political stability

The model for the reform of the European political systems after 1660 was the France of Louis XIV. This was the result of a planned reform whose basic principles were described by the king himself in the memoir he wrote to guide his successor. It had two basic purposes, to centralize all decision making in the person of the king, and to make his authority uniformly effective through the kingdom. The core was an executive council of working ministers, presided over by the king, which was drawn from the robe nobility (families whose status derived from the purchase of a high judicial or administrative office under the crown). It worked to a regular timetable and the aim was to rationalize decision making by informed free debate, from which the king could make his decisions. The results were the Louvois military reforms (see chapter 4) and Colbert's rationalizations of civil government, firmly grounded on his position as minister of finance. Colbert was able, in his first decade, to get a grip on taxation and revenue, reduce the level of the *taille* by 20 per cent, cut the cost of servicing the debt and the costs of revenue farming. When the next round of warfare began, the central budget was probably balanced. Yet the Colbertian rationalization was always limited. The amalgamation of revenue farming in one farm, the *cinq grosses fermes*, did not extend beyond the core provinces around Paris. It could not be extended to the whole kingdom, any more than it was practical to abolish internal tolls, or establish a uniform law code for the whole kingdom. The Colbertian codifications of law were largely restricted

to procedure rather than content. Similarly his mercantilist programmes were often more appearance than substance. Royal manufactures like the Gobelins tapestry works were real enough, but many
of the foreign trading companies led a brief and troubled existence,
while the campaign for regulating manufacture, through uniform
guild control, was often distorted by fiscalism and always subject to
the attrition of local particularism. The ideal of total central control
was unrealistic and Colbert knew it. This is not to deny that the
effectiveness of government was greatly enhanced. The king and his
ministers were better informed, the public revenues more efficiently
collected and administered, and the authority of the royal government more vigorously enforced. That had been the point of the legal
punitive expeditions into the provinces, the *grands jours*, to correct
banditry and noble anarchy, which made examples to demonstrate
that the king's law applied to all his subjects.

But there was another side to government, as Louis well knew, the
king was not just a chief executive, but also the living symbol of
lawful authority. The great palace of Versailles, which became the seat
of government after 1680, embodied this aspect. The symbolism was
not just in the structure, but in the public protocol of the king's daily
routines. At its peak, Versailles was home to some 10,000 of the king's
subjects, only a minority of whom were professional administrators.
Unlike them, the servants of the royal rituals were drawn from the
upper ranks of the sword nobility, (the hereditary feudal landowners,
dedicated to military service under the crown), for whom personal
access to the king compensated for their exclusion from government.
In fact it gave them an input, they could lobby for favours for themselves and their clients, and the more succesful became wholesalers,
purveying royal patronage, through which they could recoup the
expenses of living in the palace. Versailles was the working interface
between the divinely appointed monarch and his elite subjects, and
kept them occupied, under the king's eye and out of mischief. A
nobleman who earlier would have built his influence by developing
his provincial power base could now do better by being seen at Versailles, and having the right to hand the king his shirt during the
rituals of the royal toilet.

The image of the Sun King in complete control of his kingdom did
not correspond with reality. Rulers could command, but implementation did not necessarily result. Louis XIV could do more than most of

his contemporaries, particularly after the consolidation of the national intendancy in the 1690s had created a central government machinery entirely under its own control. But the *intendants* had to work in parallel with the existing local institutions, *parlements*, Estates, urban oligarchies, companies and guilds, and to succeed they needed to negotiate rather than command. The army depended on the readiness of sword nobles to invest in commissions and the whole financial structure depended crucially on the banking syndicates who provided public credit. The institutions, anchored in the purchase system, certainly embodied the investment of the propertied in the government of the kingdom, and they were not going to endanger their investment. But they had immense power to delay or obstruct what they did not like, and their cooperation had to be purchased by consideration of their interests by the royal government. Louis spent most of the reign trying to silence his Jansenist critics in the church, but even with the pope in support never fully succeeded, while his handling of the Huguenots and the revocation of the Edict of Nantes were a poor advertisement for the merits of rational decision making.

The purpose of the state-building carried out under Louis XIV was his need to participate in the European power game. The policies were designed, and largely succeeded, in extracting from French society the money, manpower and materials for waging war. Down to 1700 it succeeded, and Louis XIV's military machine was the most powerful in Europe. The subjects payed for it, but more efficient administration, and careful handling of the elites, enabled this to be done without causing the political instability characterized by the Fronde. When severe distress returned to the common people in the 1690s, the habit of compliance with lawful authority prevailed, the elites were supportive, and the suffering poor appealed to the *intendants* for relief, instead of lynching them as their ancestors might have done.

The experience of the Spanish monarchy made an illuminating contrast. The decline of Spain under the stresses of war had been real, marked by economic recession and falling population. But the death of Philip IV and the end of the costly struggle with Portugal in 1668 eased the pressures, and some signs of recovery can be observed in some parts of the penninsula. Yet royal government seemed paralysed. Spain took part in all the western European wars of the period, but her role was as victim. Repeatedly the regime proved unable to organize an effective defence of its territories. The explanation lies in the downside of hereditary monarchy. The king, Carlos II, was mentally deficient and childless, and incapable of giving force to government. Capable ministers did initiate reforms, but most failed in the face of vested interests and court intrigue which the king was unable to control. Yet his legitimacy was beyond challenge, his replacement impossible and Spain drifted, while the other powers contemplated the carve up of the Spanish inheritance that must follow his death. However, the experience also showed the underlying resilience of these devolved societies. Central government almost ceased to function, but the autonomous local communities were able to survive, as the subjects waited for Providence to determine their future. The Spanish kingdoms stagnated, but they did not disintegrate.

The Westphalia settlements had ended any realistic prospect of the Habsburg emperors creating a strong imperial monarchy, though the office of emperor had not lost real political significance. He could still adjudicate within the Empire, and arbitrate over disputed successions: he could be appealed to by Estates who accused their ruler of violating their privileges: and he had the power to grant and sell titles of nobility and appointments to office which gave the emperor leverage to raise money, mobilize political support and discourage opposition. But it was clear to the Habsburgs that the main basis of their power would now be derived from their patrimonial lands, Bohemia, the Austrian duchies and Hungary. All these territories had a similar political structure, they were ruled by a landowning nobility, which had subdued the peasants and was led by territorial magnates, who developed clienteles among the lesser gentry. They had marginalized the weakly developed urban sector, and had their institutional base in the provincial Diets. The Diets controlled local administration, and taxation, and consequently controlled much of the crown revenue.

The Habsburg emperors had no consistent plan for reconstructing their government. Their one firm principle was to restore religious unity through the Catholic church and make this the unifying force in their dominions. Leopold I was the despair of his modernizing advisers—his instinctive response to crises was intensive prayer, relying on Providence to provide solutions. Reform of central government was discussed, as with the commission of 1681, but that could not even agree how to set up a unified military budget. The Habsburgs contrived to rule through the existing systems. The settlement in Bohemia in 1627, following the purge of rebel nobles and their replacement by loyal Catholics, was remarkably conservative. The crown became hereditary, the Estate of the Clergy was reinstated in the Diet, but otherwise the new nobility retained the controlling position of the old. In the Austrian duchies the Protestant nobles, still a significant presence in 1618, had proved politically unreliable. Some were expelled during the wars, and most had gone by 1700. But the provinces remained under the control of their Diets, and the powers of the ruler were correspondingly restricted.

The one serious attempt at remodelling was in Hungary. The kingdom retained its medieval constitution and had its own central administration under an elected Viceroy and staffed by native noblemen. Protestantism had a firm hold, most of the lesser nobles were Calvinists, the burghers Lutheran. The Habsburgs had prevented the elimination of the Catholic church, and supported a Jesuit-led campaign that converted several magnate families. But confessional pluralism remained. In 1670 some nobles rebelled against the Habsburgs and were defeated, and the kingdom subjected to military occupation. Leopold was persuaded to change the constitution and bring the kingdom under the direct control of Vienna. The rebel leaders were executed after show trials, rebel property sequestered, and a military government, the *Gubernium*, installed, supported by troops who lived off the country. Protestant preachers were imprisoned or expelled, Protestant communities subjected to punitive billeting. It was a regime of authorized terrorism. The result was a Magyar guerilla movement which after 1672 was supported by Louis XIV. The build up of an Ottoman threat at the end of the 1670s induced some of Leopold's advisers to recommend conciliation. In 1681 Leopold agreed, a Hungarian Diet was summoned at Sopron, and offered the reinstatement of the constitution, abolition of the *Gubernium* and the occupation, and restoration of religious liberty. After the reconquest of Ottoman Hungary in 1687, Leopold was again in a position to impose a solution of his own, but declined to use it. In a final settlement, the crown was made hereditary, but the separate Hungarian government was retained. In 1700, the Vienna Habsburgs were still ruling over a loose confederation. The emperor's university educated jurists and bureaucrats advocated a strong central government, pursuing a vigorous mercantilist policy, but Leopold was temperamentally more in sympathy with the traditionalist views of the court nobility, passionate only about promoting the Catholic religion and eliminating heresy.

The Calvinist Elector of Brandenburg, Frederick William, represented a different and idiosyncratic approach to state building. He was patrimonial lord of a string of north-German territories. The heartland was Brandenburg, an agrarian society, controlled by its noble landlords, with their bonded peasants. In the west he ruled the Rhine duchies of Cleves-Mark, in the east the duchy of Prussia, a feudal dependency of Poland. Its landlords had done well in the Baltic grain trade, and it included a major trading city in the port of Königsberg. Experience had taught Frederick William that a ruler of his status, unless he was content to be the client of powerful neighbours, needed a military force of his own. Early attempts to get agreement to this from his local Estates failed, except in Brandenburg, where in 1653, the Diet agreed to a tax for maintaining a standing army, in return for confirmation of their privileges. This army was used in the Polish wars of 1656–60, and won him full sovereignty over Prussia. The army was then used after 1660 to intimidate the Prussian Estates into surrendering control of taxation.

Frederick William's achievement was unusual. Generally a central government and an army would develop within an existing state structure. In this case a state structure that had not existed before, developed out of an army. Frederick William's subjects were generally uninterested in, or opposed to his state-building project. So once the army was established, a central administration developed from that. The General War Commissariat, established in Berlin, not only serviced the army, but developed into the general administration for all the Elector's lands. Frederick William's new creation, heavily dependent on alien experts, and sustained by hiring out the army to the major contestants in the wars, was essentially an external imposition on the lands over which he ruled. It took decades before the native elites of Brandenburg and Prussia dropped their early indifference, or hostility to the new creation, and began to take service in the army and administration as a career choice. The artificiality of this creation brought it closer to the idea of an abstract, impersonal state where the ruler was less the proprietor, more the first servant. It anticipated an idea whose time was to come in the next century.

After 1660 the two Baltic monarchies, Sweden-Finland and Denmark-Norway, both took the path of remodelling their power structures on absolutist lines, with the interesting difference that the process involved participation by the lower orders of society. The closed oligarchy of landed nobles which ruled Denmark had involved the kingdom in a series of conflicts with Sweden in which Denmark was defeated and lost territory, culminating in 1660, when Denmark lost control of both sides of the Sound. The humiliation finally undermined the credibility of the oligarchs, and led to political reconstruction. The king, Frederick III, in active collaboration with the Estates of burghers and clergy in 1660, was able, with a little threat of force, to make the nobility accept hereditary monarchy, and then remit to the king the drafting of a revised system of government. The king and his advisers drafted the first formally absolutist constitution in Europe. It combined principles from the Law of God and Natural Law, to assert the need for an absolute sovereign power to establish effective government. The king assumed powers to tax at will, the council became his appointees, he alone could confer titles and appoint to offices. The old noble families lost their exclusive privileges, and a new service nobility developed, endowed by the dispersal of crown lands, and taking service in the modernized bureaucratic structures of central and local government and the army. The reforms met no significant resistance. Only the oligarchs seemed to lose and they were thoroughly discredited. The military imperative dictated a need to rationalize and modernize the machinery of government, while the new regime, at least in its formative years, was relatively open. A Table of Ranks meant that status went with service, commoners could enter a service career leading to enoblement, and were free to buy land, formerly closed to them. The real losers were the peasantry, the new regime had to expand revenue, its military reforms involved conscription, while the new landlords took over from the old, control of local administration. The irony was that after all the changes, the absolute monarchy was no more successful than its predecessor in restoring Denmark's international fortunes.

Sweden-Finland was different. In 1544 the Estates had declared the monarchy hereditary in the Vasa family. There was a written constitution in the medieval Land Law, which established a strong executive kingship with an independent revenue from public lands, but which also provided for power sharing. Major decisions required the king to consult the 'community of the realm' and to rule with the advice of the Council. In the Form of Government of 1634, the central government was reorganized. The king and the council presided over five collegiate ministries, staffed by professional, salaried bureaucrats. Local self-government was preserved, but supervised by a network of Provincial Governors, also salaried public servants. The administration was supported by the Lutheran Church. Sweden was free of religious dissent and the clergy constituted a further arm of central government. These arrangements gave Sweden the most efficient central government in Europe. It had enabled Sweden to win recognition at Westphalia as a major international power, and to pursue policies of predatory warfare, leading to territorial expansion, down to 1660.

Sweden was basically a poor, agrarian society, that could never have sustained these policies from internal resources. Her rulers combined the profits of war with systematic dispersal of the crown lands, to raise credit. The lands passed to the nobility, mostly to an oligarchy of some thirty families, which dominated the council and the public service. In 1660 the regency was vested in the oligarchs, and they faced the problem of maintaining Sweden's status without the profits of war. They sought escape by taking subsidies from Louis XIV to intervene in his Dutch War. Sweden was set upon by her neighbours, losing most of her overseas territories and fending off with difficulty a Danish invasion. In the end, Louis XIV saw it as advantageous to demonstrate his power by insisting on the restoration of Sweden's losses. It had been a humiliating experience for the whole community, and most of all for the young Charles XI, who emerged internally strengthened by his personal leadership of the defence, but deeply humiliated by being rescued by Louis XIV. He spent the rest of his life trying to ensure it could not happen again.

When the Estates met in October 1680, the king indicated that ways must be found to make Sweden militarily secure and self-sustaining. Charles XI and his absolutist advisers knew the commoner Estates would recommend a full resumption of crown lands as the basis for budgetary reform. They also knew many among the lesser nobles resented the power and profiteering of the oligarchs. The combined strength of the commoner Estates with the lesser nobility carried the programme through the Diet. When the oligarchs tried to use their position in the council to obstruct the reform, the king appealed to the Estates to define his authority. They responded by declaring that, as an hereditary, Christian monarch, the king had unlimited discretionary power to rule his kingdom, according to law, and was answerable only to God. The council oligarchs submitted. The reforms could then proceed, the first element being the maximum possible recovery of alienated public assets. The result of this resumption was a massive transfer of assets from the nobility back to the crown. A Budget Office was set up to establish a fixed state budget, in which all the regular public expenditure was met by the recovered revenues. By 1693, the king could announce that the budget was balanced. The complementary part of the reform was the establishment of a large standing army and navy which was funded by the budget reform. The officer corps and the cavalry were settled on properties made available by the resumption. The property provided their accommodation and basic salary. The infantry and seamen for the navy were raised by direct contracts with local taxpayers. The inducement was the abolition of conscription, a burden rightly feared by the peasantry on whom it fell, for its disruptive impact on the labour force. The result of these measures was to create a standing military establishment, permanently funded from local revenues, yet also integrated into the communities, so that the manpower remained available for employment and could contribute to, instead of being a drain upon, the local economies.

Charles XI had got the stability he sought. He had a sustainable military establishment, considerable enough to deter potential enemies, and attract allies. The absolutism was clearly based on a broad measure of consent. The nobility suffered heavy loss of property, and some felt aggrieved, but their status as the leading Estate remained unchallenged, and in compensation, they could enjoy reasonably paid careers in state service. The commoners carried a heavy load of taxation and services, but the lottery of conscription was lifted, and their obligations were legally fixed for all time. Further the public service was meritocratic, and able commoners could enter and rise into the nobility, while the majority who remained in subordination, never lost sight of the reality that the alternative to royal absolutism was aristocratic oligarchy, and they knew what they preferred—the old common wisdom, 'better one master than a hundred'.

Alternative roads

Some parts of Europe did not go down the absolutist road. In the British Isles, the collapse of army rule enabled a renewed consensus to be built through the Restoration of 1660. In appearence the old balance of a central royal government working with a federation of self-governing local communities was reinstated. The British elites, who had been split during the interregnum, reunited to ensure that it would not recur. The monarchy was reinforced by formal confirmation that the executive powers were in the king alone, he commanded the armed forces, directed foreign relations, made all public appointments, controlled the judiciary and the church, and was granted an improved financial settlement that incorporated the modernized fiscal system evolved during the wars. Since it was correctly believed that the original breakdown had been grounded in religious dissent, the episcopal Church of England was restored to exclusive authority and all religious deviance outlawed. The political significance of this was stressed by reserving all public offices to church members. One further factor ensured that England would not become a military state like the continental absolutisms—the memory of the political dictatorship of the New Model Army over the traditional elites made them resolved there would be no standing armies in England. It was soon apparent that religious divisions had not gone away. After two decades of religious freedom, the Protestant dissenters proved too strongly rooted to be eliminated by legal harassment, particularly because some within the elites still sympathized with and protected them. Then the restored Stuart dynasty was openly sympathetic to Catholicism, and was willing to accept some toleration for all dissenters, if that secured relief for the Catholic community too. This kept alive the paranoia about popish plots that had been so damaging in the 1640s. In 1670, Charles II allied with Louis XIV to attack the United Provinces (the seven member-states comprised: Friesland, Gelderland, Groningen, Holland, Overijssel, Utrecht, and Zeeland), and subsequently in the Declaration of Indulgence, claimed the power to exempt religious dissidents from the current persecuting laws. There was a powerful public reaction, which linked fear of royal absolutism to fear of Catholic plotting, and forced on the king the Test Act of 1673, specifically barring Catholics from any public functions.

When in 1673, the king's brother and heir, James, revealed he had converted to Catholicism, the court faction opposing the royal policies, an aristocratic grouping led by the Earl of Shaftesbury, saw how this could be linked to a popish plot scenario to arouse populist feeling, influence parliament and force the king to admit them into government. This created the first national political party—the Whig party—intended to lobby parliament and influence elections. They attacked the foundations of hereditary monarchy with the demand to exclude James from the succession. The exclusion crisis of 1678–83 showed how religious passions, and the experiences of the interregnum, had raised the political consciousness of common people, making a novel style of populist politics, manipulated from within the ruling elites, possible. The outcome showed the king's control of executive power was strong enough to resist. Charles II made skilful use of the dissolution of parliaments to deprive the opposition of their main public platform, he appealed succesfully to the House of Lords to defend the hereditary principle by rejecting exclusion, he cultivated an antidote to panic over the threat of popery by cultivating fears of a new civil war. In addition to using propaganda and patronage, he could use royal power to influence the law courts and the selection of juries, enabling the Whig leaders and organizers to be prosecuted successfully for sedition. He could purge local government, filling county and borough authorities with sympathizers. And he discovered that with careful management, the royal revenues could be increased sufficiently to dispense with parliaments. When Charles II died in 1685, it seemed that England, and with it Scotland and Ireland, could follow most of Europe in a quest for political stability built around a strong, authoritarian monarchy.

That this did not happen seems due mainly to contingency. The new king, James II, did not conceal his wish to see Catholics admitted to public positions and to strengthen the royal government by the establishment of an enlarged standing army. He discovered that the supporters rallied to the crown by Charles II would not accept this, as the otherwise loyalist parliament of 1685 made clear. Intensive personal lobbying by the king could not shift them. The king then sought to organize a new royalist coalition around a programme of religious liberty for all. Local government was purged and borough charters were modified with a view to controlling elections and securing a compliant House of Commons. Whether or not the campaign could have succeeded cannot be known. The programme was aborted in 1688 by the military intervention of the Prince of Orange, invited by opposition elements among the English elites, motivated by his personal drive to enlist England into his coalition to oppose Louis XIV, and enabled to succeed by the passive non-cooperation of the elites with James' government.

The revolution of 1688, made an open break with the principle of hereditary divine right, by declaring that James had abdicated and the throne was vacant. Only then were William and Mary declared sovereigns. But the subsequent settlement was content to make adjustments to the provisions of 1660, as set out in the Bill of Rights of 1689, together with a grudging acceptance of Protestant religious dissent in the Toleration Act. This would not have precluded, with skilful political management, a revival of strong executive kingship on the lines Charles II had developed by 1685. That was rendered impossible by England entering the European war against Louis XIV. It required unprecedented raising of credit on the security of taxation voted in parliament. When this was institutionalized in 1694 by the creation of the Bank of England, and a permanent funded public debt, government without active participation by parliament became impossible. This was signalled when William III surrendered the independent revenues of the crown for a parliamentary Civil List. The independent control of the executive went with it, and the subjects who had put their money into the public funds would see that it did not return.

The other deviant society was the Dutch Republic. The United Provinces had managed to play a key role in European and world affairs without a strong central government. The Union was based on the sovereignty of its seven constituent provinces, with the maximum devolution of power from the centre. The key to this was finance. The United Provinces, in reality Holland and Zeeland, dominated the economy of Europe as the major suppliers of goods, services and advanced technology, and controllers of international commerce and banking. The Dutch were the only urban-led society, driven by market economics, not by the values of noble landlords. The society was, like all the others hierarchical, and oligarchic. Holland was ruled by the Regent corporations of the eighteen cities represented in the

Holland States. The Regents were a closed group of the wealthiest citizens, who were recruited by cooption. But though they might buy country estates, they maintained a burgher lifestyle, remained resident in their cities, could not aspire to nobility, since there was no sovereign in the Union empowered to grant titles. There was a landed nobility in the inland provinces, which was powerful locally, and had an important role in the maintenance of the armies of the republic. But they were always junior partners with the Holland Regents and their national influence came through the position of the pre-eminent noble family, the princes of Orange, who commanded the armed forces, and as Stadholders, had some powers of patronage in the government of the republic. The power of the United Provinces rested on the ability of Holland, throughout the century, to borrow unlimited amounts of money on the public faith, at rates of interest below any of their rivals. With this they could fight Louis XIV or England on level terms. A society that could pay cash for the military resources it needed, derived from the voluntary investments of its citizens, did not need a central authority to extort taxation and services from them. Investors were so confident of their returns, that by 1700 there was more capital invested in public securities in the United Provinces than in land and property combined. The Regent oligarchs, holding office for life, were like kings by divine right, they too answered to no earthly power.

Europe's Slavonic eastern frontier zone was covered by the kingdom of Poland-Lithuania, and the realms of the tsar of Russia. Poland was Europe's most important elective monarchy. It was a devolved society, where a weak king governed with an unusually numerous landed nobility. At all levels of government, the nobility dominated decision making. In an agrarian society, the villagers were bound by law to the will of their landlords. Otherwise at all levels, power rested in public assemblies of the nobility, culminating in the central Diet. The king was elected at a mass assembly of the entire nobility and bound by his accession charter. He was legal head of the executive, but nearly all his functions were subject to external restraints and under constant supervision by a council elected at the Diet. The crown revenues were quite inadequate in peacetime and for war, which was the normal condition of Poland, the king, although nominal commander, was totally dependent on the collaboration of the Diet and the provincial assemblies. If the king should endeavour to break free of his constraints, the nobility had the right to form a Confederation to defend the constitution, in effect a legalized right of rebellion. The Polish-Lithuanian nobility were legally of equal status, and included feudal princes with estates as large as many small European principalities, down to rural gentry who lived in dire poverty and owned little beyond the family homestead. In reality, the nobility was structured hierarchically into factions, grouped under the great families. The magnates ruled the kingdom and negotiated as equals with their king. The pattern of politics under the three Vasa kings who ruled until the 1660s, was repeated efforts by the kings to contrive, or negotiate, a strengthening of the royal authority, each of which ended in failure. Polish society was vigorously expanding to the east, in conflict with Russia, and extending landlord settlement into the largely empty lands of the Ukraine. It was also reluctantly caught up in the running dynastic feud of their kings with the Swedish Vasas. As evidence mounted that the kingdom's military power was overstretched, it might have been supposed that proposals to strengthen the government, and fund modernized armed forces would have found support, but they did not. Instead, the various attempts to strengthen central government were met by aggressive assertions of noble power, culminating in the final paralysis of the central Diet by the insistence on a rigid unanimity rule, the claim that any one deputy, by objecting to the proceedings, could nullify a Diet session. This was the *liberum veto* that so caught the imagination of European observers, and subsequent historians, first exercised in its extreme form in 1652. Thereafter it guaranteed that no proposal, seen as threatening the liberties of the nobility, could be enacted.

This trend in Polish affairs has always seemed to outsiders as wilfully perverse, yet it is clear that to the nobility themselves it was a matter of pride. In practice, the consequences could be tolerated. The Diet could not legislate, but Poland did not need legislation, the nobility wanted to keep things as they were. It was difficult to organize military campaigning, but given Poland's vast size, and the absence, in an extremely decentralized society, of any key points that an enemy could capture and bring the kingdom to its knees, the military resources of the magnates, with their private armies and provincial militias could usually see off even such catastrophes as the great Ukrainian peasant uprising under Chelmnitsky, the 'deluge' of 1648–52. Such peasant mutinies could be neutralized in the end by bribing the leaders to desert their followers. Poland's relative weakness suited its more powerful neighbours. Poland could not threaten them, and they did not seek its collapse. For one thing the elective crown was always an attraction to ambitious dynasts, and for another a collapse would upset the political balance in central Europe. They tended to use the ample opportunities for external interference in politics to prevent the success of reform proposals. So Poland survived the seventeenth-century with only peripheral losses of territory, mainly in White Russia and the Ukraine. The nobility gloried in their difference from the rest of Europe, and cultivated the distinctive historical mythology of Sarmatianism, which asserted their cultural and racial superiority, and despised nobles in the rest of Europe who were increasingly submitting to the restraints of absolute monarchies.

The distinctive feature of the Russian tsardom was that, after the fall of Constantinople, it was the only remaining independent Orthodox Christian principality. This created an ideological and cultural barrier between the Russians and all their neighbours. Russians identified their culture as Holy Russia, the Third Rome with a divine mission to guard the true faith to the end of the world. This did not preclude contacts with western society, there was trade and an interest in western technologies, but the innovatory forces, renaissance, reformation, geographical discoveries that affected the western world, had only marginal impact on Russia. Yet the structure of Russian society was similar to that of central and eastern Europe, an underdeveloped agrarian society, with a controlling elite of landlords, serviced by small urban communities of merchants and artisans, and sustained by the labours of the peasantry. The political system was a legacy of the Mongol conquests that the Christian principalities, now subordinated to the Grand Prince in Moscow, autocrat and tsar of all the Russias, had derived from the provincial agents of Mongol despotism. The western concepts of private or corporate property rights, secured by a rule of law, had not developed. Instead the tsar-autocrat was a patrimonial lord, absolute proprietor of all the Russian lands and all who lived in them. His subjects, whatever their status, were his servants. The basic social distinction was between those who served the tsar directly, and were rewarded with allocations of land, they formed the ruling elite, and the common people who were taxpayers.

Russia was a frontier land, thinly settled and labour was scarce. For the taxpaying classes, there was the possibility of flight, to the free

Cossack communities who held the Ukraine, or eastwards into Siberia, which was steadily penetrated by hunters and settlers through the seventeenth century. By its second half these pioneers had reached the Pacific. The tsar was autocrat by divine right, sustained by the endorsement of the autonomous Orthodox church under its patriarch. He was assisted in government by a council, the Boyar Duma, in which an elite group of princely families maintained a predominant voice. A professional bureaucracy, which staffed a mosaic of departments and temporary commissions, the Moscow *prikazi*, supervised the collection of the dues and services of the subjects, and handled relations with the external world.

In 1600 this whole system suffered from the chaos arising from dynastic failure, the 'time of troubles'. It was religion, the overriding need to preserve the purity of Orthodoxy, that enabled the church and its leader, the patriarch Filaret, to organize the resistance that drove the Polish interventionists out of Moscow in 1611. It led to the calling, in 1613, of an Assembly of the Land, in which all groups above the peasantry were notionally represented, and which recognized the patriarch's son, Michael Romanov, as tsar and made the office hereditary in the Romanov family. The early years of the Romanov dynasty were threatened by Polish aggression, as the Polish-Lithuanian magnates sought new lands and peasants to exploit in the Ukraine. This produced the most significant change of the century in Russia. The poor success of the Russian armies against Poland forced the adoption of western military techniques. Foreign mercenary officers and technicians were hired, and the service gentry and their serfs organized in western-style regiments, with appropriate equipment and discipline. By the 1660s the new style formations formed the front line of Russian armies, and turned the tide against the Poles. Russia gained territory in White Russia, and the Ukraine was divided along the Dnieper, with the tsar taking Kiev and east-bank lands.

Michael's son Alexis was a pious and educated ruler, with a clear intention to strengthen crown authority. In 1648, Alexis instructed an Assembly of the Land to draft a law code for the whole Russian land, the *ulozhenie* of 1649. This laid down the guidelines for Russian society, spelling out the duties and obligations of the different groups. The code confirmed the institution of serfdom, the peasantry were legally bound to the land in perpetuity, paying taxation to the ruler and owing open service obligations to their landlords. The urban sector taxpayers were fixed into corporations, responsible to the tsar for delivering their taxes, and given limited powers of self-government. The code placed the church under closer supervision by the tsar. The *ulozhenie* established a framework for a strongly authoritarian government and placed no limitations on the powers of the autocrat. Alexis also encouraged reform in the church, patronizing elements in the clergy, often influenced by western ideas, or by renewed contacts with the Patriarchate of Constantinople. The aim was a more evangelical approach, to bring the ordinary believer closer to the church, and incidentally raising its effectiveness for the tsar as an agency for controlling society. But the first cautious measures, promoted by the patriarch Nikon, to upgrade and standardize church ritual were instinctively rejected by religious fundamentalists, who would not accept any change in the last remaining true church. The Old Believer movement was soon in schism and proclaimed Nikon an agent of Antichrist.

By the later seventeenth century, the future development of Russia was still an open question. The limited western influences could suggest that Russian society was converging with developments in the west, and for the same basic reason, the need to enhance its war-making capacity. After 1686, Russia was admitted to the Habsburg coalition against the Ottomans, suggesting it was becoming accepted as part of the community of European powers. But the evidence of continuing, implacable conservative rejection of western modernity was also strong. The stubborn ferocity of the Old Believer schism expressed the strength of anti-foreign, chauvinist fundamentalism in the population, as a barrier to the acceptance of change inspired by external influences. In some respects, Russian society was as close to the Ottoman model as it was to the monarchies of the west. Events had confirmed that if Russia was to become fully inegrated into the European political structure, the necessary changes would have to be forced from above on a largely hostile population.

If 'absolutism' be accepted as a convenient shorthand for the trend towards the strengthening of central governments at the expense of local autonomies and sectional privilege, it is obvious that each individual absolutist project had its special features. However, the common driving imperative is clear, it was to improve the war-making capacity of society, which took priority over all other considerations. These were military states, Brandenburg perhaps an extreme example, and the business of kings was war. Beyond that, the drive to create a strong central administration, able to impose its authority uniformly through the society, appears to reflect a general European trend, in reaction against the instabilities that had seemed to threaten in the post-Reformation world. The aim was described by Louis XIV himself, a government that systematically applied human reason to the solving of problems, in place of traditional reliance on established custom and precedent. The adoption of mercantilist programmes, which sought to generate economic growth through government intervention, to strengthen society as a whole, was an example of this. So was the attempt to define a 'Law of Nations' to moderate the anarchic international order. The lengthy wrangles over diplomatic precedence of the period were part of the attempt. So was the idea of an internal Table of Ranks, introduced first in the Scandinavian kingdoms, setting out the precise relative status of all office-holders, or the complex protocols controlling life at Versailles. Men like Colbert and Charles XI had an almost manic compulsion to draft written codes, rule books prescribing in great detail how public affairs were to be conducted. The aim was best expressed in the drive for complete budgetary control, never fully achieved by Colbert, but eventually realised in Sweden. Such were the aspirations of rulers, in reality the old world of cutomary practices proved remarkably resilient. For example, in France the king no longer negotiated levels of taxation with the provincial Estates, he prescribed what he required, and the Estates accepted. But since it was the Estates that actually assessed and collected the money, they could contrive a condition of being permanently in arrears, in effect, the full precept was never paid. The movement towards what the eighteenth-century German Cameralist thinkers called a 'well-ordered police state', had begun in the later seventeenth century. But the gap between the aspiration and social reality was still a wide one. There was still a lot of life left in the *ancien régime* in 1700.

4

War and international relations

David Parrott

A painting by Peter Paul Rubens hanging in the Kunsthistorisches Museum, Vienna, depicts the meeting of two Habsburg cousins, Ferdinand, King of Hungary, and the brother of the king of Spain, the Cardinal-Infante, in September 1634 on the eve of the battle of Nördlingen. In the deepening shadows behind each of them stand the commanders of their armies, united to challenge the Protestant forces campaigning in southern Germany. The large-scale work deploys a full repertoire of baroque allegorical devices to celebrate the Habsburg triumph: in the foreground a river god personifying the Danube holds a stone jar from which run water and blood; beside him sits the captive Germania, soon to be freed by the Habsburg cousins, whose imminent victory is symbolized by descending eagles bearing laurel crowns. Rubens' painting presents a luminous statement of the triumph of Habsburg arms in one of the key engagements of the Thirty Years War, all the more striking in that the battle which it depicts has received little attention from historians.

The Thirty Years War and European conflict to 1634

By September 1634 the war which had begun with the ill-fated decision of Frederick V, the Palatine Elector, to accept the royal throne offered him by the rebellious Estates of Bohemia, had lasted for fifteen years. Before Frederick's intervention, the opposition of the Bohemian lesser nobility and towns to Habsburg governmental and religious policy, which had culminated in the 'defenestration' of two of the Emperor's ministers in Prague on 23 May 1618, had remained a matter of internal concern to the Austrian Habsburg dynasty. The revolt had been no more likely to involve external powers than the previous, and in some ways more serious, revolt of the Hungarian nobility in 1606. However, the prospect of an alliance between the Bohemian Protestants and the militantly Calvinist Palatine Elector changed the situation dramatically. If Frederick were successful, he would acquire a central European territory considerably more powerful and prosperous than his present dynastic holdings, and would dominate a block of lands running from the Rhine to the borders of Poland. Even more significant for the future balance of religious and political power in central Europe, Frederick would gain a second seat in the Electoral College, the body of seven princes who assembled to elect the Holy Roman Emperor. Hitherto, although there had been Protestants in the College—the Palatine himself, and the Saxon and Brandenburg Electors—the balance had been held by the four Catholic Electors—the block of three Rhineland arch-bishops of Mainz, Cologne and Trier, and the king of Bohemia. Were Frederick to hold two seats in his own person, the process by which the Habsburgs had consistently been elected to the Imperial throne would be in jeopardy, as indeed would be the inevitability of a Cath-olic emperor.

It was these implications for the political and religious control of the Holy Roman Empire which ensured that the Bohemian revolt provoked a graver and far more extensive conflict. Both the Palatine Elector and his rival, Archduke Ferdinand, by 1617 the ruler of the majority of the central European Habsburg lands, called upon outside supporters to provide troops and money for a struggle which each was convinced he could not afford to lose. In the case of Ferdinand, this search for allies gained him the support of the Span-ish branch of the Habsburgs, whose previous relationship with their Austrian cousins down to the mid 1610s had been none-too fraternal. Additionally, and at a price which later seemed exorbitant, Ferdinand was able to buy the military support of those Catholic German states which after 1609 had formed the Catholic League under the leadership of Maximilian I, Duke of Bavaria. On the other side, Frederick of the Palatinate turned to his co-religionaries, gaining offers of support from the rulers of Transylvania, the United Provinces of the Netherlands, Brandenburg and a number of smaller Calvinist territories. He also believed that he had the backing of his father-in-law, James I of England, of his wife's maternal uncle, Christian IV of Denmark, and of France, whose policies had previously been determined more by dynastic rivalry with the Habsburgs than by solidarity with other Catholic powers. But while Archduke Ferdinand's supporters provided substantial military support for the Habsburg reconquest of Bohemia, with the exception of Transylvania and a handful of smaller Calvinist territories, support for Frederick's enterprise melted away. France, the lynch-pin of an anti-Habsburg coalition, proved hostile to the revolt. Fearing the possibility of a Spanish Habsburg candidate for the Imperial throne, French negotiators encouraged the election of the Austrian Archduke Ferdinand as Emperor Ferdinand II in 1619, and acted to ensure the neutrality of most of the German Protestant states in the approaching military conflict. Although the outcome of the battle of the White Mountain, fought just outside Prague on 8 November 1620, was by no means a foregone conclusion, with parts of the Habsburg high command strongly opposed to risking an engagement against a Bohemian/Protestant army drawn up on the defensive, in the event the outcome was a shattering defeat for the Protestants.

The political consequences of the campaign were equally decisive: the Bohemian defeat was followed by one of the most far-reaching political and social reconstructions in early modern history, resulting in a territory that became a hereditary possession of the Habsburg dynasty, controlled on its behalf by a handful of great landed aristocrats who were supporters of militant Catholicism. The territories of the Palatine Elector were occupied, and one part, together with the Palatine's Electoral seat, was granted to Maximilian of Bavaria for his military services to the Emperor. But just as the intervention of the Palatine Elector in the Bohemian revolt had ensured that it could not remain an internal Habsburg matter, so this decisive shift in the balance of European power was equally unacceptable to those rulers who had previously been reluctant to take part in the conflict. For a decade after 1620 successive Protestant, anti-Habsburg coalitions sought to overturn a military situation which had fundamentally shifted the religious and political balance of power in favour of Catholicism and the Habsburg dynasties of Austria and Spain. Indeed, for the Spanish monarchy the great benefit of helping the Austrian branch was the credit that it established for Spain's own struggle to reduce the Dutch to peace terms which would be more acceptable and honorable than those forced upon Spain in 1609 by bankruptcy and the prospect of military overextension. This Hispano-Dutch conflict began again, as expected, with the expiry of the Twelve Years Truce in 1621, and gave an additional spur to the attempts to challenge the Habsburg military hegemony which had developed since 1620. The Dutch, aware of the strategically important gains that the Spanish had made in the Rhineland as a result of the occupation of the Palatine Elector's principal hereditary territory, now needed to reverse the consequences of the Bohemian war for their own security and survival.

None of these attempts to challenge the military ascendancy of the Habsburg/Catholic coalition succeeded. By 1629, the Emperor was sufficiently confident of his military strength, and sufficiently determined about his religious obligations, to impose the Edict of Restitution on the Protestant territories of the Holy Roman Empire, and to make a bid to reclaim all Catholic ecclesiastical and monastic territories secularized since the Peace of Augsburg of 1555.

The Edict caused deep resentment amongst Protestant princes who had previously been loyal to the Emperor, most notably the Saxon Elector. Moreover it coincided with the despatch of a large portion of the Imperial army down into Italy to fulfil obligations to the Spanish crown, now locked in conflict with France over the succession to the duchies of Mantua and Monferrato. This enabled a Swedish expeditionary force, led by King Gustavus Adolphus, to land on the coast of north Germany and establish a military position strong enough to beat off the first Imperial attempts to push them back into the Baltic. When the bulk of the Imperial and Catholic League armies had finally reassembled and marched northwards to engage the Swedes, the resulting battle of Breitenfeld (17 September 1631) marked a dramatic break in the virtually uninterrupted pattern of Habsburg Catholic victories. Unexpected and overwhelming military success was followed by an expansion of Swedish war-aims: as his much-enlarged army occupied swathes of western and southern Germany, Gustavus Adolphus planned a series of campaigns which would bring him to the gates of Vienna. However, in November 1632 the prospect of an outright Swedish triumph and the definitive reversal of the Habsburg Catholic agenda abruptly collapsed with the death of Gustavus at the indecisive battle of Lützen. Although the Swedes were far from defeated, their seemingly unstoppable progress had been checked. The next two campaigns saw a piecemeal process of consolidation in those areas which the Swedes and Protestants had dominated since 1631–32, but they also provided evidence that their opponents were beginning to regain confidence. In 1633 a remarkable campaign conducted in southern and western Germany by the commander of the Spanish army of Lombardy, the duke of Feria, revealed the fragility of Sweden's military ascendancy, threatening strong points and placing the main Swedish army on the defensive. In 1634, Spain sought to capitalize on Feria's success in reopening communications northwards by moving a large force of Spanish troops from Lombardy to the Spanish Netherlands, where their commander, Ferdinand, cardinal and brother of King Philip IV, was to assume the governor-generalship. These troops linked up with the main Imperial army under the command of the emperor's son, Ferdinand of Hungary, and the combined forces began to mop up local Protestant forces in Bavaria and around the Catholic free cities of southern Germany. On the afternoon of 4 September 1634, the combined armies of Spain, the Holy Roman Emperor and the Catholic League succeeded in breaching the walls of Nördlingen after a 24-hour bombardment. A subsequent assault was repulsed by the Swedish garrison, but the fall of the city was obviously imminent. The news was received with consternation by the main Swedish and German Protestant campaign army, camped only three miles away from the Catholic forces. The supreme commander of the German forces, the Duke of Saxe-Weimar urged an immediate attack on the Spanish-Imperial army in order to preserve the credibility of the allied position in southern Germany already threatened by the loss of Regensburg and Donauwörth. As the fall of Nördlingen appeared imminent his counsels prevailed over the more cautious Swedish field marshal, Gustav Horn. By nightfall on 5 September, the two armies were drawn up, and the Protestant forces prepared for an all-out assault on the following day. Past experience suggested that there was nothing particularly foolhardy about this gamble: although the Swedes and German Protestants were outnumbered, with some

26 000 troops against 33 000 in the Habsburg/Catholic army, their troops included a large proportion of veterans from earlier campaigns, while the constricted zone of combat would counteract any obvious advantage brought by greater numbers.

Early seventeenth-century warfare and the 'military revolution'

What did the two armies drawn up outside Nördlingen look like? Much has traditionally been made of the tactical and organizational innovations of the Swedes. Their army has been presented as the exemplar of the 'military revolution', a thorough-going bid to combine the benefits of firearms, especially the musket, with the shock-value of direct assaults by infantry or cavalry. Deployed in lines only six to ten soldiers deep, smaller infantry units (squadrons) with a high proportion of officers and NCOs were brought together in elaborate, mutually-supporting groupings (brigades) which sought to combine tactical flexibility with cohesion in the face of an enemy assault. One third of the infantry were still armed with twelve to fourteen foot pikes, deployed by the fittest and most experienced of the soldiers as both a defensive weapon, to protect the vulnerable musketeers, and as the thrusting-force of follow-up assaults. Infantry may have dominated these new-style armies, but cavalry could still be effective, especially when they abandoned manoeuvres based on the use of pistols and light muskets (calivers) in favour of direct charges with edged weapons. More numerous and lighter artillery pieces were deployed in closer coordination with the infantry. These changes, it has been argued, ensured superiority over the supposedly obsolete tactics of their opponents. These, the traditional armies of the Spanish and Austrian Habsburgs and the Catholic League, still persisted in drawing up their infantry in huge squares as many as sixty troops deep, sacrificing firepower to weight of numbers. Such armies, whose tactics had not changed since the advent of the Swiss pike phalanx 150 years earlier, simply aimed to push the enemy off the field, crushing less resolute opponents under a human steam roller. Against the carefully deployed lines and reserves of the new style of armies, such deployment of very large units seemed hopelessly inflexible.

This picture of radically contrasting tactical styles and army organization needs considerable qualification. Above all, it gives a wholly false picture of armies dominated by long-serving, quasi-professional troops who could be drilled in elaborate deployments, and whose experienced officers and NCOs could coordinate their soldiers' movements effectively since they understood these more complicated and sophisticated tactics. For a small core of veteran troops in all of the major armies in the Thirty Years War, Protestant and Catholic, a reasonably high level of cohesion and discipline under fire, moderate tactical sophistication and *esprit de corps* were attainable. But the armies of this period were not, in the main, raised through the direct agency of the state. Historians have frequently commented upon the considerable expansion in the size of armies during the 1620s and 1630s. While the military establishments of the Habsburg and Valois great powers of the mid-sixteenth century had rarely exceeded 50–55 000 men, the army of Gustavus Adolphus in 1632 is claimed to have contained up to 175 000 troops, and in the same period that of his formidable Imperial opponent, Albrecht Wallenstein, well over 100 000 men. Yet this scale of military activity was beyond the administrative and financial resources of even the greatest powers of the early seventeenth century, so that the increase had to be sustained by a system of military contracting: units, and sometimes whole armies, were raised by private entrepreneurs, prepared to recruit, equip and provide initial pay for specified numbers of troops in return for full rights of command and promises of later repayment. The most usual means of repayment was a licence to levy military taxes, 'contributions', on enemy, neutral or, in the last resort, home territory. Collected under direct military pressure, these allowed exactions of money and payments in kind at considerably higher rates than any civil system permitted. Reliance on contributions to fund entrepreneurial armies had important consequences: it led to the delegation of state power to military commanders, who usurped the role of the civil authorities both in extracting taxes and adjudicating consequent disputes, and who frequently constructed their strategies to maximize contributions rather than to pursue coherent campaign objectives. Above all, it drove up the number of soldiers under arms without significantly increasing the number of troops actively campaigning and on the battlefield. For the military entrepreneur, the primary concern was not the recruitment of an elite, veteran core (though no commander turned down the possibility of experienced, battle-hardened troops if these were available), but to raise large numbers of recruits whose primary task would be to undertake the garrisoning and extortion on which contributions depended. While they might be drawn into a campaign, the great majority of such units had no experience of battle, their soldiers had little or no training, and the entrepreneurs had no illusions that desertion, sickness and death (usually through disease) would ruin most such units within one or two campaigns. There was neither time nor resources to drill such soldiers in elaborate tactics and discipline, and for the most part their function made this unnecessary. When they were deployed on the battlefield or, much more frequently, in siege warfare, such infantry would be drawn up in the simplest formations—blocks of pikemen flanked by musketeers, the size of the unit depending more upon the number of troops available than on any tactical theory—and it was hoped that by placing them in the second or third lines, or sandwiching them between the small number of experienced veterans, they would add to the overall weight of the army, but not be placed in a position where their unreliability or inexperience would lead to disaster. As these troops were raised at the expense, and were under the control, of individual entrepreneurial commanders, there was little standardization of weapons, no uniforms, and widely varying standards of discipline and leadership.

The real difference between armies lay not in different methods for the deployment of troops, but in the number of *experienced* troops who could be deployed on the battlefield. A state whose sustained military activity gave it the chance to maintain an elite core of troops, usually separated from the entrepreneurial bulk of the army, enjoyed an overwhelming advantage over forces which comprised raw recruits, or troops who had served no more than one campaign. Spanish armies consistently triumphed in the field against the newly-levied troops of the German Protestants, and indeed even over the French down to and beyond the celebrated French victory of Rocroi (1643), just as the Swedish forces who mauled the Imperial and Catholic armies at Breitenfeld in 1631 were no ordinary army, but a hardened veteran force which had fought its way down along the shores of the Baltic and into Prussia under Gustavus Adolphus. It is no surprise that the Bavarian field army was a great deal more formidable than any of the other armies of the major German princes; by 1648 over 50 per cent of the troops had five years or more of combat experience.

The armies which encountered each other around Nördlingen on the morning of 6 September included a large proportion of the most experienced troops in Europe, and the battle reflected this fact more obviously than any tactical or organizational distinction. Although both sides possessed artillery, this played a relatively minor role in the battle. There was no preliminary bombardment, and the fighting was at such close quarters that field pieces could not be deployed effectively. The Swedes, justifiably confident of their prowess in Germany since 1631 and concerned to force the issue of a battle, took the offensive: their elite brigades hurled themselves against the fortified Spanish and Imperial positions on the heights above Nördlingen. This was not a struggle determined by firepower, but by brute force—the 'push of pike'—as successive waves of Swedish infantry advanced up the slopes against the Habsburg positions and after forcing their way through the first Imperial positions were held by the disciplined endurance of Spanish veterans. Fifteen unsuccessful assaults on these positions wore down the Swedish troops, and started to reveal weaknesses in coordination between the two corps of the Swedish and the German Protestant forces. By early afternoon, as these troops were visibly weakening and starting to pull back from their positions, the Habsburg princes saw their chance and launched relatively fresh infantry and cavalry in a counter-attack against the weak point between the two corps of Saxe-Weimar and Horn. The allied armies collapsed under this pressure, and by mid-afternoon a rout had begun in which the fleeing Protestant troops were cut to pieces by Spanish and Imperial light cavalry, losing some 6000 dead, compared with some 1600 Imperial and Spanish troops. A further 6000 Swedes and German Protestants were captured, including the Swedish commander, Horn, together with their entire artillery of 54 cannon and the complete baggage train.

Peace deferred

The battle of Nördlingen was as decisive as any in the Thirty Years War, and at first it appeared that the political and diplomatic consequences would prove equally important. Although the Swedish casualties would appear small in comparison with the overall size of their military presence in the Holy Roman Empire, the core of highly-trained veterans had suffered disastrous losses. This severe damage to the military effectiveness of the army was combined with mounting political hostility in the Swedish representative assembly, or Estates, which, even before Nördlingen, had been questioning the benefits and costs of a Swedish presence deep in Germany. In consequence, the Swedish army pulled out of most of its positions in southern, central and western Germany, leaving only a few garrisons in the Rhineland which gradually fell to Imperial counter-attack, or were placed under French military control. The Habsburg armies went their separate ways after Nördlingen: the Cardinal Infante continued his slow march northwards into the Spanish Netherlands, while the King of Hungary profited from his enemies' disarray to drive the remaining Swedes out of Bohemia and Saxony. The Protestant German forces, the remnants of the Duke of Saxe-Weimar's army, were powerless to resist the re-establishment of effective Habsburg/Catholic control across most of southern and central Germany.

For the major German Protestant princes, the Saxon and Brandenburg Electors in particular, the battle was a clear indication of the political future. The Emperor himself, chastened by the failure of his previous attempt to impose an ultra-Catholic settlement on the Holy Roman Empire, was prepared to negotiate a peace which, while leaving him with more power in the Empire than any of his predecessors since Charles V, renounced the aim of wholesale recatholicization. As a result the major Protestant, and indeed the Catholic, German states moved towards the peace which was agreed at Prague in June 1635, a peace which could have offered the possibility of a lasting German settlement on the basis of the post-1634 balance of military power.

The significant obstacle to such a settlement was the France of Louis XIII, whose government had been headed since 1624 by the militantly anti-Habsburg Cardinal Richelieu. Louis had profited from the military embarrassment of the Habsburgs in the early 1630s to consolidate claims over north Italy and the Rhineland, taking advantage of circumstances to undertake a piecemeal occupation of the duchy of Lorraine, and gaining control over a series of Rhine fortresses by offering 'protection' from Catholic and Protestant armies. Contrary to traditional interpretations of Cardinal Richelieu's foreign policy in this period, which assume that he considered an all-out conflict with the Habsburg powers to be inevitable, and was seeking to place France in the best possible position to wage this struggle, there is no evidence that Richelieu anticipated the dramatic overturning of the existing military balance brought about by the battle of Nördlingen. His policies down to mid-1634 were based on the assumption that since the death of Gustavus Adolphus the Protestant allies and the Habsburgs were locked in a military stalemate which would last for the forseeable future. Neither side, Richelieu considered, would seek a major battle which might jeopardize their existing territorial control.

Moreover, Richelieu accepted the commonly-held contemporary view that wars were no longer about pitched battles. Most contemporary commanders used their troops in a slow, expensive, attritional warfare based on sieges of selected fortified cities or fortresses. This style of warfare, with its double lines of siege works often constructed on a scale almost as elaborate as the defences of the place being besieged, could frequently consume entire campaigns. This was almost exclusively the type of warfare experienced in that part of Europe which military theorists and practitioners had since the 1590s termed the 'school of war'—the Spanish and Dutch Netherlands. Such warfare was slow, unlikely to bring any dramatic overturning of the military *status quo*, and was envisaged in the context of future peace negotiations when the captured places would serve as bargaining chips.

In Richelieu's conceptual world, the battle of Nördlingen should never have occurred, and its consequences left his earlier policies exposed and France vulnerable to an attack by the victors. Having previously resisted all the blandishments of his Swedish and Dutch allies to get fully involved in the war against the Habsburgs, Richelieu was now aware that Sweden might well have been definitively disabled by the outcome of Nördlingen. In the event, the Swedish armies were not to retake the military initiative for another half decade; meanwhile the Dutch were inclined to strike a hard bargain for cooperative military activity against the Spanish, given France's reluctance to lend them substantial military support earlier in the war.

Initially Richelieu remained confident that French intervention in conjunction with her allies would tip the military balance, allowing France both to maintain her new territorial gains and to achieve a revision of the Peace of Prague. But by the summer of 1635 it was clear that this confidence had been misplaced, and that France had become locked in a protracted and large-scale conflict which was characterized by the indecisive style of siege warfare which Richelieu had accepted as the typical pattern of European conflict. Habsburg determination to push back the French from all of their advanced positions led to an over-ambitious French response, consisting of campaigns in six or seven separate theatres from Flanders down to the Pyrenean Atlantic frontier, while simultaneously maintaining fleets in both the Mediterranean and the Atlantic. Thus, from 1635 the war was being fought by the French on an unprecedented and unsustainable scale. French military resources were spread thinly between campaign theatres, while the systems of recruiting and maintaining troops were as rudimentary and reliant on private enterprise as those of any other European state. Both Richelieu and his successor from 1643, Cardinal Mazarin, gave priority in successive campaigns to the pursuit of set-piece sieges, above all on the frontier with the Spanish Netherlands, depriving the remaining army corps of even the minimum resources required to sustain their military position. The war between the Habsburgs and France became a stagnant, inconclusive, but massively expensive struggle which seemed to offer little chance of a decisive outcome.

Finally, in the course of the 1640s, the combined pressure of Swedish and French forces operating in the Holy Roman Empire began to make gradual headway against their Austrian and Bavarian opponents, and this pressure persuaded the Emperor to begin serious negotiations for peace. From the late 1630s an influential body of privy councillors advising the new Emperor, Ferdinand III, had been urging him to make substantial concessions within the Holy Roman Empire in order to focus Habsburg control upon the dynastic territories, reinforcing political and religious control over the Austrian archduchies, Bohemia and Habsburg Hungary. This argument had been considerably strengthened by the defeat of the Imperial forces at Jankow in 1645, a hard-fought, two-day battle which opened up Bohemia to the Swedish army, and signalled that subsequent campaigns would only with difficulty be kept off the Habsburg's own lands. The forum for peace discussions already existed. Ever since 1643, all of the major—and most minor—belligerents had maintained representatives at the conferences taking place in the towns of Münster and Osnabrück in the Westphalian Circle, although the first years of these negotations had been characterized more by diplomatic manoeuvres and quarrels over precedence than by constructive bids to achieve a general settlement. After 1645 these negotiations assumed greater seriousness, and after many vicissitudes were to culminate in the 1648 Westphalia peace treaties.

But while the major powers agreed to a settlement in the Holy Roman Empire, and while Spain and the United Provinces finally ended their Eighty Years War on terms which confirmed Dutch independence and commercial ascendancy, the Spanish refused to make terms with Mazarin's France, leaving the Franco-Spanish conflict to drag on for another eleven years during which neither side appeared to have the capacity to force a peace settlement which would represent an acceptable return from twenty-five years of war. The Peace of the Pyrenees, which finally ended the conflict in 1659, owed more to the additional military, and above all naval, power which an alliance with the English Republic had brought to France, than to any perception of a shift in the military balance between the two rivals. Just as Ferdinand III's councillors had urged peace in the Holy Roman Empire in the 1640s in order to consolidate and protect Habsburg dynastic possessions, so Philip IV of Spain came to identify his highest priority as the reconquest of Portugal, where a well-organized rebellion had stubbornly defied Castilian efforts at suppression since its outbreak in 1640. On the other side, Mazarin and his diplomats were well aware of the fragility of the alliance with the crumbling English Republic, and were anxious to conclude a settlement before France once again found herself without military support.

The view that the resulting Peace of the Pyrenees represented an unambiguous French diplomatic triumph is one based entirely on hindsight. The rise of Louis XIV's France to an apparently unassailable military and diplomatic position by the late 1660s has too easily suggested that the foundations of this hegemony were laid in the previous decade. At the time, however, the peace simply represented a welcome respite from a seemingly endless war which offered few glimmers of hope to either power that their rival could be worn down if the struggle was continued.

Malplaquet and military change in Europe after 1660

Seventy-five years after the battle of Nördlingen another engagement of equally decisive importance but very different character took place. The battle of Malplaquet, fought on 11 September 1709 between French forces commanded by the marshals Villars and Boufflers and an allied army of Austrian, German, Dutch and British troops under the command of Prince Eugene of Savoy and the Duke of Marlborough, has a distinctive resonance in the history of war between the states of the European *ancien régime*. Comparisons with the major battles of the First World War are not unjust. Proportionally the level of casualties for a six-hour engagement were as high as anything suffered in a particular assault on the Somme or at Verdun. Immediately after the battle, a military elite who generally cultivated an aristocratic ethos of reckless courage and disregard for suffering seemed appalled by the sheer scale of the death and mutilation around them. Called upon to sing the Te Deum, the victorious allied soldiers, who had suffered a conservative 20 000 casualties out of an army whose real strength was around 85 000 men, sang in tones 'more redolent of a funeral procession than a triumph'.

Malplaquet offers the spectacle of a battle in which the nominal victors suffered heavier casualties than the defeated force. The French, who themselves lost some 12 000 men—heavy casualties even by the normal standards of engagements during the later wars of Louis XIV's reign—withdrew from positions that they had held on the morning of 11 September but in good order, losing only 16 pieces of artillery and no significant baggage or supplies. There was little enthusiasm in France for celebrating Malplaquet as a strategic victory, but it was soon recognized that the battle had brought the allied advance to a halt and saved the north-eastern provinces from invasion. As Villars wrote to Louis XIV in his report of the day: 'If

God grants me the grace to lose another such battle, Your Majesty may rest assured that the enemy will be entirely destroyed'.

The practical and psychological significance of Malplaquet can only be grasped in terms of the dramatic shifts in military and political fortunes that had taken place on the battlefields of Europe in the second half of the seventeenth century. A number of armies before 1660 had possessed a significant proportion of veteran troops; yet the great mass of these forces continued to be made up of rapidly recruited and ill-trained units, raised by entrepreneurs and owing more loyalty to their commanding officers than a distant political authority. The dangers for civil governments of such a system had been revealed with brutal clarity during the affair of Wallenstein's alleged treason in 1633–34. The Imperial Generalissimo was suspected, probably with reason, of trying to negotiate a peace with the Swedes which would consolidate his own princely position in the Empire at the expense of his notional employer and overlord, the Emperor. As Wallenstein controlled the army, the only means of meeting this threat was to hold a secret trial in absentia and to arrange his assassination by dissident and ambitious army officers. The French government of Cardinal Mazarin, on the other hand, was unable to find any solution to the problem of the prince de Condé who opposed Mazarin during the Frondes, then in 1652 took his army into Spanish service and fought against the troops of Louis XIV. Supported by the Spanish king, he was fully restored to his governorships and territories in France after 1659 as one of the key, non-negotiable Spanish demands at the Peace of the Pyrenees.

Rulers at the end of the various conflicts which had lasted down to 1660 had good reason to regard the self-financing, self-sustaining military organization as pernicious and dangerous to established authority. To escape from this decentralized system became a high priority for rulers, though the precise chronology and extent of this escape varied considerably. The rulers of some second and third-rank powers, notably the Brandenburg Elector and a number of the Italian princes, started systematically to develop small standing armies in the years immediately after 1648. However, it was only after 1680 that Sweden made a definitive break from an army largely based on mercenary contracts, with the wholesale expansion of the *indelningsverk* by Charles XI. This system permanently assigned land revenues to permit the upkeep of a professional standing army, maintained in constant readiness for action. It laid the foundations of the substantial native army that came close to outright victory over the grand coalition of Sweden's enemies in the first years of the Great Northern War (1700–21).

The most dramatic example was, however, provided by France. Although peace had been achieved with Spain in 1659, it was not followed by a significant reduction in real levels of taxation. Taxes continued to be collected at war-time levels, with substantially less wastage and evasion, and the bulk of these financial resources were used to maintain a standing army of around 55 000 troops. This was around two-thirds of the number of effectives inadequately funded and supplied during the war decades after 1635, but some five times more than the previous number of troops historically maintained by France as a permanent military 'core'. From a standing army that had previously been numerically insignificant, France passed to having the largest permanent force in Europe outside the Ottoman Empire. These troops were regularly funded from the centre, drilled and subjected to levels of discipline and control that had been entirely impractical when the great majority of the troops were recruited for each campaign. The French army created in the 1660s by the minister of war, Michel Le Tellier, and by his son, the marquis de Louvois, became a formidable military machine. Even when the army was expanded by short-term recruitment to meet the demands of European warfare, the core of professional, maintained troops was large enough to ensure that their military qualities predominated.

The wars of French expansion, 1667–97

The effect of these French military reforms was immediate. In 1667 French troops invaded the Spanish Netherlands in pursuit of Louis XIV's claims that part of this territory had 'devolved' to him through the dynastic rights of his wife, Maria Theresa, elder half-sister of the new Spanish king, Carlos II. The justification for this territorial aggression was threadbare; it involved claiming that customary private law in parts of the southern Netherlands, which allowed female rights of inheritance, could override the public, dynastic law for the general succession of the territories of the Spanish monarchy. Yet the French claims were made good with an army which gained more cities and surrounding territory in a single campaign than the armies of Richelieu and Mazarin had obtained in twenty-five years. Admittedly part of the success was due to the demoralized and weakened state of the Spanish Army of Flanders, but it was no less the case that the French army had been transformed into an instrument of aggressive policy-making unrecognizable from the earlier decades of the seventeenth century.

Rapid military success in 1667–68 profoundly altered Louis XIV's perception of European politics. Where he had previously been prudent and anxious to avoid military confrontation, the king was no longer inclined to avoid war as an instrument of policy. Indeed the prospect of further rapid and glorious military triumphs appealed far more than victories won by diplomacy and the simple threat of force. Sieges under the cardinal-ministers had been a grindingly expensive, slow and ultimately ineffective means of prosecuting warfare. Louis had discovered that if his army enjoyed outright military superiority on the ground, and could block any possibility of organized relief, few governors and garrisons would resist to the point of starvation or assault. In the calculations of defenders, state-of-art fortifications, which had developed substantially in scale and expense since the later sixteenth century, were far less important than the possibility that a relieving force would drive the besiegers off before food, ammunition and morale were exhausted. When that was not a possibility, fortified cities and their fortresses surrendered in waves. In 1667, aware that the remaining Spanish forces in the Netherlands were incapable of throwing back the French army of invasion, the cities of Flanders opened their gates after little more than token resistance.

Louis XIV's confidence that he could dominate European battlefields began a new phase of seventeenth-century political and military history. Despite an Anglo-American historiographical tradition which proposes that Louis XIV was pursuing essentially defensive and reactive policies in the decades after 1660, the period to the end of the century could more convincingly be characterized as the wars of French expansion. That the conquests of the 1670s and 1680s were territorially modest in comparison with the gains made by the Austrian Habsburgs in the east after 1683, does nothing to qualify the ambitions of those who, from the king downwards, were formulating

French policy. The period was marked both by the systematic elaboration and assertion of dynastic claims and, when these were not sustainable, by straightforward opportunistic annexation. The treatment of second-rank states such as the duchies of Lorraine and Savoy, the Rhineland Palatinate or the Archbishopric of Cologne, leaves little doubt that Louis and his most influential ministers regarded their independence and sovereignty with contempt, and had no hesitation in using force to reduce them to the status of tractable clients or occupied territory. The notion that the systematic intimidation of such rulers on the borders of France was part of a territorially disinterested strategy to achieve France's own security is as unconvincing as the view that his treatment of the major European states reflected a concern to achieve a balance of power. The extent of Louis XIV's ambitions grew rapidly to the point where his opponents had no difficulty in depicting him as intent on the achievement of *monarchia universalis*, not the outright conquest of every state in Europe, but the achievement of a position of territorial, dynastic and military hegemony so great as to overwhelm any likely opposing coalition.

Paradoxically, what slowed the process of French military assertion in the first decade of the reign was the prospect of a territorial prize so great as to justify compromise and short-term concession. The succession of Carlos II of Spain in 1665 sent the European diplomatic system into overdrive. Rumoured to be sickly, deformed and incapable of producing heirs, Carlos was widely held to have only a few years to live. With his anticipated death the question of the succession to the extended Spanish Empire would open up. Louis XIV, like most European contemporaries, had little doubt that Carlos' testament would pass the Empire intact to the Austrian branch of the Habsburgs, and would thus recreate the 'world empire' of Charles V. In the immediate aftermath of the Peace of the Pyrenees this was a chilling prospect for the French crown: eleven years of war from 1648–59 with Spain alone had brought little military progress and the near-collapse of government at home. Yet such French views began to change after the success of the campaign of 1667. The new ruler of the Austrian lands and subsequently Holy Roman Emperor, Leopold I, also had little doubt that he would inherit the Spanish empire *de jure* if Carlos was to die without heirs. He was far less certain that he would be able to make good his practical claims to this inheritance in the face of a belligerent France, intent on blocking the re-establishment of the great Habsburg *monarchia*. At best he would find himself locked into a protracted war in western Europe at a time when the revival of Ottoman pressure on the borders of Hungary was already placing his military system under strain. The alternative in these circumstances was to negotiate an agreement for the orderly partitioning of the Spanish inheritance, probably in defiance of whatever testamentary arrangements had been made by Carlos and his ministers, but providing both the Emperor and Louis with sufficient territorial gains to stave off conflict.

Despite his new-found confidence in the effectiveness of his army, the first partition treaty presented Louis XIV with an offer—the peaceful acquisition of the Spanish Netherlands, Franche-Comté, Naples, Sicily, Navarre, Rosas and the Philippines—so attractive and bringing such prestige to the Bourbon dynasty that it was worth sacrificing some of the immediate *gloire* of military success to achieve. This was especially the case, as was noted by Louis' more perspicacious ministers of finance and foreign affairs, Jean-Baptiste Colbert and Hughes de Lionne, in that French military aggression was beginning to cause wider unease amongst previously unaligned powers. These latter were showing signs of overcoming their differences and negotiating alliances aimed specifically at halting the increasingly threatening prospect of French territorial expansion.

Even disregarding the potential dangers posed by these coalitions, there was moreover little point in launching a further campaign into the Spanish Netherlands or the Franche-Comté when the secret partition treaty would hand these over to France anyway after the remaining few months or years that it would take Carlos II to die. As a consequence of this treaty with Leopold, therefore, Louis was prepared to negotiate the Peace of Aix-la-Chapelle in 1668, settling for his previous gains in the Spanish Netherlands but renouncing further conquests, obviously pending the great division of the spoils.

However, Carlos did not die. During the next few years he gave every indication of robust health, and indeed the widely disseminated stories of his sickliness and imminent mortality seemed less and less convincing. The Peace of Aix-la-Chapelle, which at the time had seemed to Louis a rational deferral of gratification, now appeared a maddening waste of a winning hand. He was not prepared to wait indefinitely—or even for a matter of decades—for the Spanish succession to fall in. Louis' growing predilection for the pursuit of military *gloire* was abetted by the young minister-of-war-in-waiting, Louvois, and found support from marshal Turenne, whose ambition to hold supreme command of the French armies was unlikely to be achieved while France was at peace.

The result was the war against the Dutch, launched after a flurry of diplomatic initiatives in 1672. Unwanted by all of Louis' senior ministers, it represents a prime example of an unnecessary and ill-considered war. The existence of the large standing army, the king's restlessness, and an inchoate desire to 'punish' a power felt to have insulted France by opposing her earlier expansion into the Spanish Netherlands, all underpinned a campaign that was meticulously organized at the tactical and logistical level, yet devoid of any wider strategic coherence. After the initial military successes, which revealed the French army's clear superiority over the demoralized and isolated Dutch forces, the States General of the United Provinces decided to flood the open country in the provinces of Holland and Zeeland, in order to preserve the main cities including Amsterdam from the French advance. At the end of 1672 the French had gained spectacular initial success, but were now prevented from achieving the final conquest of the political and economic heartlands of the Republic. As the aims of the war had never been fully established by the king's ministers, the question of whether these initial successes would justify making a treaty on extremely favourable terms with the Dutch was simply not given proper discussion. By default, the decision was taken to continue the war into 1673, though the means by which the next campaign was to be prosecuted, and even the targets of this campaign, were still unresolved.

The decision to continue the war with the Dutch into 1673 can be regarded as the military and diplomatic turning point of the reign. A rapid war, preceded by a well-conducted diplomatic offensive to ensure the isolation of the Dutch, should have been followed by a swift peace. This would have achieved the obvious French objective of intimidating the United Provinces sufficiently to prevent them opposing the French annexation of the Spanish Netherlands, whether by partition treaty or conquest. By continuing the war, the diplomatic initiatives to achieve the isolation of the United Provinces fell apart, and France found herself confronted by a growing body of European states—Spain, England, the Emperor and a number of the German princes, notably the Brandenburg Elector—prepared to act against an outright French annexation of the Republic. Louis' response to this was predictably aggressive; far from seeking to divide and buy off his opponents, he prepared to wage war against all of them. The next campaign would involve an invasion of the United Provinces, but unlike that of 1672 it would be launched directly across the territory of the Spanish Netherlands. By violating previous guarantees, this act would ensure that Spain would have no choice but to mobilize her armies to resist the French. Meanwhile, a further French army was to be despatched into Germany with orders to engage the forces of the Emperor and the Brandenburg Elector. France's old client, the king of Sweden, was to be bullied into launching an attack against the Elector's own territories as a warning to him not to meddle in France's affairs.

On the military level, Louis' armies did encounter some setbacks. They were outmanoeuvred and driven off German territory during the 1673 campaign. Unable in consequence to maintain their lines of communication, French forces were also obliged to evacuate the United Provinces. Despite the original aims of the war, they never returned. Elsewhere though, in the Spanish Netherlands and the Franche-Comté, the French armies swept all before them, and these military gains were ultimately to be rewarded with substantial territorial concessions at the Peace of Nijmegen in 1678. But a high price was paid for this in the ever-growing suspicion and animosity which had brought together a European coalition committed to opposing further French expansion.

Emerging from the 'Dutch' war even more confident of his military capacity to intimidate and assert his power over other European states, Louis began to pursue the policy of *réunions*, the use of largely spurious jurisdictional claims to advance France's eastward frontier up to and beyond the Rhine. By 1684 these policies had succeeded in antagonizing all of the German princes and in generating an unprecedented willingness to accept Imperial authority and leadership in what was seen as an imminent and necessary war to halt French expansion. A year previously, in 1683, Leopold had faced and overcome the most spectacular threat of his reign, the Ottoman siege of Vienna. The collapse of the overextended Turkish forces in the face of the Polish and German princely relief army was to reveal the structural weakness of the Ottoman system in the Balkans.

Henceforth, Leopold's forces would continue to be engaged in the East, but as an army of conquest, pushing the frontiers of Habsburg territory from Buda (1686) to Belgrade (1688). In these radically changed circumstances, he was prepared to take up the leadership of a German struggle against Louis XIV.

This struggle had been given additional sharpness by a religious factor. In 1685, systematically misled by Catholic provincial elites and a court-ministerial faction, and jealous of Leopold's great blow against Islam, Louis XIV acted to revoke the 1598 Edict of Nantes— the measure by which Henri IV had conceded toleration to the French Protestants. During an epoch when it is widely and errone-ously asserted that confessional issues had ceased to be a factor in international politics, Louis' action stigmatized France in the eyes of Protestant Europe, and brought to an end a long period in which France had consistently sought to maintain Protestant alliances against the more inflexible confessional-political stance of the Habsburgs. From 1685 to the end of the reign of Louis XIV, no Protestant power was prepared to ally with France.

Moreover after 1688, Louis XIV was seeking to hold on to his territorial gains in the face of growing hostility not just from the German-speaking lands, but from a new and formidable composite political entity, Britain and the Dutch Republic, now united in the person of William III of Orange. One of Louis XIV's most spec-tacular own-goals by the invasion of the Republic in 1672 had been to revive the power of the House of Orange as Stadtholders to the Republic, which had seemed in terminal decline since William II's sudden death, following his *coup d'état* in 1650. William III's implac-able hatred for Louis XIV inevitably influenced English foreign policy after the Glorious Revolution of 1688, when William led a substantial military operation against James II's Catholic regime, and made good the claims to the throne of his wife, Mary Stuart. While neither state would bind itself unconditionally to the other's interests, the capacity to coordinate military and fiscal activity in pursuit of a broadly-perceived threat to political, economic and religious security brought a formidable force into the arena against France.

The expected coalition war against France began in 1689, and lasted for nine years down to the Treaty of Ryswick in 1697. Thanks to the almost complete neglect of diplomacy and concession in the preced-ing decade, France found herself entirely isolated, supported only by a reluctant and bullied duchy of Savoy, whose ruler, Victor Amadeus II, took the opportunity to defect in 1690. Although the French armies continued to hold the military advantage in successive battles, the entire military machine was coming under strain. The first casualty was the navy. Although it had enjoyed a brief flourishing under Cardinal Richelieu in the 1630s, Mazarin had allowed the navy to sink into decay. From the 1660s, Jean-Baptiste Colbert had built up a new fleet to unprecedented proportions, in part, obviously, as an alternative family fief to the army, dominated by the rival ministerial clan of the Le Tellier. By the 1670s the French navy had become a match for the Dutch or the English, and in 1690 won the greatest French naval victory of the century, over the English navy in the Channel at Cap de Bézeviers (Beachy Head). Yet within three years of this victory the costs of sustaining a high-seas fleet had become unsustainable, and the French naval effort had been reduced to licensed piracy, undertaken by private entrepreneurs against allied merchant shipping. The costs of creating and maintaining a navy had risen exponentially during the seventeenth century. Tourville's fleet off Bézeviers had consisted of seventy-five ships of the line manned by 28 000 sailors and marines, and armed with 4600 cannon—fifty times more artillery than a comparable-sized field army. In the desperate financial circumstances of the Nine Years War, the French crown could not sustain this level of expense in parallel with the costs of some 300–350 000 soldiers on land. The only alternative was to lay up the fleet, which literally rotted away once deprived of the constant maintenance and repair essential to wooden ships. On land as well, the burdens even of victorious warfare were becoming unsustainable. The army's professional core was increasingly diluted by short-term recruiting, by a wholesale willingness to sell military office to those prepared to pay for the upkeep of their troops, and by more and more frequent incidents of indiscipline and disorder. The problems on the home front were even graver: harvest failures, famine, a crumbling tax system and spiralling indebtedness. France desperately needed to reduce the scale of her military commitments, and the crown was prepared to pay a heavy price to achieve this. It became clear that France was in danger of winning most of the battles but losing the war, and indeed the terms of the Treaty of Ryswick marked the surrender of much that France had extracted by force since 1679. That the terms were not harsher still reflected her continued success in the field. But the allies were aware that France simply could not afford to keep fighting much longer, and they drove the hardest bargain that their own battered armies and economies could justify.

The Spanish succession

Ryswick ought to have marked a dramatic watershed in the structure of international relations. Louis recognized that he needed to pursue a period of prudent, unconfrontational diplomacy, at least until his enemies had grown more suspicious of each other than of France. Yet it was in precisely these circumstances that the long-anticipated issue of the Spanish succession finally erupted. Ever since 1668 the most obvious means to avoid a general war over control of the Spanish territories once Carlos II was dead, had remained a partition treaty drawn up between France and the Emperor. However, the intervening decades had seen a great increase in the power of both France and the Austrian Habsburg dominions. Each now regarded the possibility that the other could make very substantial gains from a partition of the Spanish Empire with far more apprehension than they had felt in the 1660s. The convenient solution in the years immediately following Ryswick, a solution that was also strongly backed by William III, was to pass the great bulk of the Spanish inheritance to a third party with a dynastic claim on the succession, Joseph Ferdinand, son of the Bavarian Elector. But Joseph Ferdinand's sudden death in February 1699 upset this neat plan, and forced the powers back towards a further partition treaty (March 1700) which divided the full inheritance between Austria and France, albeit on the basis of a diplomatic settlement between Louis and William III which excluded the Emperor from the negotiations. Yet when Carlos II did finally die on 1 November 1700 the terms of his will explicitly repudiated these convenient dispositions. Against general expectations, Carlos' testament offered the entire Spanish empire in the first instance to Louis XIV's second grandson, Philippe, duc d'Anjou, on condition that he accepted and defended the totality of the inheritance. If Philippe refused this offer—if France opted for the existing partition agreement—then the entire inheritance would automatically be offered to archduke Charles, second son of emperor Leopold.

As numerous historians have pointed out, Carlos' testament placed Louis in an impossible position. The worst possible scenario for French interests was that the entire inheritance would pass into the family of the Austrian Habsburgs; but this left Louis the choice between accepting the will, and probably having to fight the Emperor who would never accept the Bourbon succession to the Spanish throne, or rejecting the testament and trying to impose the terms of the partition treaty by force, given that in the eyes of the Spanish grandees, Archduke Charles was then automatically the legitimate heir to the empire. The advantage of the first choice was that although it would antagonise the other European powers more than adherence to the partition treaty, it would ensure the support of Spain for the French in any ensuing conflict.

Even after accepting the testament of Carlos, and recognizing his grandson Philip V of Spain, it might have been possible to avoid a European conflict. William III was no more anxious than Louis to see his territories drawn back into a major war, and Leopold was unlikely to fight France without the support of his traditional allies. Yet the dynastic *gloire* reaped from the achievement of the succession, the sense that at last the Bourbons were a dynasty more than equal to the Habsburgs, seems to have filled Louis and his ministers with their old arrogance and contempt for European opinion. Trampling on the sensibilities of both the British and the Dutch, Louis had by 1702 managed to recreate a hostile alliance which, if not so comprehensive as that of 1689, was a formidable threat to France's political aims. France was not isolated as she had been at the beginning of the Nine Years War, since she could count on the support of the Spanish territories and had managed to gain an alliance with Max Emanuel II, the Bavarian Elector. But the coalition of her enemies represented a formidable aggregation of resources, and it remained to be seen whether France, still bruised and battered from the 1690s, would be able to mobilize her military resources effectively enough to compensate for the allies' commercial, financial and manpower superiority.

The opening two years of the War of the Spanish Succession suggested that the 1690s would repeat themselves. French armies would continue to hold the tactical and strategic initiative, and though in the long term France would be trapped in an ultimately hopeless struggle to mobilize resources, the end result would be closer to stalemate than abject defeat. Indeed as Louis was fighting to maintain the terms of the pre-existing Spanish inheritance, it was reasonable to think that the gamble might pay off.

In 1704, it even appeared that a concerted Franco-Bavarian campaign pressing down the Danube towards Vienna might succeed in knocking Austria out of the war altogether, producing a far more favourable outcome to the war than Louis and his ministers had dared hope. However, on August 13, the combined forces of Marlborough and Prince Eugene inflicted the first of their crushing defeats on French armies, destroying the Franco-Bavarian force at Blenheim. After Blenheim, the French military situation started to deteriorate alarmingly. Two years later, in 1706, France suffered the double blows of the battle of Turin, which threw the French out of Savoy-Piedmont, and opened up Dauphiné and Provence to invasion, and the defeat at Ramillies, which cleared the French forces from the Spanish Netherlands. The pattern of French military victory was irrevocably broken. From initial optimism that France might be able to gain something from the war over and above the maintenance of Philip V as ruler of Spain, the situation by 1708, after a fourth catastrophic defeat at Oudenarde and the fall of the key strategic fortress at Lille, was the blackest of the reign. It was followed by a set of allied demands which included not merely the removal of Philip from the Spanish throne—if necessary with French military assistance—but calls for a restructuring of domestic French politics to weaken the absolutist authority of the king, the restoration of Protestant worship and the predictable sweep of France's previous territorial acquisitions. Louis rejected these terms, specifically because of the affront that assisting in the deposition of Philip offered to his dynastic pride, and in the winter of 1708–9 Marlborough and Eugene laid plans for the invasion of France that would follow in the next campaign.

In retrospect it is easy to see that France's conduct of international relations ever since the mid-1670s had been a tightrope walk, in which the critical factor was military success. Despite her huge population and agricultural wealth, France's governmental and administrative system made the efficient financing of protracted war impossible. She was fighting against coalitions of powers whose total available resources far outweighed those of France. Moreover, an important factor in this disparity of resources had become manpower itself. War in the later seventeenth century was becoming a bloodier business, with considerably higher casualties sustained not just by the defeated army but also by the victors. This process was to climax, as we have seen, at Malplaquet in 1709, but it had become a significant factor from the 1690s. In the first place, the armies involved on the field were substantially larger. As early as 1691, the battle of Steenkirk had seen 57 000 French pitted against a coalition army of 70 000. A higher proportion of available troops was committed to a particular engagement, so that heavy losses, sustained by military systems which were already trying to mobilize a much larger proportion of the adult male population, were more difficult to replace.

With new weaponry, larger armies became more lethal. The invention and proliferation of the ring bayonet in the 1690s led to the disappearance of the pike as a standard infantry weapon. All musketeers were now equipped with a bayonet, turning their firearm into a defensive weapon which could also be used by entire units in attack. The firepower of an infantry company was increased by a third as the pikemen were phased out and issued with muskets and bayonets. Still more important was the proliferation of cheap, reliable flintlock muskets, using a flint-generated spark rather than a hand-held smouldering match to ignite the powder in the cartridge. Eliminating the match speeded up fire-drill significantly, but it also allowed the musketeers to be packed far more closely in their units. Whereas 'closed order' at Nördlingen still implied soldiers standing three feet apart from each other—to avoid the danger of accidentally igniting a neighbour's cartridges with the match—by Malplaquet closed order meant shoulder to shoulder. The effects of a musket volley fired by these close-packed troops was devastating, and the numbers of deaths and wounds from gunshot increased dramatically in the later seventeenth century. These increases in the number and deadliness of infantry firearms were accompanied by a slow increase in the number of artillery pieces deployed on the battlefield. By Malplaquet the French army had some 80 cannons, the allied forces around 100. This artillery was more manouevrable than that of seventy years earlier, and was deployed more effectively to support the infantry and to reinforce defensive positions.

When the tide of battle turned against the French, therefore, it was in circumstances in which defeats in the field were much more costly. The defeat at Blenheim involved losses of 34 000 for the Franco-Bavarian army, though a very large proportion of these were prisoners. Marlborough and Eugene's aggressive tactics, which deployed frontal assaults by infantry followed up by knockout blows launched by massed cavalry, were not sparing of the lives of their own troops. The justification was that such battles really did seem capable of deciding the outcome of a campaign, and thereby possibly of the war. What had spared the allies from the horrific levels of casualties that could be expected from massed frontal assaults had been a combination of divisive French military leadership—a characteristic of Blenheim, Ramillies and Oudenarde—and the confusion and panic that such tactics had created amongst the French units when first practised by the allies.

At Malplaquet, however, the French had strong, confident leadership, and the troops were expecting an all-out allied assault. Despite the terrible winter and famine of 1708–9, which had deprived the army as well as the wider population of adequate supplies of food and had precipitated the worst financial crisis of the reign, Villars had been able to maintain the army's morale and to channel whatever resources were available towards his troops. They were poorly fed, ill-clothed and short of munitions for a long campaign, but were nonetheless prepared to fight. Moreover, in all the previous battles since 1704 the French had been operating beyond their frontiers; they were concerned to safeguard their communications and had limited choice about where and when to give battle. At Malplaquet, Villars and Boufflers had one objective: to stand their ground and to repel an allied invasion. The precise siting of the French army, and the possibility of exploiting unexpected allied disarray by taking the offensive, had been a matter of uncertainty and debate in the days immediately before the battle. By nightfall, however, all debate halted, and the French took the opportunity to dig themselves into defensive positions and to await the allied attack.

This began at 7.30 a.m. with a forty-cannon bombardment of the French positions on the left flank, followed by the first of a series of allied infantry assaults. By 11.00 a.m., and at heavy cost, the allies had pushed the French back and forced Villars to reconstitute the forces on his left wing. Further ferocious assaults on the right flank proved unable to break through the French defences, but Marlborough and Eugene noted that the price of maintaining these two flanks had been a steady weakening of the centre. A major attack by fresh allied troops took the French centre by surprise, forcing the infantry out of their defences, and threatening the complete collapse of the French line.

The situation was saved by a mass counter-attack of French cavalry, checking the allied advance, though failing to break through the allied lines. Between two and three in the afternoon, Boufflers, who had taken command after the wounding of Villars, and was aware that his troops were tiring and running out of amunition, decided to conduct an orderly retreat.

Unlike Nördlingen, artillery played a substantial role throughout the battle, being deployed at close quarters both to facilitate assaults and to bolster defensive positions. Though the final outcome of the battle was shaped by massed cavalry, the major part of the engagement had been fought between infantry, and coordinated musket-fire had been decisive in determining the success and failure of these assaults. Of those French soldiers admitted with wounds to the hospital of the Invalides after the battle, 13.7 per cent were the result of artillery fire, 64.7 per cent came from musket shot. Fewer than one quarter of the Swedish casualties at Nördlingen were the result of wounds sustained from firearms.

Malplaquet ensured that France would not be exposed to a full-scale invasion in late 1709, and it soon became clear that it had weakened the allied determination to force Louis XIV into an abject surrender. Marlborough and Eugene might remain hopeful of continuing the struggle into 1710, but the political consensus which had sustained the allied military commitment was fragmenting. In England, the electoral successes of the Tories in 1710 and their domination of the new parliament, while not removing Marlborough from his command, considerably reduced his freedom of action. Only overwhelming military success in the subsequent campaigns could have stifled the barrage of criticism of the war-effort; but Malplaquet was followed by campaigns in 1710 and 1711 which proved expensive and indecisive. The tide which had turned so catastrophically against France since 1704 had been halted in 1709, and time increasingly appeared to be on the side of the French if they could avert military disasters or financial collapse. It was in this climate that the path was opened to the peace negotiations at Utrecht (1713), where the bill for a settlement was paid not by France but by the Spanish empire. Philip V was confirmed in possession of the Spanish crown, but the price of this was a series of territorial and commercial concessions required to buy off the allies. It had been the desire to avoid a division of the Spanish empire which had led the dying Carlos II and his councillors to draft the succession arrangement that had precipitated the war; ironically the outcome of the ensuing conflict was precisely this partitioning.

Conclusion

Can any general conclusions be drawn from the study of war and the conduct of international relations in the seventeenth century? If any one factor can be isolated as the dominant theme of seventeenth-century international relations, it is undoubtedly dynasticism. Policy was for the most part formulated, not in accordance with concepts of 'national security' or *Realpolitik*, but to facilitate the family interests of ruling houses. Most hereditary princes, and even some elected rulers, saw their territories as resource-bases, a means by which family honour and the long-term interests of the dynasty could be sustained and advanced. International politics was attuned to the assertion and resolution of territorial claims based upon the dynastic connections of European ruling families, whether these were acquired through blood relatives or marriage. The currency of international relations and diplomacy was based upon this system of personalized claims—claims which often flew in the face of strategic or territorial logic, but which emphasized the sacrosanct nature of personal and family sovereignty at the heart of the European state system. Throughout the seventeenth century, for example, the French crown remained obsessed with the territorial claims that it had acquired over parts of Italy, notably Milan and Naples, although the practical problems of making good these claims were all-but insuperable. The composite monarchies which still straddled seventeenth-century Europe were testimony to the precedence given to inherited family rights over territorial contiguity, and economic, cultural or linguistic identity.

Moreover, a diplomatic system which gave priority to dynastic rights would respect these even when they were asserted by second- or even third-rank rulers, and when they implicated the major powers in unwanted conflicts on their behalf. Such was the case of the 1628–31 War of the Mantuan Succession, fought because of the determination of Charles de Nevers, the closest heir to the last of the principal line of the Gonzaga, to claim all of the Gonzaga territories without making concessions to lesser claimants. A French duke as well as a sovereign prince, Charles de Nevers appealed to Louis XIII to support his claims to the inheritance, which ultimately pitted a French army against the Spanish-backed forces of the lesser claimants, the Dukes of Guastalla and Savoy. Neither major power wanted a conflict in north Italy, but the strength of appeals for support in the face of an apparently unresolvable dynastic dispute proved irresistible.

Just as the Peace of Westphalia is too often taken to mark the end of conflicts based upon religion, so its character as a dynastic settlement can be missed in the concern to identify it as the first 'modern' peace treaty. In some respects it was innovatory: the negotiations were of unprecedented length and complexity; it did contribute to the development of permanent diplomatic representation; it did aspire to resolve a multitude of different disputes in the interests of a general European settlement that would provide some form of lasting international order. But for the Austrian Habsburgs the great gain of the peace was the confirmation of the status of Bohemia as an inherited possession of the monarchy. The creation of the eighth Electorate for the restored Elector Palatine was a belated solution to the rivalry between the Palatine and Bavarian branches of the Wittelsbach, a family connection which had originally facilitated the Imperial transfer of the Palatine Electorate from one branch of the family to the other back in 1623. Although the Brandenburg Elector was in no military or political position to assert a strong bargaining position at the Westphalia negotiations, above all against the Swedes, he nonetheless received the larger share of the duchy of Pomerania, simply because he had been the strongest claimant to the territory after the death of Bogislav XIV in 1637. Sweden had shown no wish to hand over any of Pomerania before 1647, but alarmed by European support for the dynastic claims of Frederick William of Brandenburg, resolved to give up the bulk of the territory to avoid isolation over this issue.

As the account of the western European wars after 1660 clearly reveals, dynasticism remained the primary motive force in diplomacy, territorial assertion and peace negotiations in western Europe from the War of Devolution down to the War of the Spanish Succession. The naval struggles of the English and the Dutch in 1652–4, 1665–7 and 1672–4 provide an exceptional example of warfare between economic rivals. Even in the East, in the wars with the Ottomans, rhetorical claims to the 'Byzantine inheritance' kept alive a dynastic element at the same time that the realities of the conflict were governed by *Realpolitik* and by a continued confessional fervour.

A second obvious characteristic of the seventeenth century was the length of the wars into which the European powers were drawn. From the 'Long Turkish War' fought on the frontiers of Austrian and Ottoman Hungary between 1593 and 1606, to the eleven years of the Spanish Succession, and the twenty-one years of the Great Northern War fought between Sweden and her Baltic enemies, the century was one of exceptionally long conflicts. It took twenty-eight years of war before Castile finally conceded recognition to neighbouring Portugal. These were, moreover, conflicts which, unlike their lengthy medieval precedents, involved annual campaigning; there were few years of respite or undeclared truce, and the burdens of fighting on this scale were entirely unprecedented. It is tempting to propose that these lengthy conflicts simply reflected the state of weaponry and military organization in the seventeenth century. States could raise armies, but they lacked the resources and organization to turn them into effective instruments of policy. Armies might become larger, their killing-power might become greater, but neither battles nor sieges offered the possibility of achieving decisive results quickly. Though the victories of the Swedes and the French in the Empire in the 1640s, or the victories of Marlborough and Eugene after 1704, could gradually tip the military balance, it required whole series of campaigns to bring an enemy power to the point of negotiation. Even then, a costly victory like Malplaquet, still more a clear defeat, could check the momentum towards a decision by restoring a balance of advantage in which the enemy would feel able to fight on.

All this is certainly true, and explains the protracted nature of many of the peace negotiations during the century. Such negotiations were already complicated by the involvement of multiple powers around the table; peace settlements even as late as Vervins in 1598 had tended to be negotiated as bipartite arrangements. But it was also the case that few rulers had lost hope that their military fortunes might experience an upturn, more probably because of the fiscal or organizational difficulties of their enemies than because of their own success in the field, and so long as this was the case there was a tendency to procrastinate and buy time at the negotiating table. There were of course occasions when armies were able to bring about decisive results: two campaigns in 1643–44 were sufficient for the Swedish armies to force Christian IV of Denmark into a humiliating peace settlement; the French armies campaigning in 1667 offered Louis XIV the real possibility of absorbing the entire Spanish Netherlands; Cromwell's New Model Army could crush both Irish and then Scottish military and political resistance in the campaigns of 1649–50 and 1650–51. Where military forces of unequal quality were pitted against each other, the results could still be rapid and decisive. It may well be that such examples were too often taken by rulers as the likely outcome of seventeenth-century wars, and that in this sanguine frame of mind they ignored the harsh fact that most wars were ended, whether they were won or lost, at the price of huge commitments in men and money, requiring great political and economic endurance.

Finally, in terms of the future pattern of international relations, it is relevant that not one but two critical battles took place in 1709. In September, the troops of Villars and Boufflers managed to bring the allied invasion of France to a costly halt. In late June, a Russian army of some 42 000 had taken advantage of the overextended lines of communication of Charles XII and his Swedish force of around 19 000 effectives, to win an overwhelming victory at Poltava, deep in the Ukraine. The consequent collapse of the Swedish Baltic empire and the Russian occupation of Livonia and Lithuania marked the opening of a new chapter in European diplomatic and military history, one in which a new and major power would fundamentally alter previous political alignments and shift the centre of gravity in international relations firmly eastwards during the eighteenth century.

5

The age of curiosity

Laurence W. B. Brockliss

The Augustinian landscape

Old man   Threescore and ten I can remember well;
           Within the volume of which time I have seen
           Hours dreadful, and things strange; but this sore night
           Hath trifled former knowings.
Ross   Ah! good father,
           Thou see'st, the heavens, as troubled with man's act,
           Threatens his bloody stage.

(*Macbeth*, 2. IV, 1–6)

The universe depicted in Shakespeare's plays of the late sixteenth and early seventeenth centuries was one of magic, mystery and wonder. Unnatural events bore witness to human sin, ghosts walked, and statues came alive. It was a world where men had only a limited control over themselves and even less over their environment. They were the toys of a wild, pitiless nature and the sport of malign and invisible spirits who could conjure storms and turn humans into animals. Only the cunning few, witches and warlocks, had the measure of this unforgiving landscape and could bend its forces to their own desire. Such an awesome ability to command the winds and read the future, however, was in its turn dehumanizing. Prospero regained his dukedom through his knowledge of the dark arts but he had to break his staff to re-enter his Milanese inheritance.

How far Shakespeare believed in the reality of this universe will never be known. It is certain, on the other hand, that his rich but pessimistic vision was a cultural commonplace shared by the large majority of his contemporaries and by generations of their ancestors. For most of the seventeenth century, virtually all Europeans regardless of homeland, class or education, saw themselves inhabiting a material world where the natural and supernatural and the sub- and superlunary were interwoven. They were the hapless spectators on a cosmic battlefield where God, the devil and their agents inter- vened continually in the natural order, and the planets through their adverse or benign conjunctions brought mayhem or prosperity. Even nature herself was full of tricks and surprises, as the frequent accounts of monstrous births, vampires, werewolves, and talking animals revealed. Inevitably in such an unpredictable universe people of all backgrounds leaned heavily on the papier mâché shoulders of the legion of astrologers, soothsayers, necromancers and alchemists who claimed to be able to understand and even manipulate the chaos.

The Reformation of the sixteenth century had done little to under- mine this world-view. Although the first reformers and counter- reformers had declared war on certain aspects of contemporary culture, which they considered pagan superstitions, they and their seventeenth-century successors remained wedded to the principal assumptions of the Shakespearian vision. By and large their ire was reserved for those who claimed to be able to harness the forces of nature and the spirit world for their own profit or others' ill. In fact, Catholic and Protestant theologians had helped to strengthen the cultural commonplace by placing a novel emphasis on the omni- presence of the devil and his agents in human affairs. By stamping witchcraft, both black and white, with the mark of Satan, the post- Reformation theologians confirmed the impossibility of mere mor- tals gaining the power to control their environment by their own efforts and for the first time made the village wise-woman an object of suspicion. The unprecedented number of witches murdered by the state in the century 1550 to 1650—far more than the number of heretics—was testimony to the pervasiveness of this Church-fostered belief in diabolism, which only exceptional figures, such as the Bra- bant physician, Johann Weyer (1515–88), withstood. Some Protestant churchmen, anxious to emphasize the power of God over his creation, even promoted judicial astrology, the art of predicting the course of people's lives from the position of the planets at their moment of birth. While Catholic theologians did their limited best to put court astrologers out of business, insisting that God had given humans free will, the Lutheran Philipp Melanchthon (1497–1560), for one, believed that a successful astrological prediction would confirm that our choices were predestined by an omnipotent and omniscient deity.

The confessional churches of the first part of the seventeenth century, moreover, underpinned the pessimism of the Shakespearian vision with the bleakness of their doctrine of salvation. Theologians in both camps accepted without demur the limited view of human nature which had dominated Christendom since the time of St Augustine of Hippo (354–430). Man was an irreparably fallen creature ultimately only redeemed in God's eyes through the saving power of Christ on the cross. Their differences turned around whether or not men played any part in their own salvation through the performance of good works. Neither side believed that performing good works was easy, given the rotteness of the human condition. On the contrary, both agreed that without specific divine grace performing an action pleasing to God was impossible. Only a handful of Jesuit theologians who took their lead from the Spaniard, Luis de Molina (1535–1600), believed that such grace was man's for the asking. Indeed, according to the wing of the seventeenth-century Catholic Church which identified with the opinions of Cornelius Jansen bishop of Ypres (1585–1638), the bestowal of divine grace was arbitrary. Catholic theologians then were often as austere and anti-humanist as their Protestant counterparts. All Christian confessions stressed that life was a vale of tears, the much deserved punishment of God for human disobedience.

Augustine's negative view of mankind was also used to justify the fact that the majority of Europeans were daily subject to 'the proud man's contumely' and 'the insolence of office' as much as the cruel indifference of nature. As frail fallen vessels in an age where the state's arm was still relatively short, seventeenth-century Christians had to be imprisoned within the confines of a gendered, hierarchical and deferential society to ensure that the divine moral order was passably upheld. Make men too comfortable and they would have too great an opportunity to sin. Punish too leniently and they would sin with impunity. Put men in a state of nature or equality and they would tear themselves apart. An Augustinian view of human nature also sustained the penchant of seventeenth-century theologians and lawyers for divine-right absolute monarchy. While Christian political thought had always emphasised the divine origin of political power, many theologians and lawyers in the sixteenth century had followed the Paris Dominican Thomas Aquinas (1225?–74) and other medieval scholastics in allowing the possibility of overt popular resistance to a usurper or tyrant. Most commentators after 1600 allowed subjects no such luxury. Anxious, especially in France, to outlaw the *frondeur* behaviour of the aristocracy, theorists such as Richelieu's *créature*, Cardin le Bret (1558–1653), insisted unequivocally that the prince was both sovereign and inviolate, answerable only to God for his behaviour whatever his sins. Only certain Jesuit theologians, members of the libertarian wing of the Catholic Church, continued to preach the traditional political doctrine.

In Orthodox Russia where the study of non-religious literature was forbidden, literacy extremely low, and schooling for the laity virtually non-existent before the reign of Peter the Great, this Augustinian vision went completely unchallenged within establishment culture. In contrast, in Catholic and Protestant Christendom, even at the beginning of the seventeenth century, some Europeans at least were introduced to a more positive view of human potential through their encounter with pre-Christian classical culture in the course of their schooling. Thanks to the propaganda of sixteenth-century humanist educationalists, an increasingly large proportion of Europe's elite, noble and non-noble, spent its formative years in newly-founded grammer schools, colleges and gymnasia studying Latin (and to a lesser extent Greek) from the belief that a knowledge of the language and literature of classical antiquity was the hallmark of a Christian gentleman. In the course of poring over the poets, orators and historians of the Late Republic and Augustan Empire, especially Virgil and Cicero, the schoolboy was transported into a very different cultural universe, where a man chose to follow his fate and where he could and should be virtuous by his own volition.

This positive message was further reinforced when or if the tiro humanist proceeded to study philosophy at school or university. Although the curriculum in the first half of the seventeenth century was still dominated by the Ancient Greek philosopher, Aristotle (384–322 BC), the study of the Aristotelian corpus offered an equally important corrective to contemporary Christian pessimism, since it provided a rational, secular account of God, man and nature. Aristotle's logic supplied the tools for understanding the cause of things; his metaphysics explained the nature of causation, including the essence of the first cause or God; while his ethics explained how the individual could achieve the greatest good. Above all, Aristotle's natural philosophy provided a coherent material and naturalistic account of the behaviour of natural phenomena that eschewed astral influences and the miraculous or diabolic. All corporal bodies were deemed to be the product of two principles—primary matter and an added 'something' called form—but an absolute distinction was made between the unchanging heavens and the corruptible sublunary universe. In the terrestrial world the body's form determined its sensible properties and qualities, and was related but not reducible to its peculiar and unstable mix of the four elements (fire, air, earth and water).

The handful of philosophy students who went on to study medicine at university encountered a similar naturalistic doctrine of man, expounded in the teaching of the neo-Aristotelian Roman physician, Galen of Pergamum (c.130–200). Students learnt that an individual's health depended on maintaining the proper balance of the qualities or faculties inherent in the forms of the body's solids and fluids. As that balance was principally upset by the corruption or abuse of the non-naturals (air, food and drink, sleep, sex and so on), good health was largely an individual's responsibility.

However, the corrosive effect of such exposure to classical culture must not be exaggerated. It is quite plausible that most schoolmasters were good Augustinians who taught their charges that classical literature was to be read for its literary worth—as a source of tropes and bons mots—rather than for its moral wisdom. Certainly, professors of philosophy were careful to reconcile Aristotelian ethics and metaphysics with Augustinian orthodoxy. Indeed, some Calvinist educational institutions were so nervous that philosophy students would gain the wrong idea of God and his relations with man that they limited the philosophical curriculum to the study of logic and physics. Aristotelian physics, too, was suitably Christianized. Working for the most part within the Thomist Aristotelian tradition of the late Middle Ages, professors stressed that there were many aspects of the natural world that the Greek philosopher, deprived of the insights of Revelation, had misunderstood, most obviously its divine creation and preservation. By insisting that Aristotelian forms were spiritual substances distinct from matter, professors equally made room for the logical possibility of bodiless invisible spirits at work in the universe. Many medical professors, influenced by the sixteenth-century Paris physician, Jean Fernel (1485–1558), even argued that many qualities, especially those present in the body's fluids when an individual fell victim to a major disease like the plague, were unknowable and occult, the result of planetary influences.

Moreover, even if the student of Aristotelian natural philosophy had gained an understanding of the behaviour of natural phenomenon, he was no better equipped than anyone else in his society to survive the hazards of daily existence. Aristotelianism was not a worker-science: it did not teach the adept how to control the natural world. Even physicians trained in the Aristotelo-Galenic medical tradition made only limited claims for the practical utility of their knowledge. They always stressed that their prognosis in the particular instance was uncertain and that God alone decided on the efficacy of medical treatment.

Augustinian values were also more prevalent in the artistic culture of the elite than they had been in the previous century. The period was one of extensive artistic patronage. Interest in court, religious and domestic art and architecture was no longer primarily the preserve of Italians but spread all over the continent, even to England. But increased artistic investment did not reflect a growing confidence in the human condition. Although seventeenth-century art and architecture bore constant witness to the pervasive influence of the pre-Christian era—especially in the continued fascination with classical architectural style, history, mythology, buildings and dress—the art of the Baroque was seldom a Renaissance hymn to human beauty, dignity and potential.

As in previous centuries, religious art, architecture and music were used in Catholic countries to emphasize the peculiar mediatory role of the Church in reconciling fallen man to God. As so many of the more grandiose constructions were built for the new religious orders, religious archictecture in the period also pointed up the dominant role of the Jesuits and their allies in the preservation and extension of Catholic Christendom. Even at the parish level this theologically correct art left its mark, as thousands of new altar pieces were commissioned for the edification of the faithful. Their subjects were as wide and varied as their more spectacular and select Renaissance ancestors, but one theme was particularly privileged—the Madonna and Child. Befitting in a Counter-Reformation Church that aimed to concentrate the worshipper's attention on the redeeming divinity of Christ and the peculiar sanctity of his mother, the holy duo were the religious commonplace of the century. Madonnas and Child came in all styles and moods—from the saccharine sweet concoctions of the Spaniard, Bartolomé Esteban Murillo (1617–82), to the ethereal beauty of *The New Born* of the Lorraine artist, Georges de La Tour (1593–1652).

Secular architecture primarily served to bolster and celebrate the inviolability and grandeur of divinely-constituted authority. This was an era of ever larger palaces and private houses, a trend which culminated in Louis XIV's Versailles and its many imitators, such as William of Orange's *Het Loo* at Appeldoorn. Much secular art served a similar end. Classical allegory and simple portraiture were constantly used to underpin deference and obedience throughout society—in the humble Dutch hospital as much as the royal court. Masters of illusion, court painters such as the Fleming Peter Paul Rubens (1577–1640), the Spaniard Diego Velázquez (1599–1660) and the Frenchman Philippe de Champaigne (1620–74) worked steadfastly to boost the image of the divine-right monarch and his leading henchmen. Charles I of England was a tiny man with a stutter; his wife, Henrietta Maria, had buckteeth. The Fleming Anthony van Dyck (1599–1641) turned them into gods. In the form of genre, landscape and still-life painting, less grandiose secular art was dedicated to revealing the baseness of human nature and the vanity of human wishes, as in *The Arcadian Shepherds* (1638–9) of the Frenchman, Nicolas Poussin (1594?–1665), where the rural idyll is destroyed by the subjects' discovery of a classical tomb bearing the legend 'Et in Arcadia ego'.

For the most part, then, high and low in the period 1600–1660 inhabited the same cultural universe. Although tensions existed between popular culture and contemporary Christianity, and between Christianity and classicism, they were of little significance compared with the deeply engrained consensus that corrupt mankind was powerless in the face of a hostile animate nature. Only the redeeming power of Christ offered a way out.

Curiosity, observation and measurement

As the previous section made clear, the philosophical and theological assumptions underpinning the dominant mindset of the seventeenth-century were not a recent creation. Augustinian values had held the Church in thrall since the fifth century, while their integration with Aristotelian philosophy was principally the work of scholar-priests of the twelfth and thirteenth centuries. However, in any study of this broader Augustinian moment, the seventeenth century must occupy a privileged position as it was the first time in over a thousand years that this traditional world-view was seriously challenged. Throughout the century a small but growing minority of educated Europeans refused to accept the Augustinian analysis of the human condition, if only in part, and developed an unusual, and to Augustinian contemporaries unhealthy, interest in both the material manifestations of the human spirit (past and present) and the abundant and complex variety of the natural world. Augustinians saw the world as a snare and the enjoyment of its fruits (artificial or natural) as vanity. In contrast, this growing minority had an obsessive and insatiable aesthetic and intellectual interest in their environment: they sought more and more information about its treasures, and, where possible, appropriated, collected and examined its wonders themselves. In their hands, the private cabinet ceased to be a space for personal devotion and became a theatre or museum of nature sometimes intentionally modelled on Noah's Ark.

Such people were known to contemporaries and each other as the 'curious', a sobriquet that immediately suggested unorthodoxy. Their appearance was closely associated with the genuine opening-up of the non-European world to European travellers in the previous century. By 1600 the continent, thanks to the printing revolution, was awash with descriptions of ever-more varied flora, fauna and cultures. Educated Europeans for the first time had access to a world much bigger and brighter than their own. However, the desire to own, handle and examine not just exotic objects but even the commonplace specimens of their own natural and historical environment reflected the more positive and subversive inheritance of Renaissance humanism. Renaissance textual scholarship by the middle of the

sixteenth century had engendered a more critical and 'curious' mentality. Later humanists, hungry for tangible evidence that might solve
conflicting points of detail in the recovered Latin and Greek texts or
fill in chronological gaps in the history of the Ancient World, began
to hunt for coins and artefacts with the same enthusiam their predecessors had hunted manuscripts. Some of their number, usually
physicians, were even inspired by reading the scientific texts of the
venerated masters to imitate their original research and look for
themselves, only to find the classical record uncomfortably
insufficient.

Throughout the seventeenth century the most splendid cabinets of
curiosity were built up by princes and great aristocrats. Some, like
Emperor Rudolf II of Austria, had a genuine passion for the study of
nature and drew to their courts a retinue of like-minded enthusiasts.
The majority, though, built up their collections as a symbol of their
power and authority and were only interested in owning the choicest
marvels and treasures. Their cabinets of curiosity became public evidence of their wealth and contacts rather than private spaces in which
they could entertain and instruct their personal friends. In this guise,
collecting might have been vain, but it was scarcely subversive. Princely collections, however, were only the tip of the iceberg. What made
the culture of curiosity so dangerous to the Augustinian establishment was the increasing number of educated and professional
people—lawyers, medical men, clerics, monks—and even the
occasional woman, who caught the bug from their betters and
transformed its significance.

The truly curious in the seventeenth century had catholic and
eclectic collecting tastes. A prime example in the early century was
the Provençal lawyer Nicolas-Claude Fabri de Peiresc (1580–1637)
who was a passionate cultivator of exotic flora such as Indian jas-
mine, and collected local minerals, fossils, shells and corals, and a
wide variety of classical and early medieval remains (coins, weights,
utensils, armaments, vases, and statues) indiscriminately. The truly
curious, too, were not passive collectors but dedicated investigators.
Surrounded by their books and instruments, they turned their
cabinet into a 'laboratory', where natural phenomena and human
artefacts could become sources for study.

In this regard the seventeenth-century cabinet of curiosity had a
close affinity with the medieval and Renaissance alchemist's cell.

Alchemists belonged to an ancient and subversive scientific tradition that the Augustinian establishment had never been able to eradicate. Eternally optimistic in their endeavours to transmute base metals into gold and frequently protected by avaricious princely patrons, they were the inevitable role model for the first generation of curious, despite their artisanal and morally suspect status. Indeed, many alchemists were themselves curious and vice versa.

The curious who specifically concentrated their attention on exploring the structure of the natural world were called in English 'experimental philosophers' or more contemptuously 'virtuosi'. In the privacy of their cabinet, these proto-scientists dissected animal and human remains, subjected organic and inorganic material to chemical analysis, and, much to the dismay of the pious, developed a variety of vivisectional and experimental techniques to discover how nature behaved in unnatural conditions. Initially their experiments were simple and uninspiring. The first generation of experimental philosophers lacked the necessary instrumentation and the collective experience to 'torture' nature convincingly. Their one novel scientific instrument was the low magnification telescope (invented c.1608 by a Dutch lens-grinder) with which they explored the heavens. From the mid-seventeenth century, however, the microscope, the air-pump (courtesy of Otto von Guericke (1602–86)) and the reflecting telescope of Sir Isaac Newton (1642–1727) were added to the experimental repertoire.

The most imaginative and influential experimental philosopher of the decades after 1650 was the Englishman Robert Boyle (1627–91), who is particularly remembered for devising a series of elegant experiments which explored the properties of air and air pressure. Boyle also helped to stabilize a 'protocol' for the performance and description of experiments. In the first part of the century the authenticity of an experimenter's results was continually open to question. Not only was the replication of another's experiments difficult because scientific instruments were poorly constructed and often idiosyncratically calibrated, but there was also no consensus as to how experiments should be conducted. Some were content with announcing the results of 'thought' experiments. Most lacked our modern belief in the need to repeat and refine their observations. The so-called 'crucial' experiment whereby the brother-in-law of the French mathematician, Blaise Pascal (1623–62), proved the existence of air-pressure by observing the different heights attained by a column of mercury at the bottom and top of the Puy-de-Dôme, a mountain in central France, was only performed once. Pascal's purported confirmation of the experiment using the tower of the Paris church Saint-Jacques was wishful thinking: given the altitude of the building there should have been no measurable difference between the readings. Boyle's solution to the anarchy was not to invent and popularize a rigorous set of experimental procedures. Rather, the younger son of the earl of Cork fittingly popularized a 'protocol' based largely on contemporary court etiquette where the authenticity of a fact was guaranteed by the word of a gentleman. An experiment or observation was written up using the active not the passive case in the form of an eye-witness testimony, and its veracity judged by the social class of the narrator.

Through the efforts of the curious, mankind's factual knowledge of the universe, the terrestrial world and the structure of matter (organic and inorganic) was greatly extended. The most spectacular achievements—such as the discovery of Jupiter's satellites in 1610 by Galileo Galilei (1564–1642), or the annunciation of the circulation of the blood in 1628 by William Harvey (1578–1657)—were inevitably the work of the most committed and ingenious experimental philosophers. The majority lacked the necessary imagination, enthusiasm and time (curiosity was a hobby not a vocation) to turn their cabinet into a space for creative and original observation. None the less, even the most inconsequential anatomist, botanist or astronomer contributed some factual titbit to the culture of curiosity and aided the work of the handful of mega-stars, if only by bringing to their attention peculiar examples of nature's fecundity or confirming their observations.

The most original coterie within the community of the curious was the small group of experimental philosophers who brought a novel precision to their investigations through using mathematics. Many virtuosi recognized the deficiencies of classical Latin and contemporary vernacular languages as vehicles for accurately recording and transferring their ever-more complex observations. Most, though, thought that these deficiencies could be remedied by constructing a transparent universal language that could be used as the *lingua franca* of the burgeoning scientific community. It was necessary either to recover the original language of Adam and his successors that was believed to lay hidden in Hebrew, or invent a completely new tongue, as the English clergyman don, John Wilkins (1614–72), tried to do. Only a handful of the curious, especially in the first half of the century, considered that a better solution to the accurate linguistic rendition of the bounties of Nature lay in the adoption of the language of mathematics.

The science of mathematics and its application to the study of the natural world had not been unknown in previous centuries. The late middle ages had inherited from the Greeks and the Arabs, a complex science of astronomy, optics and harmonics based primarily on Euclid (active 300 BC) and Ptolemy (active second century AD), while a better acquaintance with the writings of Archimedes (c.287–212 BC) in the Renaissance had led to a revitalized science of statics and the first attempt to create a science of dynamics. Traditionally, however, natural philosophers considered mathematics unrelated to physics, on the grounds it dealt with abstract not corporeal objects. It was a useful tool for predicting the movements of incorruptible heavenly bodies, and hence an important aid to navigators. It was of little value for studying the behaviour of corruptible and ever-changing sublunary phenomena.

The coterie of mathematical experimental philosophers rejected this Aristotelian assumption, arguing that sublunary natural phenomena could be as effectively studied mathematically as celestial ones. The fact that terrestrial bodies were continually subject to changes of place did not mean that their movements could not be successfully measured and their trajectory and end-point predicted. The most significant exponent of the possibility of a mathematical physics in the first half of the century was Galileo, who single-handedly perfected the nascent science of dynamics, in particular through his study of the movement of balls down inclined planes and the oscillation of pendulums. Galileo's findings, announced in his *New Science* of 1638, were the inspiration for the rapid mathematization of the sciences of ballistics, fortification and horology in the second half of the century by figures such as Christiaan Huygens (1629–95), who invented the pendulum clock in 1656.

The achievements of the first mathematical physicists would have been undoubtedly even greater had they been able to use a more sophisticated form of analysis. There were a number of important developments in mathematics over the century. François Viète

(1540–1603) adopted modern algebraic notation; René Descartes (1596–1650) invented coordinate geometry; while Newton among many mathematical triumphs discovered the binomial theorem. But it was only towards the end of the century that Newton and Gottfried Wilhelm Leibniz (1646–1716) independently invented the mainstay of modern mathematical physics, calculus. Speedy advance in the mathematical study of terrestrial motion in the seventeenth century therefore was constrained by the limitations of Euclidian geometry. Only Newton seems to have had the extraordinary intellectual dexterity required to bend traditional mathematics to the solution of the more complex problems of dynamics. Newton, too, chose to work principally in the more traditional field of planetary astronomy. Although he believed that his mathematical theory of interplanetary attraction discussed below had a universal and hence terrestrial application, he never got further than enunciating the hypothesis and mooting the possibility that capillarity and other forms of apparently motorless motion might be reduced to some form of inverse square law.

For all their achievements, the seventeenth-century curious never constituted a church, a visible, independent community with a powerful institutional base. Those able to teach mathematics often found a safe haven to pursue their enthusiasm within the university world: Newton for instance was Lucasian professor of mathematics at Cambridge from 1669 and was able to turn his rooms in Trinity into a laboratory. Others, again usually mathematicians who in the first part of the century at least were willing to dabble in astrology or act as military advisors, gained patronage at court, like Johannes Kepler (1571–1630) with Rudolf II or Galileo with the grand-duke of Tuscany. Yet others in Catholic countries found space in convents. Most, though, were professional men or gentry forced to pursue their intellectual interest in the confines of their own home, often in relative isolation.

On the other hand, from the beginning of the seventeenth century the curious were always more than a motley band of princes, nobles, priests, lawyers and medical men, only occasionally made aware of each other's endeavours when observations were committed to print. As Europe's economy and society were relatively integrated, intellectual intercourse was easier than it seemed. Letters were continually carried to and fro in merchants' knapsacks, while the popularity of the Grand Tour ensured that even relatively indigent members of the community in northern Europe could easily visit their counterparts in the south by offering their services as amanuenses or tutors to noble travellers. Key figures quickly became the high priests of the movement by deliberately fostering correspondence networks with themselves at the centre, such as the one run from Paris by the Minim, Marin de Mersenne (1588–1648), in the 1630s and 40s, embracing 300 people. Mersenne too invented the role of scientific impresario. Discoveries imparted in secret were passed on shame-lessly to rivals for comment, while, more acceptedly, third-parties were encouraged to suggest solutions to correspondents whose research programmes had run into the sand.

From the beginning of the century, too, the curious in several Italian cities formed themselves into informal clubs in imitation of existing literary societies, the most famous being the *Accademia dei Lyncei* at Rome, which Galileo attended. These early gatherings, how-ever, had a transitory existence. It was only in the 1650s, when similar clubs began to meet in Paris, Florence, Oxford and London, that the nascent community took its first hesitant steps towards more formal organization. Unlike their predecessors, a number of these new soci-eties or their offshoots quickly gained princely patronage. The French crown had already given official backing to a society for the promo-tion of language and literature with Richelieu's foundation of the *Académie de France* in 1635, but it was only with the establishment of the Tuscan *Accademia del Cimento* in 1657, the London Royal Society in 1661, the embryonic Paris *Académie des Inscriptions* in 1663 and the Paris *Académie des Sciences* in 1666 that Europe's princes gave official institutional backing to the activities of the curious. The Royal Society was by far the most important of these early foundations. An incorporated society with its own charter and freedom to recruit its own members, it rapidly became the governing body of European experimental philosophy with an ever-growing fellowship of London residents and English and con-tinental correspondents. Through the assiduity and contacts of its secretary, the German-born Henry Oldenburg (1618?–77), it became the institutionalized hub of the first truly European correspondence network. With the concomitant establishment of its own organ of publication, *The Transactions*, the Royal Society was quickly the favoured forum to which the curious reported their observations in the hope that they would be immediately disseminated at minimal cost to themselves.

By the final quarter of the seventeenth century private scientific clubs were beginning to appear in cities as far apart from the economic heartland of Europe as Dublin and Naples. From the beginning of the eighteenth century, too, the number of permanent societies increased exponentially with the foundation of a new wave of princely academies: Berlin and Seville in 1700; Bologna, 1714; St Petersburg 1724; Uppsala 1728; and so on. Although many of these new foundations were devoted to the promotion of the arts and the sciences indiscriminately, all tended to privilege experimental philosophy and provide experimental facilities. Such facilities were particularly important for the development of the life sciences, where individual research was often stymied by limited space and access to specimens, especially human cadavers. While Europe's faculties of medicine had accepted relatively early on that there was a need to provide courses in the burgeoning sciences of anatomy, surgery and botany, they seldom had the wherewithal to provide such facilities themselves. By 1700 only a handful of faculties, such as Leiden and Montpellier, had a purpose-built anatomy theatre and a well-stocked botanical garden.

However, the establishment of princely-sponsored scientific societies was not the only factor raising the profile of the culture of curiosity at the turn of the eighteenth century. The novel phenomenon of the literary journal, pioneered by figures on the fringe of the movement, also helped to place its activities more solidly in the cultural mainstream by reviewing its achievement alongside the publications of orthodox theologians and *littérateurs*. Far the most important was the *Nouvelles de la République des lettres*, begun in Rotterdam in 1687 by the exiled French Huguenot, Pierre Bayle (1647–1706). So powerful was its influence at the turn of the century that its imaginary territorial provenance was adopted by the curious as their spiritual home. Henceforth they were the citizens of the Republic of Letters, a self-conscious, cross-confessional community dedicated to the extension of worldly knowledge.

Even at the end of the seventeenth century, the curious were still only a minority among the educated. Probably active members of the Republic numbered no more than a thousand, though many more associated themselves with its endeavours and followed its triumphs.

Furthermore, despite their high profile and princely support, the curious were always an object of suspicion to the Augustinian majority. At best their activities were viewed with scorn and ridicule as pointless and hubristic—witness the satirical portrait of the experimental philosophy in *The Virtuoso* (1676) of the English playwright, Thomas Shadwell (1642?–92). At worst they were feared as free-thinkers and atheists for daring to challenge the Augustinian conviction that man was doomed to know no more than his forebears. However, it was not just the apparent irrelevance of the culture of curiosity that raised the Augustinian's ire. What unnerved the orthodox in particular was that an increasing number of the community—particularly those primarily interested in the experimental philosophy—were also ideological subversives, in thrall to a variety of anti-Aristotelian philosophies, and seemingly intent on displacing part or all of the Augustinian world-view.

The disenchantment of nature

In the first half of the seventeenth century there was no necessary conflict between the activities of the curious and Aristotelian natural philosophy. The Thomist Aristotelianism taught in the schools and universities was not a totally closed philosophical system but one which proved extremely successful in absorbing much of the new observational data, such as superlunary comets and new stars. Professors in introducing Aristotelian physics always insisted that Aristotle's (or Galen's) views were not sacrosanct. 'It is in this manner that Aristotle should be supported in the schools', dictated the Paris professor of philosophy, Jacques Du Chevreul (1595–1649) in 1629. 'We should seek out his opinion, but on the occasions where his opinions are faulty, we should only embrace what he ought to have thought'. Professors even cited the Horatian tag 'in nullius verba' ([we rely] on the words of no one), which became the motto of the Royal Society. Provided that a new fact about the natural world could be explained in terms of fundamental Aristotelian principles about the structure of the universe, the educational establishment was happy to accept its authenticity and integrate it into the physics curriculum.

For this reason, most of the first generation of experimental philosophers could be described as creative and critical Aristotelians, who were quite happy when talking about the theoretical implications of their work to use the traditional language of forms and qualities. Of the leading experimental philosophers in the first half of the century the most unequivocally Aristotelian was Harvey, whose doctrine of the circulation of the blood depended on a conception of the constant motion of the heart explained in terms of the organ's substantial form. But Harvey's prejudices were shared by hundreds of lesser mortals. The absence of any necessary incompatability between Aristotelianism and the experimental philosophy explains why so many Jesuits were connected with the movement. As an order, the Society was sworn to sustain Thomist and Aristotelian orthodoxy. Yet over the century the Society protected and encouraged many innovative experimenters. Athanasius Kircher (1602–80) helped to found the new science of magnetism, while Ignace-Gaston de Pardies (1636–73) was asked by Huygens to replicate Newton's prism experiments.

This said, there was always a coterie of virtuosi who did reject their Aristotelian inheritance and embraced alternative natural philosophies apparently more congenial to their enterprise. For the first three-quarters of the century most anti-Aristotelian experimental philosophers took refuge in some form of neoplatonism. This was a primarily pagan gnostic and magical tradition largely created in the early Christian era from a variety of classical and pre-classical cultures and given a new lease of life from the late fifteenth century with the publication of a Latin version of the *Corpus hermeticum*, a series of texts purportedly written by the mythical Egyptian prince-god, Hermes Trismegistus. Neoplatonism differed from the Aristotelianism of the schools in two significant ways. First, it replaced the explanatory concept of form with a doctrine of spirit. The universe was deemed to be filled by a hierarchy of spiritual beings or souls who temporarily occupied material shells and gave them the characteristics of natural phenomena. Secondly, it had no place for the fundamental division between the super and sublunary worlds favoured by Aristotelians. As souls could migrate, their potency be affected by 'higher' spirits, and their material shells be invaded by rivals, everything in the universe was interrelated.

In important respects, the neoplatonist conception of the world as a cosmic battlefield of warring and mobile spirits had much in common with the Augustinian world-view. None the less, there were other aspects of neoplatonism which made it peculiarly attractive to experimental philosophers. By the very fact it was an inchoate, unsystematic philosophy, neoplatonism gave much greater room to observational autonomy. Aristotelianism may have been a plastic and adaptive natural philosophy in the seventeenth century but so many of its assumptions about the structure of the universe encouraged people to doubt the evidence of their own eyes, not privilege it. Too many experimental discoveries—such as the apparent space above an inverted column of mercury discovered by Evangelista Torricelli (1608–47)—controverted non-negotiable Aristotelian principles (in this case that nature abhorred a vacuum). For the curious anxious to make sense of their discoveries, the spiritualized neoplatonic universe offered an infinite resource. A process as bemusing as chemical bonding or dissolution, for instance, could be easily attributed to the attractive or repulsive power of spirit agents. Although the extent to which experimental philosophers came under neoplatonism's power has been exaggerated, there can be no doubt that supporters included luminaries such as Newton and Kepler.

The most visible group of virtuosi to be profoundly indebted to this resurrected philosophical tradition were the followers of the Swiss German physician, Philipp von Hohenheim, called Paracelsus (c.1493–1541), who in the first half of the sixteenth century had constructed a novel philosophy of health and disease based on the heady mix of personal experience, folklore, and alchemical and hermetic ideas. In his life time Paracelsus was an isolated figure. A century later he had many supporters among practising physicians who in the interim had developed his inheritance in a more specifically chemical direction. His leading apostle was the Brussels-born Jean-Baptiste van Helmont (1579–1644), who in 1648 in his posthumous *Ortus medicinae* was the first to explain human physiology and pathology in terms of benign or adverse chemical reactions.

Augustinian theologians objected to neoplatonism on the grounds it encouraged hubris and folly. Neoplatonist concepts of the human soul suggested that mankind was potentially more in control of his fate than traditionalists allowed. Moreover, whereas Aristotelianism was specifically not a worker science, the hermetic corpus intimated that natural philosophers could not only understand but manipulate this spirit universe for their own ends. At a time when theologians of all confessions were asserting that only those in league with the devil had the key to nature's secrets, neoplatonism gave a spurious legitimacy to witches, magicians, alchemists and astrologers. To the Augustinian, there was a narrow dividing line between neoplatonism and heresy, and a number of prominent members of the first generation of curious stepped across it. The most spectacular boundary-breaker was the Italian Giordano Bruno (c.1548–1600), who was burnt in 1600 for equating the Holy Spirit with the *anima mundi*, calling Christ a Magus, and declaring Christianity a perversion of the original true religion of the Egyptians.

By the end of the seventeenth century, however, it was not neoplatonism that had found favour with the majority of curious, but another rejuvenated classical natural philosophy—atomism, the brainchild in particular of Epicurus. Known in the Renaissance world primarily through the rediscovery in 1417 of Lucretius's atomist poem *De rerum natura*, it offered a far more radical alternative to the Aristotelian tradition. Classical atomists conceived the universe as nothing more than an eternal congeries of material particles of different shapes and sizes perpetually in motion and continually coalescing to form unstable natural bodies. They had no place for superadded substantial forms or internal spirit entities. In the first half of the seventeenth century only a handful of anti-Aristotelian experimental philosophers associated themselves with the doctrine in print. Whatever its attractions, its Epicurean roots associated it with materialism and atheism. Atomism only became a plausible philosophical alternative once appropriately sanitized in the mid-century by Descartes and the Provençal philosopher-cleric, Pierre Gassendi (1592–1655).

Descartes's rendition of the atomist philosophy was announced in his *Discours de la méthode* of 1637 and fully developed in the *Principia philosophiae* of 1644. Starting from the assumption that the universe contained only two distinct substances, mind and matter, he constructed a physics that was both completely atomist and anti-materialist. Set in motion by a creator God, matter was inert, lifeless and continually being reshaped. Its constant motion, collision, separation and coalescence explained the structure of all natural phenomena. Only the totally separate human soul, divinely created in each individual case and whose essence was pure thought, had self-knowledge, the power to act independently, and a permanent existence beyond the collapse of its corporeal shell. Gassendi's atomism in contrast, only fully enunciated posthumously in his *Syntagma philosophicum* of 1658, was far more eclectic. While Descartes was uncompromisingly atomist, insisting that natural phenomena could only be explained in terms of matter in motion, Gassendi endowed some atoms with various active powers such as attraction or self-regulation to explain the more complex facets of the natural world, especially life.

Of the two forms of the mechanical philosophy (as the new atomism quickly became known), it was the Cartesian that eventually won the allegiance of the largest part of the community of experimental philosophers. Descartes's physics was more succinct and coherent and better packaged by his followers. Gassendi's philosophy, moreover, for all its orthodox pretentions, still carried too many materialist implications to attract the God-fearing Christian. Only in England was Gassendist atomism particularly popular in the second half of the century, where the idea of particles with active powers gelled with a home-grown atomist tradition which derived from the astronomer and mathematician, Thomas Harriot (*c*.1560–1621). Gassendi's failure to underpin his mechanical philosophy with a rigorous metaphysics also gelled with a peculiarly English distrust in aprioristic natural philosophy. The idol of the majority of English experimental philosophers was Francis Bacon (1561–1626), who in his *Great Instauration* or *Novum Organum* of 1620 and other works had argued for the need to build an entirely different type of natural philosophy based on the slow collective accumulation of observational knowledge and its analysis by a process of classification. Although English experimental philosophers were unwilling and unable to follow Bacon's inductive method to the letter, they did take to heart his empirical emphasis. Gassendi's mechanism was appropriated for its non-dogmatic flexibility. It afforded experimental philosophers such as Boyle and later Newton the luxury of causal speculation in a mechanist framework, but allowed them to maintain an absolute distinction between the truth of their experimental discoveries and mathematical analysis and the hypothetical and contingent nature of their physical theories.

Yet, if Descartes came to be favoured as the more godly option by continental experimental philosophers, his philosophy found no more favour among mainstream Augustinian theologians than neoplatonism. The Cartesian world was totally disenchanted. By removing all spiritual entities from its midst except the human mind, angelic visitations, satanic pacts, even thinking animals became a nonsense. Indeed, as Descartes declared that God had endowed the universe with a finite amount of motion at the Creation, it was impossible to find any room within it for divine miracles. If all changes of state were only transfers of pre-existing motion, how could God ever intervene supernaturally? Catholics were particularly worried about the implications for the miracle of transubstantiation. Moreover, Descartes's mechanical philosophy was ultimately no different from all other forms of atomism. Just like the neoplatonists, atomists were this-worldly philosophers who believed that a knowledge of nature could be harnessed to improve mankind's lot. Believing that the principles informing the behaviour of visible and invisible matter in motion were exactly the same as those that governed the operation of man-made machines, they argued that it was possible not just to understand but replicate and master natural phenomena. Thereby the key Aristotelian distinction between science and art was completely eroded. In Descartes's opinion, his mechanical philosophy would bring particular benefits to human health. Writing in conclusion to the *Discours*, he promised his readers:

To devote the time left to me to no other occupation than that of trying to acquire some knowledge of Nature, which may be such as to enable us to deduce from it rules of medicine which are more assured than those we have had up to now.

The utilitarianism of seventeenth-century neoplatonism and atomism can only have enhanced their appeal to the curious. The claim that the pursuit of curiosity would eventually pay material dividends must have been psychologically comforting to a small community of social deviants. As a rhetoric it was also politically rewarding and an insurance against state-backed Church persecution. Anxious to fill the state's coffers by fair means or foul or ensure that they chose the most apposite time to go war, Renaissance princes were always ready to patronize alchemists and astrologers, regardless of the objections of their confessors and chaplains. Seventeenth-century experimental philosophers courted princely patrons with even more enticing promises. Before 1650, as the Augustinians feared, the curious at court peddled dreams that were scarcely to be distinguished from those of traditional natural magicians. But in the second half of the century both neoplatonists and mechanists usually promoted more practical projects. This was the hey-day of the experimental projector, wandering from court to court, irrespective of confessional allegiance. Typical was the early cameralist, Johann Joachim Becher (1635–82) of Speyer, who in the 1660s and 1670s served in turn the Elector of Mainz, the count of Hanau and emperor Leopold of Austria, then died at the court of the King of England. Promising to solve the longtitude problem, build a perpetual motion machine or improve the court's water supply, such figures were the impermanent representatives of anti-Augustinianism at the heart of the state. Indeed, in France their presence was institutionalized. It was primarily for its potential utility that Louis XIV, under the mercantilist Colbert's guidance, founded the Paris *Académie des Sciences* and agreed to stipend a number of leading experimental philosophers, such as Huygens and the Italian astronomer, Giovanni Domenico Cassini (1625–1712).

The this-worldliness of anti-Aristotelian experimental philosophers only reinforced the Augustinian belief that cultivators of curiosity were atheists. Although this jibe was totally unfair at any time in the period, as we will see below, it is true that some of the supporters of the utilitarian value of the experimental philosophy in the first part of the century were religiously unorthodox. Their commitment to improving the human lot through a fuller knowledge of nature was closely connected with their millenarianism. All Augustinian Christians believed in the Second Coming and many Protestants in the first half of the seventeenth century believed that the Thirty Years War was Armageddon. Orthodox Augustinians, however, assumed that Christ's return and the subsequent end of the world would be unannounced. Millenarians argued conversely that the Second Coming would be initiated by an era of peace and posterity in which the godly would inherit the earth and love hold sway for one thousand years. This belief was embraced by many Calvinist members of the community of the curious who had an unprecedented access to and interest in Jewish rabbinical literature. At one point on the eve of the Thirty Years War, a group in Germany seem to have formed themselves into a shadowy secret society, the Rosicrucian Brotherhood, but in general millenarians maintained a low profile. Their window of opportunity only opened with the outbreak of the English Civil War, which gave Puritan millenarians, such as Samuel Hartlib (d. 1662) and the Bohemian exile Amos Comenius (1592–1671), much needed space to air their views.

Millenarianism was a powerful liberating force. Far from waiting around resignedly for Christ's arrival, millenarians believed the godly Christian must prepare for Christ's advent by building paradise on earth. Gathering, disseminating and applying observational knowledge of nature thus became a Christian duty. Some millenarians were convinced that the source of all knowledge was hidden in the Bible and used the techniques of the Kabbala and cryptography to hunt for the key. Others, most famously the Transylvanian-based Johann Heinrich Alsted (1588–1638), more prosaically became interested in reducing the ever-growing corpus of information in the arts and sciences to the manageable but relatively uncritical form of the dictionary or encyclopedia. Many millenarians were also interested in discovering a universal language and using education to build the New Jerusalem. Although they seldom intended to subvert the existing social hierarchy, they did hope that the new educational system would be inclusive and provide an opportunity for social mobility. In the 1648 plan of the English father of political economy, Sir William Petty (1628–87), for *Ergastula literaria* or literary workhouses for children over seven, none were:

to be excluded by reason of the poverty and unability [sic] of their parents, for hereby it hath come to passe, that many are now holding the Plough, which might have beene made fit to steere the State.

The sun-centred and infinite universe

Despite the fears of the Augustinian traditionalists, it is likely that the majority of the curious, even those more appropriately labelled experimental philosophers, retained some form of Aristotelian allegiance until the final quarter of the eighteenth century. Moreover, it is simplistic to portray the curious dividing up into clearly defined rival camps as the century progressed. Whatever the impression given in the preceding section, it is better to imagine natural philosophical opinion in the seventeenth century as structured in the form of a spectrum that ran from uncompromising atomist materialism on one side, through Cartesian mechanism and scholastic Aristotelianism to the most outrageous neoplatonic animism on the other. That said, however, there was definitely one important respect in which neoplatonists and atomists could nearly always be distinguished from their Aristotelian colleagues. Anti-Aristotelians were supporters of heliocentricity, the theologically suspect doctrine that the sun was the centre of the universe.

The scholastic Aristotelians of the sixteenth and early seventeenth centuries had accepted, usually uncritically, Aristotle's geocentric, solid-sphere astronomy, which taught that the planets were carried around a central earth on rotating luminous globes. Although it was recognized that the observed motions of the planets suggested that they did not orbit the earth at a consistent speed or in a regular circle—Mars even seemed to go backwards at one point—the Aristotelians accepted that the principle had been successfully saved by Ptolemy in the second century AD through the deployment of various geometrical devices, notably the epicycle. The alternative heliocentric theory, initially adumbrated by Aristarchus of Samos (third century BC) and resurrected by the Pole, Nicolaus Copernicus (1473–1543) in 1543 was agreed to be simpler but rejected as physically preposterous. A rapidly turning earth would mean *inter alia* that a ball fired from a cannon against the earth's spin would be carried in the opposite direction to which it was aimed. It gradually became clear, too, that the churches, especially the Catholic Church, were hostile to the promotion of heliocentricity as a fact. An earth-centred universe was deemed consistent with commonsense, man's place in the hierarchy of being, and validated by a number of statements in the *Old Testament*. In 1616, the Roman inquisition declared Galileo reckless for declaring in his manuscript *Letter to the Grand Duchess Christina* that the Biblical passages might be interpreted metaphorically. In 1633, after demonstrating his allegiance to Copernicus more fulsomely in his *Dialogue on the Two Chief World Systems*, he was placed under permanent house arrest. Although Galileo was to be the only genuine Copernican martyr, his treatment indicated the Counter-Reformation's hardening attitude towards heliocentricity. It would be 1835 before the Catholic Church removed the *Dialogue* from its index of forbidden books.

For most of the seventeenth century the astronomy taught in the universities and schools remained steadfastly anti-Copernican. In the light of the growing observational evidence, professors were willing to modify certain aspects of traditional cosmology. They came to accept the existence of planetary satellites and superlunary comets;

they rejected the existence of solid spheres; they even admitted that Galileo's study of the phases of Venus (announced in 1613) meant that one planet definitely orbited the sun not the earth. None the less, however flexible Aristotelians could be in the face of empirical evidence, one aspect of traditional Aristotelian natural philosophy remained non-negotiable—geocentricity. In the second half of the seventeenth century, Aristotelians rejected Ptolemy's and Aristotle's own account of planetary structure, but they adopted instead the equally geocentric model of the Dane Tycho Brahe (1546–1601). Developed at the end of the sixteenth century, the Tychonic system conformed to the existing astronomical data but was complex and dynamically implausible. Twin rather than single-focused, it kept the earth at the centre of the universe orbited by the moon and the sun but had the other five planets circling the sun.

The Aristotelians' refusal to jettison the geocentric universe reflected intellectual conservatism, religious deference and an unwillingness to jeopardize their establishment credentials. As long as there was no unimpeachable observational reason for abandoning the earth-centred universe—and this would only come with the confirmation of stellar parallax in 1838—they were under no intellectual compulsion to offend the prejudices of the religious establishment. Accepting geocentricity, too, would have meant abandoning one of the fundamental and distinctive principles of Aristotelianism—the absolute division between the corruptible sub- and incorruptible superlunary universe. Neoplatonists and atomists made no such distinction, so they had no philosophical problem with heliocentricity. Indeed, neoplatonists found the doctrine particularly attractive because of the significance they gave to the virtue of the sun in their macrocosm-microcosm analogies.

Heliocentricity therefore tended to go hand in glove with neoplatonism and atomism. Moreover, as it developed in the hands of the anti-Aristotelians it became an increasingly radical and disturbing doctrine. In its initial Copernican formulation it had retained some of the essential ingredients of Ptolemaic cosmology, for the Cracow professor accepted the existence of the planetary spheres and continued to believe that the universe was finite, bounded by the orb of the fixed stars. In the hands of seventeenth-century Copernicans the original theory was significantly transformed. A number of daring souls speculated as to the possibility of extraterrestrial life and whether there was just one creation. In a work publicly praising Galileo for his astronomical discoveries, the neoplatonist Kepler even went so far as to suggest that the height of humanoids on other planets would be relative to their size. More significantly in the long term, other experimental philosophers began to question the traditional conception of the bounded universe. As the ever-improving powers of the telescope made it evident that there were thousands of stars invisible to the naked eye, some Copernicans began to jettison the notion of the sphere of the fixed stars and posit the revolutionary idea that the stars were suns at the centre of distant solar systems. The concept of a multiple universe seems to have been initially developed towards the end of the sixteenth century by the heretic, Bruno. It was first clearly and graphically set out in Descartes's *Principia* of 1644.

What divided Copernicans at the turn of the eighteenth century was whether the universe was bounded at all. Descartes and his followers argued that its extent was indefinite. Newton, however, as Bruno had done a century before, insisted that the universe was infinite. Newton, too, had a peculiar conception of the universe's material structure. Cartesians (like Aristotelians) believed that the universe was completely filled with matter. Gassendists in contrast championed the classical atomist belief that the world was full of *vacuolae*, little holes, without which, it was claimed, matter could never be put into motion. Newton took this theory and developed it in a radical direction, arguing that the universe was primarily an empty space with only pockets of matter. Even the most solid object, such as gold, was only partially material. To critics, Newton's concept of the infinite vacuous universe was theologically suspect. If Newton could hardly be accused of materialism or pantheism, it did seem to many contemporaries that he was implicitly equating God with space.

Despite the theological objections, all but the most cautious experimental philosophers had accepted heliocentricity by the end of the period. What eventually gave Copernicanism the edge over the Tychonic system was the mathematical regularities that a heliocentric universe had been found to contain. To the growing number of educated Europeans who believed that the book of nature was written in the language of mathematics (even if they usually lacked the key themselves), the true status of Copernicanism was powerfully confirmed by the discoveries of Copernican mathematical astronomy and the debates they engendered.

The ground-breaking work was done by Kepler in the first decades of the seventeenth century. In his *Astronomia nova* (1609) he demonstrated that the Copernican theory had no need of equants and epicycles to save the phenomena, if it was assumed that planets moved round the sun in ellipses. In the *Harmonices Mundi* (1619) he showed that planetary motion in a Copernican universe was complex but mathematically concordant. Planets might not move at a constant speed (as had been always thought) but a line joining a planet to the sun swept out equal areas of space in equal times and the square of the periodic time of any two planets was proportional to the cube of their mean distance from the sun. Kepler's discoveries, however, were initially poorly disseminated even within the world of experimental philosophy, where they were ignored by both Galileo and Descartes. It was only in the second half of the seventeenth century that Kepler's achievements were properly appreciated and mathematical astronomers began to develop his work in new directions. The most prominent of these was Isaac Newton, whose pioneering contribution to astronomical physics, the significantly entitled *Principia mathematicae*, appeared in 1687.

Newton used Kepler's insights to explore mathematically the dynamics of planetary motion. With the abandoment of solid-sphere astronomy the process maintaining the planets' orbit around either the earth or the sun became one of the great unsolved physical puzzles. Kepler, the neoplatonist, believed that the sun and the planets were magnets, and planetary motion affected by the mutual attraction and repulsion of their poles. Descartes, the mechanist, argued that the solar system was a vortex of circulating subtle matter in which the planets were carried. Newton, influenced himself by neoplatonism and convinced that Cartesian mechanism took God out of his Creation, began by showing that the Cartesian theory was dynamically impossible. Taking up the Keplerian idea, he then proceeded to demonstrate that the solar system could be kept in being, assuming the planets had once been given an initial straight-line propulsion by God, by an attractive power or force (his word) which operated mutually on the sun and its satellites. This force was proportional to their mass and inversely proportional to the square of their distance from the sun.

Unlike Kepler's own work, Newton's monumental development of Copernican astronomy was quickly disseminated within the world of experimental philosophy—evidence of its much greater cohesion at the end of the seventeenth century. None the less, although continental mathematicians appreciated the beauty and simplicity of the inverse square law, the majority were now Cartesians and found its physical implications problematic. Newton's mathematical law seemed to imply the existence of active powers in the universe. In the general scholium to the second 1713 edition of the *Principia*, the English experimental philosopher attempted to meet this objection by pointedly only asserting the truth of his *mathematical* discovery.

Hitherto I have not been able to discover the causes of those properties of gravity from phenomena, and I feign no hypotheses. To us it is enough that gravity does really exist . . . and abundantly accounts for all the motions of the celestial bodies and of our sea.

The Cartesians, however, were unimpressed. Newtonian mutual attraction was deemed philosophically absurd.

At the turn of the eighteenth century, therefore, if most Copernicans were Keplerians, they were not Newtonians. French Cartesian mathematicians in particular spent the fifty years after the publication of the *Principia* attempting vainly to devise a new formulation of vortex theory which would work mathematically. Before the 1730s Newton only found supporters in the British Isles, the United Provinces and the Italian peninsula. And only in Britain, where he had been able to use his power as President of the Royal Society in an age of war with France to good effect, had he become a cultural icon, lamented on his death by the general public as the genius of his age.

The ascent of man

Despite the jeremiads of the Augustinian establishment that the world was succumbing to atheism, the very large majority of the curious had no intention of subverting their Christian inheritance however far they might distance themselves from scholastic Aristotelianism. Many of the community demonstrated their Christian allegiance by living exceptionally pious lives, like Peiresc. Others went further and claimed that their experimental activity and new philosophical allegiance were far more effective props to orthodoxy than

Aristotelianism. In the eyes of the Calvinist atomist Boyle, for instance, only the mechanical philosophy did justice to the extraordinary virtuosity, wisdom and paternal concern of the divine clockmaker:

The last, but not the least, service, I hope, our doctrine may do religion, is, that it may induce men to pay their admiration, their praises, and their thanks, directly to God himself, who is the true and only Creator of the sun, moon, earth, and those other creatures, that men are wont to call the works of nature.

Such statements were deeply felt and not merely justificatory gestures. Descartes was extremely upset by the accusation of Catholic theologians that his brand of the mechanical philosophy made the miracle of transubstantiation impossible. He and several of his followers went to considerable lengths to explain how, if matter was defined as extension, bread and wine might be turned into the body and blood of Christ without losing their physical identity. Boyle was so confident that the discoveries of the experimental philosophy could be used to sustain the Christian faith that he left money in his will for the foundation of an annual series of lectures in London expressly to demonstrate the fact.

The large majority of the curious, too, steered clear of invading the theologians' own territory. The laymen amongst them and many of the clerics, too, concentrated their investigations squarely on gaining a fuller understanding of the natural world and human cultures past and present. They shied away from using their knowledge or their methodology as a point of departure for constructing independent anthropologies, ethics, economics and politics, let alone theologies, which might challenge Augustinian orthodoxy. Doubtless mindful of the fate of Bruno who had had the temerity to evaluate Christianity in the light of hermetic philosophy, the majority of seventeenth century *érudits* went out of their way to leave the great questions about the human condition to the Church. Descartes made it absolutely clear in his *Discours* of 1637 that his sceptical methodology was no threat to establishment values: it was to be used entirely for the creation of a new natural philosophy.

The curious who did attempt to draw wider conclusions from their researches, moreover, seldom came to unorthodox conclusions. The Jesuits, for instance, who were particularly responsible for introducing seventeenth-century Europeans to the religious culture and mores of non-European peoples, used their knowledge of foreign cultures to sure up existing assumptions. No people in the world, they declared, be they primitive native Americans or cultured Chinese, lacked an understanding of the existence of a creator God separate from his creation. In consequence, it could be assumed that the newly encountered pagans were the lost descendants of Noah who had retained at least a vestige of the original religious knowledge of Adam.

Even the curious unable to find any evidence of a common humanity through the study of past and present cultures did not usually rock the theological boat. Seventeenth-century cultural relativists were in the main austere Augustinians, whose cultural researches led them to conclude that human reason was a fallible instrument in most areas of enquiry and that the only reliable source for information about the human condition was the Bible. Indeed, the Catholic sceptic, François de La Mothe Le Vayer (1588–1672), believed that his cultural and philosophical relativism made him a fitter Christian:

> The soul of a Christian sceptic is like a field cleared and cleansed of bad plants ... which then receives the dew drops of divine grace much more happily than it would do if it was still occupied and filled with the vain presumption of knowing everything with certainty and doubting nothing

Yet for all the circumspection and Christian commitment of the large majority of curious, a handful of brave souls in the second half of the century did invade the traditional territory of the theologians. After Bacon and Descartes, this coterie included the half dozen or so most innovative philosophical minds of the century—the English royalist Thomas Hobbes (1588–1679), the French Oratorian Nicolas de Malebranche (1639–1715), the English philosopher-physician John Locke (1632–1704), the Dutch Jew Baruch Spinoza (1632–77), Leibniz, the French Huguenot Pierre Bayle, and Christian Thomasius (1655–1728), professor of law at the Prussian University of Halle. The group was hardly a homogeneous one—its members came from different countries and confessional backgrounds and had different agendas. If there was one common feature to their intellectual identity, it lay in the fact that the majority had been profoundly touched by Descartes's epistemology and metaphysics. Unlike Descartes himself, however, they in no way felt constrained to limit the application of his radical methodology of doubt to the field of natural philosophy.

A dominant, although not universal concern, of the group was to refashion the contemporary assumptions that the state was a divinely-sanctioned institution principally intended to uphold the true Christian religion. Confronted by the horrors of religious strife that engulfed large parts of Europe in the era of the Thirty Years War, a number of philosophers concluded that the search for confessional unity only bred anarchy and misery and that the state's *raison d'être* should be limited to the maintenance of internal peace and material well-being. The starting-point for this new, secularized conception of political authority was a hypothetical construct—the state of nature—a state in which there was no sovereign power and where the inhabitants were free and equal, governed only by their reason. The concept was initially developed, although not invented, in the early seventeenth century by the Dutchman Hugo Grotius (1583–1645), as a means of uncovering a universally applicable set of rules or laws of social intercourse which every state should enforce, regardless of the wishes of the religious establishment. The idea came of age in 1651 with the publication of *Leviathan*, Hobbes's contribution to the contemporary political debate about the re-establishment of civil peace in post-Civil War England. Hobbes was a cultural relativist whose account of the state of nature had no historical content and was based on a series of assumptions (akin to Euclidian propositions) about human psychology. These emphasized the limitations of human rationality, but also stressed the ability of all men to understand the surest way to obtain lasting security. Hobbesian natural man had no supernatural purpose outside his earthly existence: the Hobbesian state was a human construction erected by popular consent for temporal ends.

To a large extent, the natural-law theorists of the second half of the seventeenth century were all followers of Hobbes. Like the author of *Leviathan*, they accepted a rationalist epistemological foundation of political theory, agreed that the state's purpose was secular not religious, and founded the state on a popular contract. Equally and sensibly, they argued in favour of a monarchical form of government. Understandably no one built on the embryonic natural-law theory (among other arguments) evolved by the English Levellers in the 1640s in defence of their demand for the establishment of a representative democracy. Natural law theorists disagreed, however, over the precise definition of the state's role. Hobbes insisted that the primary and perhaps single duty of the state was the preservation of the individual life. Locke in his *Two Treatises on Government* (1690) extended this to include the individual's property. At the turn of the eighteenth century, Thomasius went further and suggested that the state also had the duty to promote material well-being. Influenced by the Aristotelian notion of the state as a positive institution, the Halle professor and his eighteenth-century cameralist successors even talked of the *Wohlfahrstaat.*

Natural-law theorists were also divided over the value of religious toleration. Hobbes himself was no tolerationist. While insisting that the state should be freed from the clutches of the Church, he recognized the political dangers of allowing religious competition in a fanatical age and advocated the establishment of a single enforceable religion laid down by the sovereign, irrespective of its truth. Other natural-law theorists, like Locke and Thomasius, were more liberal and argued that the state should tolerate the open existence of different Christian confessions. No natural-law theorist, however, advocated complete toleration. Locke in his *Letters on Toleration* (1685–92), for instance, justified the continued proscription of Catholics on the grounds that their allegiance to the papacy made them potentially political subversives. Among the *enfants terribles,* only Bayle was a full-blooded tolerationist, vigorously defending the sanctity of conscience in his 1686–8 anti-Augustinian pamphlet, *Commentaire philosophique sur ces paroles de Jésus-Christ 'Contrains-les d'entrer'.*

These divisions between the natural-law theorists were largely determined by their understanding of human nature. Pessimists, like Hobbes and the German academic, Samuel von Pufendorf (1632–94), emphasized that men in a state of nature were slaves of their passions: they knew what to do but always followed their selfish and socially-destructive instincts. As a result, the conclusions they drew from their secularized account of political authority were just as negative as the views of the Augustinian establishment. Human beings in a state of civil society had still to be ruled with an iron fist to ensure they obeyed the laws of their own survival; political authority had to be in the hands of an all powerful sovereign; and resistance was totally forbidden, except if the state sought your life. Optimists, on the other hand, most notably Locke, completely broke with this Augustinian framework and insisted that natural man was quite capable of obeying natural law. A state of nature then could be a working society where people respected each other's person and property and civil government was only needed to deal with exceptional malefactors. Locke, too, was quite willing to entrust the people with its own security. If the state broke the natural laws it had been erected to preserve, rebellion (as a last resort) was permitted.

The second concern of many of the radical coterie was to lay to rest the mind-body problem created by Descartes's metaphysics. Descartes's insistence that the universe consisted of two totally distinct substances left unsolved the question of their interaction. To mechanists—and all the *enfants terribles* were mechanists of some description—this was a challenging metaphysical puzzle that cried out for rational exploration, whatever affront might be given in consequence to orthodox Christian theology.

The solution developed by Spinoza, in his *Tractatus theologico-politicus* of 1670 was to collapse the two substances into one and argue that material phenomena were not separate entities but only 'modes' or manifestations of spiritual ones, a conclusion that was judged theologically suspect for not distinguishing clearly enough between the Creator and his creation. Malebranche, solved the problem by denying that interaction ever occurred. Instead, in his *Recherches de la vérité* first published in 1673, he maintained that interaction was a divine miracle. Every time the mind and body connected, God imparted the necessary motion or created the necessary image. In itself this doctrine was not unorthodox, but Malebranche's claim that the images were formed through God allowing the soul to look into His divine mind suggested, heretically, that the beatific vision was possible prior to death. The answer developed by the eclectic Hanoverian philosopher, Leibniz, in his *Monadology* of 1712, was no more orthodox. Leibniz, too, argued that interaction, was impossible, but postulated that the individual soul and every particle of matter was a monad, a clock-like engine primed by God on its creation to perform an indefinite series of actions in a predetermined order. Leibniz's doctrine was too predestinarian even for Protestants, for it implied that God was the author of sin. Even attempts to solve the mind-body problem by pretending it did not exist could land an author in trouble. Locke in his *Essay on Human Understanding* (1690) denied that either substance could be *essentially* known, but then found himself accused of materialism for speculating that matter might therefore think.

The radical coterie's readiness to invade the theological realm in these two particular areas reflected a deeper alienation from their contemporary Christian culture. Only Spinoza (obviously) and Hobbes, who claimed that the sole knowable attribute of God was His existence, were not Christians, but most were unorthodox or semi-orthodox. In the first place, they had begun to question the unimpeachability of the Old Testament. While not necessarily denying its divine status, several members of the group—Spinoza, Bayle, and another French Oratorian Richard Simon (1638–1712), for instance—believed that the text should be subjected to the same canons of literary criticism as classical literature. In particular a question mark was placed against Moses's supposed authorship of the Pentateuch, and scepticism expressed over Augustine's attempt to explain figuratively Old Testament immorality. As early as 1655 the French Calvinist Isaac La Peyrère (1596?–1676) went further still and in his *Prae-Adamitae* queried the reliability of *Genesis*. In his opinion the different cultures of the world suggested that Adam and Eve were merely the last in a series of separate and inferior divine creations.

Secondly, and even more daringly, a number of the coterie were unafraid to challenge, albeit sometimes speculatively, many of the fundamentals of Augustinian theology. Bayle, an orthodox Calvinist in many respects, frequently indulged in unorthodox musings in print. Most famously in his *Dictionnaire historique et critique*, first published in 1695–7, he pondered why the Christian God allowed evil to triumph so frequently in the world and concluded that the pagan Manichaean belief that the Almighty was relatively powerless had much to recommend it. Leibniz was equally fascinated by the problem. However, less bowed down by the world's woes, he argued in his *Theodicy* (1710) that evil was far less pervasive than it seemed. Many natural evils especially were in fact partial goods, and only evil from a narrow human perspective. Thomasius was completely unorthodox. He not only rejected all form of Church ceremonial, even a basic liturgy, but argued that the Jews and even some pagans were saved. His salvation theology seems much closer to the discredited views of Augustine's opponents in the Early Church, the British monk Pelagius (*c*.360–*c*.420) and his followers, who stressed natural man's potential for good, than to the traditional Christian position. Newton and Locke, on the other hand, leant towards the anti-Trinitarian heresy of Arius of Alexandria (d. 336) that denied Christ and God were consubstantial. According to Locke's *Reasonableness of Christianity* (1695), the doctrines of the Church had to be tested on the anvil of rationality and those found irrational, such as the Trinity, jettisoned or judged dubious.

A number of prominent Protestant figures in the Republic of Letters at the turn of the eighteenth century, therefore, hovered on the edge of heresy. However tentatively, figures like Locke were constructing an anti-Augustinian Christianity that emphasized the potential of human beings, played down the doctrinal and liturgical purity of even the early Church, and encouraged a critical, albeit devout, reading of the Bible. The significance and daring of their critique cannot be underestimated. Although anti-Augustinianism is implicit in the works of Renaissance Christian humanists, Erasmus and his friends were careful never to declare themselves Arians or Pelagians. In the sixteenth and early seventeenth centuries any deviation from Augustinian orthodoxy was suspect. Even the most fervent mystic could face accusations of Satanic possession. Avowed Arians, like Faustus Socinius (1534–1604), were completely beyond the pale.

The position was little better for the rest of the seventeenth century. Only in England in the 1640s and 1650s, which saw the temporary emergence of a variety of mortalist, millenarian and messianic sects, could anti-Augustinian views be uttered with relative impunity. The espousal of Arian and Pelagian ideas at the turn of the eighteenth century by leading members of the Republic of Letters inevitably gave anti-Augustinianism a novel legitimacy. The fact that their writings were published (even anonymously) and they escaped persecution emphasized the declining grip of the Church in some parts of Europe. In Protestant states especially the curious were too well connected and potentially too valuable to the prince to be allowed to languish in prison for theological speculation.

As opponents feared, the tacit acceptance accorded an anti-Augustinian Christianity quickly proved the thin end of the free-thinking wedge. If genuine free-thinkers, with the odd exception of a Hobbes or an Edward Herbert, first Baron Herbert of Cherbury (1583–1644) had been all but publicly invisible across the seventeenth century, the position changed rapidly with the more tolerant climate around 1700. In England and the Netherlands the publication of Locke's *Reasonableness of Christianity* was immediately followed by a trickle of much more objectionable theological works which devalued the person and mission of Christ completely, such as the deistic *Christianity Not Mysterious* (1696) of John Toland (1670–1722). In the first decades of the eighteenth century, even in Catholic France, a number of anti-Christian polemics, were circulating in manuscript. Arians and free-thinkers, moreover, made common cause against the Augustinian enemy. By the 1720s they had their own church with the establishment of the first masonic lodges. In the eighteenth century, freemasonry gave the European-wide but still small Republic of Letters an organization through which to marshal its camp followers. With its eclectic symbolism drawn from various religious cultures, Christian and non-Christian, and its optimistic and positive tone, freemasonry was the perfect organizational expression of anti-Augustinianism.

Towards the Enlightenment

As a result of the developments outlined in the previous sections, it was argued fifty years ago by the French historian, Paul Hazard, that the final quarter of the seventeenth century witnessed a 'crisis of the European conscience'. Put simply, the great expansion in the information available about the natural world, the reconceptualization of nature as a machine, the creation of a secular science of politics, and the subjection of the Bible and texts of the early Church to critical enquiry so completely undermined the traditional Christian worldview that Europeans in the eighteenth century had no choice but to evolve a new and much more secular anthropology and ethics. The Age of the Scientific Revolution and Cartesian Rationalism ineluctably gave way to the Age of the Enlightenment. Hazard's view still has much to recommend it, but is none the less flawed. Although his account of the multifaceted movement of criticism which swept the Continent in the final decades of the seventeenth century has never been bettered, it exaggerates the degree to which the critics really shook the foundations of the Augustinian edifice. The seventeenth century as a whole can be described as an 'Age of Curiosity', but to borrow the famous remark made by Immanuel Kant (1724–1809) about the Enlightenment, it was not a curious age.

As the eighteenth century dawned, Augustinian values were everywhere still in the ascendant, especially in the churches. Indeed, to the extent that the burgeoning critical activities of the Republic of Letters engendered a moral panic in the ecclesiastical establishment, traditional values were initially reinforced and old pieties reasserted. The churches were especially reluctant to harbour subversives in their own ranks. In France, French Jesuits who attempted to teach Malebranchean metaphysics were rusticated. In 1694, the Dutch Calvinist pastor, Balthazar Bekker (1634–98), was suspended for doubting the existence of the devil. Even in England, where the hierarchy at least was becoming more tolerant of unorthodox views, William Whiston (1667–1752) was deprived of the Cambridge Lucasian chair in 1710 for Arianism. In some countries, the reaction only stimulated a more austere Augustinianism rooted in the sceptical conviction that man's capacity to reason rightly had been fundamentally flawed by the Fall. In early eighteenth-century France, one of the most widely read books was the posthumous *Pensées* of the erstwhile *virtuoso*, Pascal, a threnody on the magnificence of the unknowable God and the nothingness of human kind. At the same time, the Jansenist movement to which he belonged, under a cloud for much of the reign of Louis XIV, was given a new lease of life.

Only in one—albeit important respect—were the churches willing to compromise with the interests of the citizens of the Republic of Letters. They finally accepted the inadequacies of Aristotelian natural philosophy and permitted institutions of higher education under their control to teach some form of the mechanical philosophy. However, by and large acceptance was slow and grudging. If versions of the mechanical philosophy were being promoted in the universities of Protestant Holland and England from the mid-seventeenth century, significant change in most parts of Catholic Europe did not occur before 1700. The Jesuits in particular continued to teach traditional physics far into the eighteenth century. The mechanical philosophy, moreover, was only accepted in a sanitized form. Most French Cartesian professors of physics in the early eighteenth century, for instance, denied that matter could be equated with extension and only adopted a mechanistic explanation of the universe as an heuristic device which had no ontological status.

It is difficult not to conclude therefore that, *pace* Hazard, the traditional world-view was not in crisis but merely exhibiting the first signs of sickness. The Republic of Letters was a large and growing island of curiosity in a sea of Augustinian despair and its boundaries were largely safe from the eroding tides of ecclesiastical ire thanks to princely protection. None the less, the values of optimism, tolerance and open-mindedness which pervaded the Republic had yet to be successfully exported beyond its shores. The only country where curiosity could be said to be king and not an attendant lord was the new British state with its powerful Whig establishment, which expressed its singular commitment to the cause, first by honouring Newton with a knighthood and then by interring him in Westminster Abbey.

In consequence, most educated Europeans in 1700 inhabited much the same mental universe as their great grandfathers. They saw human beings as fallen creatures; they continued to believe in the confessional state, despite the horrors of the Thirty Years War; and they applauded rulers who attempted to root out non-conformity. The savage treatment meted out to Hungarian and French Protestants at the turn of the eighteenth century demonstrates graphically how little had changed. In Portugal the inquisition was still releasing heretics to be burnt by the secular arm as late as 1750. Admittedly, witches were no longer subject to state persecution—virtually everywhere with the exception of Hungary and Poland, trials ceased in the last decades of the seventeenth century—but this did not mean the elite no longer believed in pacts with the devil. To most lawyers and clerics, the world was still peopled with good and evil spirits, but it was now deemed extremely difficult to distinguish their activities from natural causes. Admittedly, too, most educated people by 1700 were much less ready to see the hand of God in the heavens. By and large comets were no longer thought to be the harbingers of impending doom. On the other hand, credulity was still rife, even in England. In 1726 only a year before Newton's state funeral, a court apothecary unhesitatingly certified that a certain Mary Toft had given birth to rabbits.

Clearly, then, it is implausible to argue as some historians have done, such as Robert Muchembled, that the seventeenth century witnessed a novel and growing division between elite and popular culture—the one the product of the new science, the other immured in time-honoured animism. Such a division might grow in the course of the eighteenth century as the mechanical philosophy became the staple diet of classroom physics, but in 1700 this was a development that had hardly begun. Indeed, if there was any significant gap between elite and popular culture in the seventeenth century, it stemmed from the continual failure of the ecclesiastical establishment to wean the European peasantry from the neopagan beliefs and practices of late medieval Christianity. At the end of the century, as at the beginning, Augustinian confessional Christianity was still predominantly an urban and educated phenomenon.

Clearly, too, we are a long way from the Enlightenment of the free-thinking *philosophes* at the opening of the eighteenth century, even if a few anti-Christian diatribes were for the first time beginning to circulate. Although the activities of the curious can never be reduced to any one enterprise, it is evident that the lion's share of their energies was devoted to the study of the natural world not the world of man. Many members of the Republic of Letters certainly contributed to history and ethnography through their travels and collections but little was done with this material, except in the area of classical numismatics. The handful of brave souls who did attempt to create a new, independent science of man actually turned their back on an empirical approach to ethics and politics. The *philosophes*, therefore, to the extent that they attempted to produce a new observationally-based secular science of society, had to begin virtually from scratch. They may have learnt from the methodology of seventeenth-century experimental philosophers and pillaged data from earlier ethnographers, Biblical scholars and church historians, but they were engaged in a much more radical and daring enterprise than all but one or two of their predecessors.

The very large majority of adepts of the culture of curiosity were anchored firmly in a Christian world-view. Generally pious and usually anxious not to offend the religious establishment, they were much more interested in showing the ways of God to man than cutting mankind adrift from the deity. The Enlightenment may not have been possible without the Age of Curiosity, but few *virtuosi* would have recognized the *philosophes* as their intellectual descendants. Pierre Bayle was a Christian fundamentalist, suspicious of all religious establishments, including the Calvinist Church to which he belonged: he was not Voltaire *avant la lettre*. The culture of curiosity maintained and promoted Renaissance humanist values in an era of confessional strife. Most *virtuosi* even the millenarians, thought their activities would help to restore Christian unity: Leibniz for one actively worked towards it. Their target was a particular, entrenched, pessimistic Augustinian Christian tradition, only exceptionally Christianity *tout court*.

6

Europe and the wider world

Anthony Pagden

Contexts

By the beginning of the seventeenth century Europeans had already charted, if only in outline, much of the globe as we know it today. And Australia and New Zealand were still hazy conjectures. In 1642 the Dutchman Abel Tasman landed on Tasmania and the south island of New Zealand, and circumnavigated Australia itself, although he never came within sight of the eastern coast. The full extant of the *terra australis incognita*, as it was called, was therefore to remain, until the voyages of Captain Cook in the eighteenth century, largely imaginary—although in 1681, persuaded by Victoria Ricci's very unusual projection of 1676, the Vatican created a *prefectura* for it. The northern reaches of America were equally vague, and the size of Antarctica was unimaginable. But by 1600 the coasts of America, Asia and Africa had been mapped with considerable accuracy, as had sizeable areas of the interiors of these continents. Europeans—European intellectuals at least—were also coming to terms with the implications for their former world-views of the apparently ever-increasing number of peoples of whose existence they had previously had only the dimmest knowledge and about whose ways of life they knew absolutely nothing. For the great synthesizers and historians of the nineteenth century, Jules Michelet, Jacob Burckhardt and Alexander von Humboldt, who were largely responsible for the periodization which we still use, it had been the sixteenth century which had in Michelet's celebrated phrase led to 'the discovery of the world and the discovery of man'. It had been the great explorers of the Renaissance, Columbus, Cartier, Vespucci and Verrazzano, declared Humboldt who, by discovering America, by exploring the coasts of Africa, and by creating new trade routes to Asia had extended 'the circle of what is known' and thus also 'opened further the prospect of what still remains to be overcome'. That task, the seizure of literally the entire world, if not quite politically and economically, then at least scientifically had been fulfilled in the late eighteenth century, by the voyages of Cook, Antoine de Bougainville, Charles de la Condamine, Juan de Ulloa and finally Humboldt himself.

In this history the seventeenth century was a period of consolidation, a period in which the Europeans had extended their hold over the Americas, in which the British and the Dutch had slowly transformed what had once been limited trading operations in Asia into fully developed overseas empires, and in which large areas of coastal Africa came under effective European control. It had also, on a more positive note, been a period in which knowledge of the great civilizations of the East, China and Japan, increased to the point where some, like the Jesuit 'figurist' and polymath Athanasius Kircher, were prepared to argue that China, at least, had not merely a material civilization which rivalled, if not surpassed, that of Europe, but also one which possessed a religion which could be recognized as the bearer of that 'ancient theology' which had preceded, but never been annihilated, by the Gospels.

Nineteenth-century historiography which made Europe's relations with the non-European world a central feature of modernity, was overwhelming concerned with the process of discovery. It is a narrative which makes a rationalist, scientific hero of Columbus (and more improbably still of Prince Henry 'The Navigator' before him), and which prompted one admirer to describe Galileo as 'almost a new Columbus'. Discoveries in the heavens were analogous to discoveries of new lands. Both extended the range and the autonomy of human understanding. Both also implied, if only metaphorically in the case of astronomy, the power of mankind to seize and possess the world of nature. It is also a narrative which curiously detaches the process of oceanic navigation from the wider history of the development of European science, which alone made the decisive exploratory voyages of the eighteenth century possible. It is not simply that the discovery of the means of establishing longitude, or the change in rig and hull design—all of which occurred during the seventeenth century—made the final seizure of the planet possible. It is that the changes in understanding and in scientific method associated with the scientific revolution of the seventeenth century were both substantially influenced by, and contributed to, Europe's subsequent material hegemony over much of the world, and to Europe's own ineluctable transformation in the face of cultures and beliefs seemingly so different from its own. For the seventeenth century was, of course, as Laurence Brockliss explains, the period in which the established scientific and philosophical understanding of Europe was transformed. At the beginning of the century intellectual authority resided in a given canon of texts—the Bible, the Church fathers and the limited number of classical authors—and was policed by a single institution, the Church. At the end of the century the Church had lost its place as a universal arbiter in international affairs, its role as the censor of knowledge had been severely damaged, if not yet entirely erased, and the primacy of both the canon of authoritative texts, and the practice of interpretation as a mode of understanding had been wholly undermined. The philosophy of the universities—the 'schools'—built upon the interminable exegesis of the texts of Aristotle, what Thomas Hobbes contemptuously described as 'mere Aristotelity', had been replaced by something which, for all the lingering traces of ancient habits and ancient beliefs, looks recognizably like modern science.

Although the non-European world has no place in his account, Michel Foucault's conception of a 'classical age' which begins precisely in the middle of the seventeenth century, and the 'threshold of our modernity' which takes place at the beginning of the nineteenth, is a far more useful tool for conceiving the changes which led Edmund Burke to declare in 1777 that the 'great map of mankind' had been unrolled so that now there was 'no state or gradation of barbarism and no mode of refinement which we have not at the same instant under our view'.

When the poet John Donne declared that:

> Tis all in peeces, all coherence gone;
> All just supply, and all Relation:
> Prince, Subject, Father, Sonne, are things forgot,
> For every man alone thinkes he hath got
> Toe be a Phoenix, and that there can bee
> None of that kinde, of which he is, but hee.

he was thinking primarily of the destruction of the older Ptolemaic systems. But he was aware, too, that a world in which new worlds *could* be found was also a world which was in a period of rapid and alarming transition, a world in which it was necessary for all the older systems of knowledge to be re-worked, or abandoned, in which the individual, rather than society, or the political order, was increasingly becoming the focus of all moral and political concern.

The meanings of 'discovery'

The transformation which Donne had witnessed had been very largely a response to the increasing uncertainty which had engulfed European intellectual life after the collapse of Christian unity during the Reformation. From 1562—when the Religious Wars began in France—until the Treaty of Westphalia in 1648, which brought the Thirty Years War to an end, Europe had been in state of almost incessant religious and ideological conflict. Faced with such bloodletting on behalf of competing confessions, the only possible conclusion to which any reflective person could come was that there could be no certainty in the world, no undisputed authority, expect, in Michel de Montaigne's famous phrase 'that which is properly mine'. This is scepticism, and scepticism both in science, and more generally in the understanding of what constituted the world of mankind was to be the dominant mode of the century. It was not, however, only a response to religious difference. It was also the reaction to the ever-widening knowledge of the world beyond Europe. As Pascal noted in the 1650s, in a universe with such an evidently bewildering variety of customs, what was 'natural' could only ever be what was generally accepted 'on this side of the Pyrenees'. Beyond lay only the uncertainty of other places, other laws, other customs, other notions of the 'true' and the 'good'. It is not, of course, the case that any of those who responded in this way to the sceptical challenge, not even Pascal himself, became, as Pascal's observation might seem to suggest, convinced relativists. Most sought precisely to find alternative definitions of the 'natural' which would leave the assumed truth of the Christian religion and the assumed superiority of European norms intact, while still recognizing the vast range of actual and possible customs and beliefs which existed in the world. This, at least, was the project of the great natural-law theorists of the century—the English philosophers John Locke, and Thomas Hobbes, the Dutch humanist Hugo Grotius, and the Saxon jurist Samuel Pufendorf. To achieve this, however, they had to take the customs and beliefs of their disturbing non-European neighbours seriously. A knowledge of the wider world thus became a crucial part of the equipment of the new post-scholastic philosophy. For, as Locke, who was an avid reader of travel books and who had a direct involvement in the settlement of the Americas, noted, those who could not see beyond the 'smoke of their own chimneys' could never be relied upon to form a compelling or accurate vision of mankind. In 1625, Samuel Purchas, the compiler of one of the largest contemporary collections of accounts of travel narratives, described the objectives of his project, aptly entitled *Purchas his Pilgrims*, in the following terms:

What a world of travellers have by their own eyes observed in this kind is here . . . delivered, not by one preferring Methodically to deliver the History of Nature according to, rules of Art, nor Philosophically to discuss and dispute; but as in the way of Discourse by each traveller relating what is the kind he has seen. And as David provided material for Solomon's Temple or (if this be too arrogant) as Alexander furnished Aristotle with Hunstmen and Observers of Creatures to acquaint him with these diversified kinds and natures . . . so here Purchas and his Pilgrims minister individual and sensible materials (as it were with Stones, Birches and Mortars) to the universal Speculator for their theoretical structures.

Purchas' 'universal Speculator' was the new Baconian scientist, precisely he who would ground his understanding of the world upon this extensive sampling of the phenomena it contained, rather than upon the exegesis of ancient texts. For, as Francis Bacon himself remarked when men 'study words not matter', when natural philosophy is made subservient to logic—which had been Aristotle's gift to Western science—it then becomes 'useless and disputatious'. Purchas' Baconian 'Speculator', with his knowledge of a wider world, was to be both the heir to the great encyclopaedic traditions of the Renaissance and the precursor of the natural and human scientists of the eighteenth century. This meant not only the revitalization of the scientific tradition in accordance with the need to replace textual exegesis by experiment and direct engagement with the external world, it meant, too, the creation of new kinds of scientific inquiry—

cartography, astronomical navigation, hydrography, statistics, geology—which by aiming not at epistemic certainty, but at a measure of descriptive accuracy, would generate a whole cluster of new objects of knowledge. Purchas' predecessor Richard Hakluyt, no less than Purchas himself, had for this reason made the new astronomers, geographers and navigators the heroes of the modern age, as the great philosophical synthesizers had been of the Ancient. 'Was not divine Plato', he asked, '(who lived so many years ago and plainly described their West Indies under the name of Atlantis) was not he (I say) instead of a Cosmographer unto them. Were not those Carthaginians mentioned by Aristotle *lib. de admirabil. auscult.* their forerunners?'

For both Purchas and Hakluyt these modern Platos of the natural world were overwhelmingly concerned with the 'new'. They looked forward into a future of unlimited possibility, secure in their own superiority over the thinkers of the past. For Purchas the significant break between Ancient and modern geography was not only between a tradition which insisted upon Ptolemaic division of the globe into three parts—Europe, Asia and Africa—but one which recognized not merely the existence of four but possibly also five, even six continents. It was also between what the Ancients had *not* known and the Moderns did. 'Now for the *New World*', he wrote, 'we begin it at China, which the Ancients knew not, and take all the East and North parts of *Asia* from the *Caspian Sea*, the Arctoan [*sic*] regions, all *America* and *Terra Australis*, comprehending all in that *New Title*'.

The 'Old World' on this account remained still, as Hegel would later say of it, 'the place of origination', but it now shared that place with any number of others over which, at least in Purchas' imagination, it would inevitably come to triumph. All those who lived beyond Europe, however, lived still outside the dimension of 'history'. With considerable geographical generosity, 'Europe' could also, in Purchas' description, be made into the home of the only true religion, and the place where true science had had its beginnings. The use of the term 'discovery', in connection with the 'new' worlds beyond Europe, did not imply—as so many modern commentators have supposed—that the oceanic navigators believed that they had literally come across something which was altogether unknown. They knew perfectly well that both Asia and Africa had for long been inhabited, and inhabited by peoples of a very high degree of what most were prepared to recognize (despite the widespread use of such terms as 'barbarian' and 'savage') as social and technological sophistication. The true meaning of 'discovery' lay elsewhere. 'Discovering' the peoples of Africa, of America, or even, in most Portuguese accounts, of India, meant bringing them into the narrative of redemption and social and technological progress which constituted the history of the Christian world. By travelling to Asia, claimed the Portuguese canonist Serafim de Freitas (whom we shall meet again), Vasco da Gama and his followers had been the first, to 'draw these [peoples] from the eternal darkness and ancient chaos into the light of day'. History was, in this way, the *operatio dei* in time. Those, then, who had had—whether through any fault of their own or not—no share in Christendom, could also have no place on the evolving scale of humanity, a scale which was measured in terms of mankind's increasing domination of the natural world. The celebrated 'Apostle to the Indians', Bartolomé de las Casas, had made the same point in the mid-sixteenth century when he described the American Indians, before Columbus had stumbled upon them, as 'these numberless peoples who had laid in oblivion throughout so many centuries'.

Nature and its laws

The need to unite the world in this way under a single narrative, did not, however, limit either the awareness of difference, of 'otherness', or the recognition that if 'history' was a European, Christian process, Europeans had themselves once been peoples with no history. For this reason, as the great Jesuit historian José de Acosta had argued in 1590, writing about the habits and customs of the American Indians was not a merely frivolous pursuit, comparable to writing novels of chivalry. It was, precisely as Purchas perceived it, a means to understanding Europe's own past, and thus the common ancestry of all mankind. By the mid-seventeenth century the theoreticians of the new political and social sciences, John Locke, Thomas Hobbes, Hugo Grotius, all turned to a narrative of the origins of a society as a means of sustaining their own predominantly secularised descriptions of the social order, a device which, in the eighteenth century was to give rise to the famous image of the 'noble savage'. Most of these narratives were highly schematic and all were, at least in form, largely conjectural fictions. They were, however, based upon a substantial amount of ethnographical information, and part of Locke's *Second Treatise on Government* (1660), by describing America as 'still a Pattern of the first Ages in *Asia* and *Europe*', was explicitly intended to sanction the English expropriation of American Indian lands.

The purpose of such narratives had been to demonstrate that man, far from being naturally sociable, as the Aristotelians of the preceding centuries had maintained, had instead created societies as an act of will, and as a response to specific human requirements. The confessional conflicts of the sixteenth century and the ever-expanding body of knowledge about the customs and practices of non-European peoples suggested that nothing which could not be supposed to be accepted by all peoples everywhere could have any universal validity. It was no longer possible to claim, as previous generations had done, that what was 'natural' was more or less identifiable with the customary practices of Europe, and to stigmatize all those myriad customs and practices which were radically unlike those found in Europe as simply 'unnatural'. 'He that will carefully peruse the History of Mankind and look abroad into the several Tribes of Men', wrote Locke in the *Essay on Human Understanding* (1690), 'and with indifference survey their action' would see all too clearly that morality did not derive, as past generations had believed, from a set of innate principles implanted by God in the human mind. Instead it derived wholly from opinion. The only way to find some way through the labyrinth of opinion and custom which now lay before the European moral imagination was to discover some principle which might be supposed to be acceptable to all, no matter what their customs or beliefs. A thing would be truly 'natural' if a Chinese or an Amerindian were to find it just as intelligible as a Dutchman or a German, a Protestant as a Catholic. The answer provided by Hobbes and Grotius and (in a somewhat modified form) by Locke supposed that early man, finding himself in a situation of perpetual warfare in which his life was, in Hobbes' famous phrase 'solitary, poor, nasty, brutish and short', had contracted together to form societies. By choosing, in this way, to surrender their natural liberty to do as they please and by appointing a 'sovereign' to guide their ends, mankind had acquired a measure of security. Grotius arrived at this conclusion by a simple logical progression. 'The first principle of the whole natural order', he began, 'is love'. But this was not, as the Christian moralists had maintained, the disinterested love of one's fellow beings. It was instead self- rather than other-regarding. It was love 'whose primary force and action was directed to self-interest'. Anyone who doubted this had only to look at the actual behaviour of human beings in all the societies in the world. From this Grotius was able to claim that the primary laws of nature were not, as the Catholics had insisted, injunctions to sociability ('love they neighbour as they self' and 'do unto others as you would have others do unto you') but rather they were: 'It shall be permissible to defend one's own life and to shun that which threatens to prove injurious' and 'It shall be permissible to acquire for oneself and to retain those things which are useful to life'. Although Grotius does suggest that men had some obligations to their neighbours these were only expressed in terms of abstention from doing harm. The natural law which had once offered a complex argument for human sociability could now be reduced to a minimal moral core, upon which, in Grotius' view, no reasonable man, no matter what his customs, his traditions or his religious beliefs, could fail to agree.

Here then was an explanation for the origins of society which could account for all the worrying human diversity which had troubled the sceptics. The world might be filled with many different people practising a wide range of diverse cultures, but nowhere, except where the primitive 'state of nature' still prevailed, could there be found societies in which people did not live according to some rule of law, and did not recognize some form of political order. Nowhere, in short, could there be found a people who did not put their own interests before those of others and who did not value their own survival above all other goods. And nowhere did peoples live in extensive societies which were not created to ensure that survival.

The recognition of the existence of the 'new' worlds was also registered in other more sensitive areas. In particular the presence of America seemed to threaten both the Biblical account of the peopling of the earth and the Church's long-cherished suppositions about its age. By the mid-seventeenth century, the question of the origin of the American Indians had become a subject of furious debate. Hugo Grotius himself, whose status contributed substantially to the seriousness of the argument, in an attempt to save the Scriptural account of the origins of mankind, argued that America had been peopled by Viking seafarers, while the German philosopher Georg Horn claimed that the Amerindians were the descendants of the Phoenicians, the Chinese and the Scythians. The existence of disturbing others, who appeared to have no obvious links with the races of the 'old-world' led others, however, to question the authority of the Book of Genesis as a narrative of origination. The Italian polymath Giordano Bruno, for instance, argued that all life was the outcome of spontaneous generation (one of the several claims which led to his being burned by the Papal inquisition in 1600). Isaac La Peyrère argued in his *Prae-Adamitae* of 1655 for the existence of several separate sources of origination, and for the existence of races before the creation of Adam. Neither of these prevailed, if only because the belief in a single origin for all humanity was far too closely associated with the deeply-held belief in the common identity of humanity. By the late seventeenth century a consensus had emerged which posited a long migration from what is now Mongolia across a land bridge over what is now the Bering Strait to the American mainland, an hypothesis which the fossil record now appears to confirm. These arguments and counter-arguments were not the arcane, scholarly disputes they might seem to be today. For behind them was the perception of an immediate and pressing need to secure a narrative, which would preserve the essential idea that Europe and Christendom were indeed the places in which 'history' occurred, and at the same time would allow for the existence of any amount of human diversity, both known, and of course while large areas of the globe remained unexplored, still-to-be-known.

Mare liberum?

Behind all of such concerns to grasp just what it was which the emergence of 'New Worlds' meant for the cultures of Europe, there were also pressing political anxieties. The new worlds of America, Asia and Africa, were not of course, merely conceptual spaces. They were all continents rich in lands, in minerals and in peoples which, ever since the late fifteenth century, first Portugal and Spain, then England and France, and then Holland had sought to exploit for their own ends. In doing so all the major European powers inevitably came into conflict with one another. This, the struggle for mastery overseas and the corresponding quest to establish unassailable rights in far-flung regions of the globe, set a pattern for international relations which was to survive, in one form or another, well into the late nineteenth century.

The European quest for empire was not, however, without its critics. From the very moment in the early sixteenth century that it became clear that first Spain, then England and France, had not only stumbled upon a continent about which they had had no prior knowledge, but that they were in a position to colonize large areas of it, the legitimacy of their enterprise became a subject of much concern. The original European claims to exercise sovereignty in lands beyond Europe had been based on papal grants. In 1454, Afonso V of Portugal had been granted future rights over all 'provinces, islands, ports, places and seas, already acquired and which you might acquire in the future, no matter what their number size or quality' in Africa, and in 1493, Alexander VI had conceded to the Catholic Monarchs, Ferdinand and Isabella, similar territorial rights over the Americas. One year later Spain and Portugal, by the Treaty of Tordesillas, divided the entire world, of which they possessed only the most primitive geographical knowledge (even the 370 leagues west of the Cape Verde Islands—approximately 46° 30′ W—along which the Tordesillas Line was drawn could not be established with any accuracy) into two discrete spheres of jurisdiction.

Although these claims remained for both the Spanish and the Portuguese throughout the seventeenth century, the principal charter for their overseas empires, their continuing expansion soon began to raise doubts, particularly in the face of increased rivalry between European powers, as to the validity of these or indeed any other such concessions. Could any European state claim to exercise sovereignty over peoples of which, before contact, they had had no prior knowledge? Could they then go on to claim, as the papal concessions had, sovereignty over persons and places whose very existence was as yet uncertain? In 1539, the Dominican theologian Francisco de Vitoria— now hailed as one of the founders of international law—had delivered a famous lecture at the University of Salamanca entitled *De Indis—On the Indians* (or *On the Indies*)—on the legitimacy of the Spanish conquest of America. In this, which marked the entry into

European political and juridical discourse of the struggle over the nature of the rights which Europeans might exercise beyond Europe, Vitoria had asked quite simply: 'by what right were the barbarians subjected to Spanish rule?' The answers to Vitoria's question were many. But the only 'title' which seemed to be at all secure was what he called the right of 'natural partnership and communication'. 'Amongst all nations', he argued, 'it is considered inhuman to treat travellers badly without some special cause, humane and dutiful to behave hospitably to strangers'. Vitoria's claim was that a right to travel peacefully, and to be granted hospitality is precisely a right which—in common with the right of self-defence—survives the creation of civil society and the division of humanity into distinct nations. It was, he insisted 'never the intention of nations to prevent men's free mutual intercourse with one another'. The American Indians were, therefore, obliged to allow the Spanish peaceful access to their territories. The same law, Vitoria pointed out, also obliged the French not to 'prevent the Spaniards from travelling to, or even living in France and vice versa'. Laws in nature applied to all mankind, civil and barbarian alike.

Vitoria also had a further, and immensely significant, proposition to make, namely that if 'communication' was a right which transcended the division of the world into nations, then so too was commerce. Commerce is an expression of what Vitoria called 'love', and love between humans is an injunction of the natural law, as well of course as a divine command—'love they neighbour as thyself'.

Vitoria's argument marked the beginning of a long debate. It was a debate not only about the laws of hospitality and the legitimacy of restricting access to foreigners, but also one about the place and the meaning of commerce in international relations. It is one which runs via Hugo Grotius, the Saxon jurist Samuel Pufendorf, the German philosopher Christian Wolf, and the Swiss diplomat Emeric de Vattell all the way to Kant's *Perpetual Peace: A Philosophical Sketch* of 1795. For Vitoria, as later for Kant, commerce could only be free, and the means to pursue it could only belong to what was called the 'common property' of mankind. But such a claim not only ran counter to the actual practices of civil legislation, it also constituted a threat to any notion of sovereignty as, in Hobbes' phrase, 'incommunicable and inseparable'. If the new nation-states which were emerging in Europe in the seventeenth century were to be able effectively to police their borders, then they had also to be able to control the movements of persons across them.

Vitoria's thesis became of pressing importance as the rivalry between the European powers overseas escalated during the first decades of the seventeenth century. Until then, the Treaty of Tordesillas had been largely respected by the two Iberian kingdoms and the activities of the British and the French had been confined to North America and to fitful—and generally ineffectual—raids on Spanish shipping in the Caribbean. It was the emergence of the Dutch, with an extensive and powerful maritime fleet, which upset this precarious balance. The Dutch had taken their struggle with Spain (and after the union of the Iberian kingdoms, with Portugal) out into the Atlantic and then into the Indian Ocean. On the whole the Dutch East India Company—in common with most early trading companies— avoided direct confrontation. Theirs was, they always insisted, a peaceful legitimate enterprise. Its political purpose was to make Holland wealthy, and where possible to inflict economic rather than military damage on the Spanish-Portuguese empire. In 1602, however, an admiral of the Company, named Heermslerck, seized the Santa Catarina, a Portuguese vessel, in the Straits of Malacca. The Portuguese protested that this was an act of piracy, and a number of the directors of the company agreed. Some refused to have any share in the prize (which was considerable), some sold their shares in protest, some even discussed the possibility of setting up a separate trading company under the protection of Henri IV of France.

Between 1604 and 1605 Hugo Grotius (who was a cousin of Heermslerck) wrote a defence of Heermslerck's actions, and the now increasingly frequent Dutch attacks on Portuguese shipping. He called it, echoing Vitoria's 1539 lecture, *De Indis*—although now it was the East rather than the West Indies to which he was referring. The text, which has subsequently come to be known as *On the Right of Booty* (*De iure pradeae*) was never published. But in 1608, one chapter appeared anonymously under the title *Freedom of the Seas* (*Mare liberum*). It was intended to be part of the Dutch armoury in the negotiation over the Treaty of Amsterdam of 9 April 1609, which brought the struggle between the Spanish and the Dutch to a partial conclusion. And by publishing it the Dutch hoped to deflect Spanish attempts to secure a Dutch agreement to abandon their activities in the East and West Indies. But for all the specificities of its origins, it started a debate which ran on for more than a century, and has a good claim to being one of the foundational documents of most subsequent international relations.

Grotius' objective was to demonstrate that the Portuguese could not claim sovereignty over the seas and therefore could not prevent the Dutch, or any other power, from trading in the same oceans as themselves. 'Can any one nation', he asked, 'have the right to prevent other nations which so desire, from selling to one another, from bartering with one another, actually from communicating with one another?' The answer was, of course, no. Grotius begins with the same arguments which Francisco de Vitoria had used on the naturalness of hospitality and reciprocity, and the need which all humans have for communication and inter-national sociability. God, he claimed, 'has given to all peoples a right of access to all other peoples', which can be proved—if proof were required—by the fact that, as Seneca had observed, the winds 'blow from one quarter and now from another'.

The Portuguese were, as Grotius knew, unlike the other European imperial powers in laying claim to what were in effect not rights of property—although that was how they were expressed—but rights to use. For whereas the Spanish had claimed, by virtue of conquest, to exercise rights over persons, and the English, and to some degree the French, to exercise rights over lands, the Portuguese claimed rights over commerce, and by implication over the seas. For now, as international rivalry increased, it became obvious that the world beyond Europe was constituted not only by its inhabited regions, but also by its oceans. It became increasingly clear, too, that the emergent imperial powers in the seventeenth century, Holland itself and England, would be as much maritime empires as the Spanish and French had been territorial. 'The sea', declared the Scottish theorist and soldier of fortune, Andrew Fletcher of Saltoun in 1698, 'is the only Empire which can naturally belong to us. Conquest is not our Interest'. It was, of course, not quite true to say that neither power was wholly unconcerned with conquest, but it was broadly the case that, in the seventeenth century, both Holland and England saw that their interests would be best served by building up an overseas empire which was based, as the Portuguese had been, mainly upon trade. Even the Spaniards who, although they possessed a massive Atlantic fleet, regarded navies as essentially defensive, had learned from their two most loathed but increasingly successful enemies, that, as the diplomat Diego Saavedra Fajardo phrased it in 1640, in the very mobility of ships 'the strength of empire consists'. By the middle of the century it had also become obvious to many that, as Holland and England had shifted the focus of concerns from conquest and occupation to trade, then commerce would soon become the ground on which the rivalries between the European powers would be conducted. 'The golden ball', Fletcher called it, 'for which all nations of the world are contending, and the occasion of so great partiality, that not only every nation is endeavouring to possess the trade of the whole world, but every city to draw all to itself'. And in this struggle the right to control the sea-ways became of overwhelming importance. The question which now became pressing was whether the seas were regions in which men found themselves once again in a state of nature, which meant that no law could apply except that of the strongest. Or could some measure of agreement be reached over how to regulate human relations beyond the limits of established society?

In Grotius' view, as in Vitoria's before him, the seas were the common property of all mankind, and the rules which governed the relationship between ships at sea were exactly those which had governed the relationship between individuals in the state of nature. If that were the case then no civil law could apply and all men preserved their primitive rights to secure themselves at all costs from harm. On the basis of this claim, Grotius was able to mount a somewhat disingenuous argument that Heermslerck's seizure of the Santa Catarina had been, in effect, a means to protect Dutch interests and the future of the fledgling Dutch republic from Luso-Hispanic aggression.

The importance of *Mare liberum* for later discussion over international law lay, however, less in Grotius' conclusion—which had, in any case, to be largely established *a priori*—than in the nature of Grotius' initial attempt to establish that the seas were, in fact, the common property of all mankind. It was, he said, absurd to speak, as the Portuguese did, of 'conquering' or possessing the seas, not only because all mankind had the right of access to all parts of the world—a point he spelt out at greater length in his best-known work *On the Laws of War and Peace* (*De iure belli ac pacis*) of 1625—but because, and this was his key point, the ocean is inexhaustible, 'so limitless that it cannot become a possession of anyone'. For no-one can claim to have sovereignty in those things which have never been occupied, 'nor in anything which although serving some one person, still suffices for the common use of all other persons'. The sea, he continued, like all bodies of running water, was essential for human life; to claim to have conquered it was as ridiculous as claiming that you had conquered the air, for neither the seas nor the sky could be 'attached to the possessions of any nation'.

Grotius' treatise started a war of words, to which the Portuguese, the French, the English, the Spanish and even the Venetians all contributed. His argument, however, that the seas were, and could only ever be free to all those who chose to sail in them was, at best, even for the Dutch, a dangerous proposition to maintain. All the European powers, while wishing to secure unlimited access to the world's oceans for their own ships, also had ambitions to limit the commercial opportunities of their rivals. And in the 1610s and 1620s, the Dutch West India Company asserted its rights to the New Netherlands (over which the English claimed sovereignty) on precisely the same grounds as the Portuguese had asserted theirs over the Indian Ocean, namely, in the words of Adrian van der Donck 'that our Netherlanders have possessed the places from that time forward in sailing and trading'.

Unsurprisingly the first attempt to refute Grotius' claims came from Portugal. In 1625, Serafim de Freitas, Vespers Professor of Canon Law at the University of Valladolid, published a point by point refutation of *Mare liberum*. Freitas' main objective was to find an answer to Grotius' argument that the seas could not, by their very nature, be subject to ownership. Grotius had accepted that ships may be protected and pirates punished, and although he had also insisted that this could only be achieved by a merely formal agreement between nations and could have no purchase on those who were not party to the contract, Freitas pointed out that any agreement of any kind which attempted to restrict the activities of vessels at sea implied some measure of sovereignty over the sea. This also provided Freitas with an answer to Grotius' most telling observation, namely that the ocean was 'so limitless that it cannot become a possession of anyone'. This was, Freitas was prepared to concede, true. But the Portuguese were not claiming sovereignty over the *Ocean*; they were claiming the right to control access to specific parts of it, in this case the Indian Ocean, in the same way that they—and the Dutch or any other nation—might claim sovereignty in those waters where their ships were threatened by pirates. The argument from size and inexhaustibility could, he pointed out, also be applied to the land, in particular in places such as Asia and Africa which are filled with immense deserts, yet it could hardly be concluded from this that the land was similarly indivisible. As for Grotius' claim that the seas had to be free in the same way that all running water was, since like the air we breath, it was necessary for human survival, Freitas replied that the right to drink water was not the same thing as the 'right to fish from it or trade in it'. The Portuguese had no objection to the Dutch drinking from the Indian Ocean if they so wished. What they objected to was their trading in it, their benefiting, as Freitas phrased it, from the 'travails, sacrifices and the blood and lives of others'.

If, therefore, it was possible to claim some kind of dominion over the seas, then that claim could only be based upon historical fact. For although we may not, 'by reason of its vastness, and our impotence, occupy all the seas, we can nevertheless partially protect, purge, dominate and impose our authority over it so as to protect our things and to defend ourselves from enemies and pirates'. And in doing so, in demonstrating that they were able to exercise the kind of political authority implied in the term 'authority', the Portuguese had also established *de facto*—and hence on Freitas' understanding *de iure*—the rights they required to exclude other European powers. Freitas' insistence that it was historical circumstances, contingency, which could alone provide the basis for sovereignty in the worlds beyond Europe, worlds, that is, in which European civil law could have no force, was, in its pragmatism, a very Grotian type of argument. It was also one which was to have—and continues to have—considerable weight in the discussion over the rights of access to the world's oceans. Similar claims were made by the Spanish jurist Juan de Solórzano y Peyreyra, whose massive *On the Laws of the Indies (De Indiarum iure)* of 1629 was the first sustained attempt to offer a fully comprehensive juridical account of the grounds for the Spanish, and more broadly the European presence in the Americas. And when in 1636, the English jurist John Selden, came to defend the English claims to the North Sea against Grotius' arguments, in *Mare Clausum*, his conclusions followed very closely those made by Freitas.

Competing for empire

The debate over international law and international right was in part a response to the extension of older Catholic-Protestant rivalries into new areas of the globe. Even by the late sixteenth century the Dutch, in particular, had begun an onslaught upon the Portuguese possessions in Asia (far more vulnerable than the Spanish in America). By the mid-century they had taken possession of Cochin, Malacca, Sumatra, Java, Borneo, the Celebes, the Moluccas, the western end of New Guinea, Formosa and, most importantly, Indonesia. When in 1658 they succeeded in taking possession of Ceylon all that remained of the Portuguese empire in the East Indies was Goa in southern India and Macao. Similarly the English, although initially driven out of Indo-China, had by the end of the century set up factories with the co-operation of indigenous rulers at Madras, Bombay and Calcutta. All of these gains had been real ones, but they all relied to a greater or lesser extent upon the co-operation of indigenous rulers. Before the mid-eighteenth century there were few areas of Asia in which any European power was strong enough to colonize to any significant extent.

In those areas where colonization seemed at all possible, in Africa, and above all in America, the battle between the Catholic and Protestant powers took the form of border skirmishes and extended disputes over claims to territory whose full extent was generally unknown. The Dutch established the colony of the New Netherlands on Manhattan and along the Hudson River in the 1620s which, as we have seen, allowed them to make sweeping claims to control, if not the lands, then the trade of much of the eastern seaboard of North America. In 1609, when there were only a handful of settlers clinging to the malarial swamps of the St James River, the first Royal Charter for the Virginia Company solemnly laid claim to all,

territories in America either appertaining unto us, or which are not now actually possessed by any Christian prince or people, situate, lying and being all along the sea coasts between four and thirty degrees of northerly latitude from the equinoctial line and five and forty degrees of the same latitude, and in the main land between the same four and thirty and five and forty degrees, and the islands thereunto adjacent or within one hundred miles of the coast thereof.

No-one, it need hardly be said, knew anything about the real extent of these regions, nor of the nature of their inhabitants. To match this, the French Crown in 1627, at a time when there were only 107 French settlers in Canada, gathered in settlements in Acadia and the St Lawrence and completely isolated from one another, asserted its rights over a territory which reached from Florida to the Arctic Circle, nearly all of which was uncharted, and virtually none of which was in practice, either unoccupied or, given the Spanish presence in the south, 'undiscovered', nor could it possibly have been said to be so even in theory. Throughout much of the century these struggles between the British and French over their respective spheres of influence were confined in this way, largely to imaginative geography and border skirmishes. They were only resolved by the conclusion of the Seven Years War in 1763 and the final loss of Canada to the British.

The only significant conquest in the Americas was the Dutch occupation of large areas of Brazil—the only full-scale settlement which the Portuguese had established anywhere—between 1624 and 1654. Cromwell's 'Western Design' of 1654–55, an attempt to seize Hispaniola as a base for a subsequent invasion of the Spanish-American mainland, resulted in humiliating defeat, both for the English and for Cromwell's vision of the English Commonwealth as a new Rome in the west. The Scottish attempt to found a colony on the Isthmus of Darien in the 1690s, which was based on the assumption that the indigenous populations would assist the honest Scottish Protestants as a welcome change from their Spanish rulers, proved equally abortive.

Despite this ability to defend at least part of its vast American dominions, Spain had been slowly losing its grip on its own overseas empire from the late 1580s. By the mid-century much of the trade between the colonies was being carried in foreign ships, and largely to the benefit of foreign merchants. By the 1680s, the Portuguese had established a colony at Sacramento on the estuary of the Rio de la Plata, the French had moved south from Canada to found New Orleans, French and English buccaneers had sacked Panama, Cartagena and Veracruz, and Spain's naval power had fallen so low that during the War of Succession (1702–13) French warships were used to escort the treasure fleets home from New Spain.

The rise of slavery

This shift in overseas influence from Spain and Portugal, and to a lesser degree France, to Holland and England had far-reaching consequences. Not only did it extend the rivalries between European states out into the worlds beyond Europe, so that the final stages of the 'Eighty Years War' between the Netherlands and Spain—which was only brought to a close in 1648—has a claim to being the first world war, it also resulted in a huge increase in the number and kind of Europeans who now chose to leave Europe in an attempt to improve their living conditions. Certainly by the time of the Treaty of Westphalia migration had become a source of both potential wealth and considerable anxiety. It had long been recognized that colonization could provide an outlet for military, glory-seeking activities which might otherwise lead to internal unrest. Colonies also offered places in which to dump the increasing numbers of mendicants and criminals which thronged the cities of Europe. Even in Antiquity, wrote the Saxon jurist and historian Samuel Pufendorf in 1688, colonies had been one solution to the problem of what to do with all those who 'wander from want of their daily bread and who harass all whom they meet'. By the mid-century, migration (and later deportation) to the colonies had come to be seen by some as the only solution to the growing number of dissatisfied and socially restless beings which every advanced commercial society seemed destined to create. 'Many of those that go to our Plantations', wrote Sir Josiah Child, the political economist and president of the East India Company, in 1665 'if they could not go thither, would and must go into foreign countries, though it were ten times more difficult to go thither than it is; or less, which is worse (as it hath been said), would adventure to be hanged, to prevent begging or starving, as too many have done'.

Either that, he believed, or they would have 'sold themselves for soldiers to be knocked on the head'. The foundation of modern colonies was thus presented as a providential means of halting what would otherwise have been a crippling social malaise. Migration, thought Richard Hakluyt, was the human equivalent of the swarming of bees. Even the fact that so many of the migrants from England had been religious dissenters could be seen as part of God's—or

Nature's—design. The victims of religious persecution, these 'per-adventure mistaken and misled People', as Charles Davenant described them at the very end of the century, had been provided in America, he believed, with a 'Place of Refuge' by a 'Providence which contrives better for us than we can do for ourselves', so that 'several nations, which in time may grow considerable, have been formed out of what was here thought an excrescence in the body politic'. God or Nature could also be relied upon, where necessary, to prepare the new ground for the immigrants. 'It hath generally been observed', wrote Daniel Denton in 1670, with admiration at the symmetry of Providence, 'that where the English come to settle a Divine Hand makes way for them by removing or cutting off the Indians, whether by wars one with the other or by some raging, mortal disease'.

It was, however, by no means certain that Europe did have so many 'superfluous peoples', as Hakluyt called them, that it could so easily afford to export them in this manner. The greatness of states depended, or so it was widely believed, upon the number and the quality of their inhabitants. Sending people overseas, or allowing them to migrate of their own free will, while it might help to free the metropolis of some of its more obviously menacing human elements, also threatened to denude the nation altogether. Underpopulation, as the English republican James Harrington had warned in 1656, could lead even the seemingly most powerful nations to 'lose the empire of the world'. This indeed, or so it seemed, was what had happened to Spain. In pursuit of ill-conceived and uncontrolled imperial ambitions, Spain had sent to the Americas not the superfluous, but most of its more productive subjects. Spain, Charles Davenant remarked, had had 'perpetual evacuations and no recruits'.

But Europeans were not the only migrants, although they may have been the only voluntary ones. For Europe's incursion into the non-European world led also to the largest, the most sustained and the most tragic migration in human history: the overseas slave trade. Slavery has, of course, been common amongst most societies in most parts of the world, and was a necessary condition of the growth of the societies of the ancient Mediterranean. Modern slavery, however, which began with the Portuguese in the late fifteenth century (the first shipload of African slaves to reach Europe arrived in the port of Lagos on August 8, 1444), and reached its greatest extent in the early eighteenth century, was in many ways quite unlike its ancient and medieval predecessors. It was created to meet the needs not of expanding territorial states, but to provide the manpower for colonies overseas. More precisely it was created to supply the manpower for a particular socio-economic unit—the plantation—which had been unknown in the old world, and which only became a crucial component of the colonial economies in the seventeenth century. And in scale and in its long-term consequences for population distribution—not to mention sheer barbarity—it surpassed anything which had taken place before. The living conditions and the life-expectancy of plantation slaves was far below that of anything in the ancient world since, until the reduction and final suppression of the slave trade in the late eighteenth century, it was generally more economical for plantation owners to work their slaves until they literally dropped, and then to buy new ones, than it was to reduce the rates of production.

The European slave trade relied almost entirely upon the co-operation of the rulers of the states along the west-African coast. The trade had been endemic within Africa for centuries—a fact which the supporters of the trade insisted upon tirelessly—but by hugely increasing the demand, the European slavers turned what had been a local commercial practice into the greatest forced migration in human history: between 1492 and 1820 five or six times as many Africans went to America as did white Europeans. It shattered entire cultures within Africa, and constituted new ones on the far side of the Atlantic. It contributed to the creation of inter-racial communities, of Europeans and Africans, of Africans and Native-Americans, of Asians and Africans, and it fragmented and dissipated communities which were once, or believed themselves to be, solidly endogamous. It also provided vast fortunes for those who lived by it, and turned otherwise small unremarkable seaports—Liverpool and Nantes, Bristol and Newport—into thriving, wealthy, sometimes sophisticated, metropolises. It transformed small African communities, such as Dahomey, into powerful states. The slave trade also significantly changed the composition of the areas into which the slaves were transported. Brazil, the Caribbean and southern North-America all become in effect multiracial societies, in which Africans far outnumbered the dwindling indigenous inhabitants. In some areas, most notably parts of the Caribbean, they replaced the aboriginal peoples altogether.

The long-term consequences of these transformations would only become apparent in the second half of the eighteenth century. But if in the seventeenth the destruction brought about by the advent of slavery could not have been foreseen, there were nevertheless many who felt at least uncomfortable about the moral implications of this trade in human merchandise. Morally and theologically, however, the subject was a thorny one. Slavery as such had been accepted by the Ancient world as a necessary condition of existence. In the Graeco-Roman world enslavement was one of the unfortunate consequences of having fought on the losing side in war, a view endorsed by St Augustine. Similarly the Bible, and later the Qur'an accepted that individuals, and indeed entire populations, might be enslaved in pursuit of supposedly 'just' wars. The triumph of Christianity made very little difference to this view, except that it gradually restricted the degree to which Christians might themselves be enslaved by other Christians (But not by non-Christians. Luther even warned Christian slaves against 'stealing themselves' away from Muslim masters). There were voices of protests raised against the injustice and inhumanity of the whole affair, slavery and the slave trade alike, but these tended to be few and were generally swiftly silenced. The great seventeenth-century Jesuit Antonio de Vieira, for instance, abhorred the condition of the slaves he had seen in Brazil and was one of the very few to condemn all forms of slavery. He, however, saw them, and the Indians in Brazil, not so much as victims than as martyrs, and equated their sufferings to a vocation which has 'illuminated' them and for whose 'purpose is eternal inheritance as a reward'. 'Oh what a change of fortune', he told them 'will be yours at that time, and what astonishment and confusion for those who have so little humanity today!'

The justification most generally given for the purchase of Africans by Europeans was that these had first been seized in some 'just' internal African conflict. This was in all cases patently false, but it was, at least until the eighteenth century, very rarely questioned. When asked if the European traders had a moral obligation to ascertain whether the slaves they had purchased had been acquired in a just war, Francisco de Vitoria had replied, 'it is not up to us to judge of the affairs between barbarians'. Most of those who engaged in the trade shared this view. However, such objections as there were in the seventeenth century were often directed not against the legitimacy of the trade, much less of slavery as such, as against the specific circumstances under which the Atlantic slave trade was conducted. Between 1684–6 the Holy Office received a number of petitions attacking the slave trade, most from the Portuguese mulatto Lourenço da Silva, precisely on the grounds that the slaves had not been taken in any 'just war', between African nations, but seized in order to satisfy the European market. This received considerable support from the Capuchin Order which was seeking to make converts in the Congo, an enterprise which was constantly thwarted by the presence of the slave-traders. In 1686, the Holy Office condemned the slave trade, but took no actions against the slavers themselves. It therefore came to nothing. Some of Da Silva's arguments, however, in particular that free peoples of colour were to be treated as free whites, and indeed American Indians, may have inspired the *Code noir* of 1688. This remained in force in the French overseas possessions until the Revolution, and although on most issues it followed the Roman law on slavery, it did guarantee, at least in theory, a greater measure of independence to slaves than any that existed in the other European colonies.

Seventeenth-century attitudes towards slavery were always ambiguous. Slavery, associated as it was with ancient notions of dependence and degradation, was generally and widely abhorred. John Locke, for instance, passionately denounced it as 'So vile and miserable an estate of Man, and so directly opposed to the Generous Temper and Spirit of our Nation; that 'tis hardly to be conceived that an *Englishman* much less a *Gentleman* would plead for it'. Yet he held shares in the Royal Africa Company, whose main business was the slave trade, and defended slavery for Africans on the grounds that it rescued them from the worse fate of eternal damnation and barbarism. The implicit, and frequently explicit claim was that it was better for the slave to be a slave, and nominally a Christian, amongst Europeans than a free pagan in Africa. Such protests against slavery and the slave trade as there were, often tended to be more concerned with the slave-owners obligation to convert his slaves, and subsequent moral duty to treat them as fully human creatures, than with the extrinsic rights of the slaves themselves. In 1673, for instance, the English Puritan Richard Baxter condemned all those who bought human beings 'and use them as beasts for their mere commodity, and betray or neglect their souls, are fitter to be called incarnate Devils than Christians'. Similarly the Quaker, George Fox, who visited the Caribbean at the end of the century, although he was shocked by what he saw and suggested that 30 years of labour should lead to manumission, nevertheless urged slaveholders to treat their slaves with consideration because to do otherwise placed their own immortal souls in danger. Like Baxter he showed no apparent concern for any rights which the slave might have as a person, or the obligations which this might place upon his owner (But then, even William Wilberforce believed that emancipating the Africans might ultimately be less important than bringing 'the reign of light and truth and happiness among them', by which he meant primarily Christianity and British 'laws institutions and manners'). The only unqualified denunciation of slavery on record in this period is the famous memorandum by the Pennsylvania Quakers in 1688 to the Pennsylvania Meeting in which it was declared that all men were free and equal 'making no difference of what generation, descent or colour they are'. And it ended with the question, 'have there neggers not as much right to fight for their freedom, as you have to keep them in slavery?' This, however, clearly represented only the voice of a small minority, and the question went unanswered.

Then, of course, the Africans were black, and although there is only scant evidence in this period of the kind of racism which would emerge some hundred years later, black people had clearly, as early as the late fifteenth century, been marked down as an inferior race of beings. Even Aphra Benn's novel *Oroonoko: or the Royal Slave* (1688) often described as a forthright condemnation of slavery, is nevertheless the account of a slave rebellion led by an African king— something which, even in the racial hierarchies of Europe, sets him aside from the mass of the black people amongst whom he finds himself—and there is more than a mere suggestion that the ultimate failure of his revolt is due to the subservient nature of the other slaves.

Religion and civilization

Colonization, and the development of colonial political and economic regimes, also, of course, brought the Europeans into increasingly complex and changing relations with the indigenous inhabitants of the places in which they settled. These varied greatly not only because of very marked cultural differences between the aboriginal peoples but also because of the cultural, political, ideological, and above all perhaps confessional differences between the European powers themselves. The banner under which all the European nations had marched across the globe was, of course, religion. The Spanish, and to a lesser degree the Portuguese had, by the beginning of the seventeenth century, well established missionary projects throughout most of their overseas possessions. The seventeenth century, however, also saw vastly increased missionary activities by the French, English and later the Dutch in both America and Asia.

In the case of the French, and to some degree the English, evangelization was offered, as it had been in Spain, as the prime motive for the creation of overseas colonies. When in 1627 Louis XIII established *The Company of a Hundred Associates*, which was originally granted the right to settle New France, he hoped, he claimed, that the French should,

> discover in those lands and countries of New France, called Canada, some habitation capable of sustaining colonies, for the purpose of attempting, with divine assistance, to bring the peoples who inhabit them to the knowledge of the true God, to civilise them and to instruct them in the faith and Apostolic, Catholic and Roman religion.

The only means to achieve this end, he continued, was to 'people these lands with Catholic French nationals who, by their example, might dispose these nations to the Christian religion and the civil life'. Almost as an afterthought, he added that these colonists might also 'derive from the aforesaid newly discovered lands, some commercial advantage for the utility of the King's subjects'. The claim was repeated once again by Louis XIV when he informed the governor of New France, Daniel de Remy de Courcelle, that: 'The King has two main aims regarding the native Indians. The first is to gain their conversion to the Christian and Catholic Faith as quickly as possible'. The second was 'to make these Indians, his subjects, labour usefully for the increase of trade'. Not, of course, that there was any perceived conflict between these objectives. Trade, like the natural resources with which God had blessed the

Americas, was viewed as a reward for the efforts of the Europeans to bring the Indians to a knowledge of God. Trade, furthermore, was itself a vehicle for evangelization. 'The advantages of trade', pointed out the Jesuit Francois du Creux in 1664, 'begins to reach these miserable peoples and with these benefits comes the light of the gospel'. Wherever the merchants ships went, the priests went inevitably too.

The priority given to evangelization was also sustained on behalf of the French crown by the religious orders in the Antilles, although there the indigenous populations had almost ceased to exist before the French arrived. The sole purpose of the first French colonies claimed Charles de Rochefort in 1665 in his *Histoire naturelle et morale des iles antilles de l'Amerique*—the work which was to provide Rousseau with the data out of which he constructed his 'poor Carib'—had been 'the edification and instruction of the poor barbarians'.

The planting of religion, so clearly linked semantically as well as literally to the planting of new European settlements, was also adopted by the English as a motive for their continuing encroachments in the Americas. America was, as Edward Winslow remarked tartly in 1624, a place where 'religion and profit jump together'. The steady link in the Protestant English mind between profit and the work of God even made it possible for someone like John Smith, governor of the Roanoke colony from 1608 until 1609, to follow the logic of this argument so far as to celebrate the 'unparalleled virtues' of England's sworn enemies, the Spanish and the Portuguese. 'Their mountains of wealth' were, he concluded, due to the 'plants of their generous endeavours'. God, it seems, even if he was not Himself a Papist was willing to recognize and reward Papist efforts on His behalf.

These English voices are by no means exceptional; but they are partial. Unlike New France, or indeed the various Dutch settlements in both the East and the West Indies, the English colonies in America had been founded by men holding a wide variety of religious beliefs. As Sir Josiah Child noted in 1665, the Spaniards had achieved unity between the colony and the mother country by imposing a rigid code of religious uniformity, whereas the English who 'vainly endeavour to arrive at a Uniformity of Religion at Home', were prepared to 'allow an Amsterdam of Liberty in our

Plantations'. Whatever the nature of these differences, however, all the British colonists, with the exception of the Catholics in the short-lived settlement of Avalon in Newfoundland, were either Anglicans or Protestants whose religious beliefs might be broadly described as Calvinist. Such men, as Anglicans at home frequently complained, had little real interest in converting Native-Americans. 'I would to God', wrote Richard Eburne, in 1621, 'that there were among *Protestants*, that profess and have a better religion than the *Papists*, one half of that zeal and desire to further and dispense our good and sound religion as seems to be among them for furthering theirs'.

Eburne, however, seems to have misunderstood the profoundly isolationist pull of most of the settlers' beliefs. The views that the majority of these men had on the origin of all civil law in Mosaic Law, and on the dependence of natural law on the divine will, inevitably translated religious communities into national ones. 'Whereas the way of God hath always been to gather his churches out of the world', wrote the Puritan John Winthrop in 1637, 'now the world or civil state must be raised out of the churches'. For most of these colonists their colonies had been founded for no religious purpose other than their own perfection. The Puritan 'Cities on the Hill' were to be *their* cities. They were to contain no aliens. English Protestantism, therefore, despite its continuing claim to be converting Indians, and sporadic attempts to establish mission stations and even schools for native clergy became, as the century advanced, increasingly isolationist. Charles II's charter to settle Carolina characteristically refers to the Native-Americans as 'savages' and places them in the same general category with 'other enemies pirates and robbers': persons who are to be displaced, not incorporated. 'Our first work', Governor Wyatt had written in 1623, 'is the expulsion of the savages . . . for it is infinitely better to have no heathen among us, who were at best but as thorns in our sides, than to be at peace and league with them'. In general this was to remain the dominant position of most of the English colonies until Independence.

The differences in religious conviction led inexorably to widespread differences in political and social behaviour by the European powers with respect to the aboriginal populations of their colonies. The Portuguese in Brazil and the Spanish elsewhere in America had always attempted to integrate the Indians into a miscegenated society, albeit at the lowest possible social level. The French, by contrast, sought to 'Frenchify' their indigenes, and frequently went native themselves. Under the terms of the creation of *The Company of a Hundred Associates*, both the French settlers, their descendants and those Native-Americans, 'who have come to an understanding of the faith and have made a profession thereof, should be supposed and held to be French nationals, and as such might come to live in France whenever they wished.' No Huron or Iroquois, so far as we know, took advantage of this provision. But a pattern had been established, a pattern which, with the exception of the French occupation of North Africa in the nineteenth century, has determined the course of the French overseas dependencies until this day.

The English, as we have seen, did their best to exclude the Indians from their settlements. The grounds on which this piece of 'ethnic cleansing' was conducted—and continued to be conducted into the nineteenth century—widely accepted the view that the American Indians did not, or so they claimed (in defiance of all the evidence), cultivate the land but merely foraged over it. They could not, therefore, claim to possess it. For, as the poet John Donne told the members of the Virginia Company in 1622, 'In the Law of Nature and of Nations', 'a land never inhabited by any, or utterly derelicted and immemorially abandoned by the former inhabitants, becomes theirs that will possess it'. By settling, by 'maturing, gathering, ordering etc.' the English had acquired rights of possession in the land which their original inhabitants could not claim. The settlers had then made good those rights by 'improving' through agriculture what were frequently described, whatever the realities of the situation, in Locke's words, as the 'vacant place of America'. The consequences of these beliefs was to create a world in which there was always a firm, impassable demarcation between the settler populations and the native. Only the occasional captive crossed the line. Famously these sometimes refused to be 'rescued', preferring a life of 'savage' freedom to the claustrophobic world of the colonial settlements. But they were few. For the most part, the British looked upon the Indians only ever as 'savages'. Gradually these were driven further and further westwards as the colonial frontiers expanded, until finally, in the late nineteenth century, they vanished into carefully prescribed 'reservations' where, it was widely believed, they would one day vanish altogether.

Relations between the English, the French, and the Dutch in Asia and Africa were far more tenuous. The European presence, however, was largely confined to fortified 'factories', trading stations similar to those which the Portuguese had established in the fifteenth century. These were generally held by agreement with the indigenous rulers to whom rent or tribute was paid in most cases and in no sense could they be described as 'colonies'. Most of the European factories in Asia in this period were established with active native support, and constituted mixed communities of both European and Asian merchants.

From this a belief, however cynically exploited on occasions, grew up that the English, the Dutch, and the French, by contrast with the Spanish, operated a kind of reciprocal and thus beneficial relationship with the peoples with whom they had dealings of any kind. The Europeans would bring civilization in the form of technology and the Christian religion to undeveloped peoples who, in exchange would provide raw materials, land, and where necessary labour. Empire was a form of exchange, a mode of helping the miserable indigene. The great seal of the Massachusetts Bay Company in 1629, even bore the image of an Indian with the logo 'come over and help us'.

Rivalry between the European powers was also played out in a series of futile bids to win over native peoples. Both the Dutch during their brief occupation of Brazil and the failed Scottish attempt to create a colony in the Isthmus of Darien in the 1690s assumed that the indigenous populations would welcome them as saviours from the ferocious Portuguese and Spanish so that, as one Scottish propagandist of the Darien scheme explained, the colonists would 'peaceably enter upon their new Colony without either Fraud or Force' so as to deliver 'their Brethren, the sons of Adam, from such hellish servitude and oppression'. Even in India where by the end of the century their record for benevolence was none too good, the English proudly contrasted their own trading practices with the alleged violence employed by their Portuguese and Dutch rivals. Had not the Dutch, asked one champion of the East India Company in 1685, 'killed thousands of *Indians* for one that ever died by the *English* hands'. Some, especially amongst the more republican of English political theorists, in accordance with this image of empire as a society for the mutual benefit of all, sought to recast the rapidly expanding British empire as a protectorate in which the more powerful states who participated in the laws of nations would impose order upon those uncivil peoples who lived still in the state of nature.

'This is a commonwealth', wrote Thomas Harrington in 1656,

of the fabric that hath an open ear and a public concernment; she is not made for herself only, but given as a magistrate of God unto mankind, for the vindication of common right and the law of Nature. Wherefore saith Cicero of the like, that of the Romans 'nos magis patronatum [sic for patrocinium] orbis terrarum suscepimus quam imperium', we have rather undertaken the patronage than the empire of the world.

However remote this may have been from the social and economic realties of life in the colonies and the complex relationship between colony and metropolis, it was, and remained an aspiration which was to last until the final collapse of what have come to be called Europe's 'first overseas empires' in the second half of the eighteenth century.

Conclusion

It is possible to see the relationship between Europe and the 'wider world' in the seventeenth century as one of rapid and often chaotic change. It was the period from the 1590s until the 1720s when the recognition that Europe *was* indeed part of some wider world, became part of the calculations, ethical, scientific, political of almost every reflective educated person. It was the period which saw the recognition of the need for a body of international law, and more urgently for a set of principles by which to regulate international relations, as the earlier cruder bids for overseas empire settled down into sustained and systematic attempts to build new societies over-seas. By the end of the century many of those societies had become sufficiently unlike their respective 'mother countries' as to constitute independent, and generally dynamic cultures, cultures which, in the following century would bring about the greatest political and cul-tural revolution the European world had witnessed since the collapse of the Roman Republic.

But the consequences of the European migrations overseas had also a profound impact upon Europe itself. During the course of the century, and still more markedly in the next, the slave trade, together with the terrible diseases which the Europeans carried with them and the devastating effect even their most well-intentioned efforts at 'improving' both the lands and the life-ways of those who they came to colonize, slowly bore in upon even those who had never left Europe. As Montesquieu was to observe, no overseas empire could be set up in such a way that what took place in the colonies could be insulated from what happened in the metropolis. Empires, as Samuel Pufendorf observed in 1688, were always in this way perilous entities, 'shapeless, huge and horrifying' which were far more likely to destroy their builders than to enrich them. Yet this sense that the exposure to wider worlds, and in particular the ambition to possess and subjugate them, was a potentially dangerous business, did not prevent Europeans from becoming ever more concerned with 'discovery' and conquest, both as a means to extend their, often slender, economic resources and as a means of securing political hegemony. It was this contact with worlds beyond, some violent, some, such as the increasing recognition of the depths and range of Chinese civilization, instructive and, as Voltaire was later to observe, ultimately chastising, which established the basis for what we today call 'modernity'. Chronologies are always treacherous. But if we must divide time into discrete periods—and all Europeans seem inexorably driven to do so—then it is probably safe to say that the moment of our historical experience which is now drawing, or on some accounts has already drawn, to a close, has many of its cultural and intellectual origins in the experiences which the 'long' seventeenth century provided of the 'wider world'.

Conclusion:
the ancient and
the modern

Joseph Bergin

If anything can be seen to signal the end of the seventeenth century and the commencement of its successor, it was probably the comprehensive raft of treaties signed after several years of interrupted negotiations at Utrecht between 1713 and early 1715, complemented by those of Rastadt and Baden in 1714. Between them, they brought to an end the War of Spanish Succession, the biggest European (and indeed extra-European) conflict since the Thirty Years War. The transition was sealed, so to speak, by the death shortly afterwards, in September 1715, of Louis XIV whose policies, if less overtly aggressive than historians once believed, had nevertheless done so much to precipitate as well as perpetuate the conflicts of the four previous decades. These epic struggles terminated, the century tiptoed off the stage in a manner wholly dissimilar to the upheavals—the French Revolution and World War I—which successively heralded the end of the next two centuries that followed. How can we best—and briefly—characterize and measure the changes which occurred during the century and which constituted its legacy to the eighteenth? The question will be looked at from a limited number of perspectives.

For one thing, as the scale of the Utrecht settlement suggests, the European state-system had evolved in line with the intensification but also the 'extensification' of the century's military conflicts across ever more parts of the continent. Seventeenth-century Europe was like a galaxy at whose core were fragmented political entities which generated a disproportionate number of conflicts which gradually, through a sort of 'gravitational pull', drew in the larger powers which were mainly to be found on its peripheries. The duration and intensity of the ensuing conflicts depended in turn on the political stability, resources and ambitions of those larger powers, which grew, peaked and declined according to different timescales. Peace conferences, if not an actual invention of the seventeenth century, were an increasingly used mechanism for resolving conflicts, which were gradually becoming more extensive and, more tentatively, the wider issues lying behind them. It was a sign of the times that just as ruling princes, with a very few exceptions, no longer led their armies into battle, neither did they meet face-to-face any more to resolve their differences, but left the business of peace-making to plenipotentiaries, ministers, career diplomats, and assorted spies. First mooted in 1636, a peace conference to end the Thirty Years War only came together at Münster in 1644, but for a long time it was dogged by disputes over precedence, ceremonial, safe passage and the refusal of recognition to certain belligerents. However, in the end the diplomats had their day, and the cluster of peace treaties of 1648 followed. By contrast, the Treaty of the Pyrenees of 1659 ending the Franco-Spanish war was a more traditional bi-lateral agreement, unspectacular in itself, though it was lent some glamour by the lavish festivities laid on for the betrothal of Louis XIV to the infanta Maria Theresa. The European conflicts which subsequently punctuated the king's long reign also gave rise to more or less elaborate peace conferences, ranging from those of Aix-la-Chapelle (1667), Nijmegen (1678), and Ryswick (1697), to Utrecht (1712–15), all of which in varying degrees functioned as sounding boards for wider inter-state disputes and in some respects even acted as international tribunals. The consequences of these shifts were both short- and long-term.

The redrawing of the political map of Europe in 1713 was unprecedented in its scale, looking forward in some respects to those of Vienna and Versailles in later times. The French Bourbons might now reign in Madrid, but the rest of Europe was not prepared to accept promises, however solemnly sworn, that there would never be a united Bourbon power bloc in the future, and insisted at Utrecht on redistributing the non-peninsular European lands of the Spanish Habsburgs—Naples, Milan and the Southern Netherlands—to the

Austrian branch of the dynasty, with Sicily (later exchanged for Sardinia) and its royal title going to the house of Savoy. At about the same moment, a no less major shift in the balance of power in northern and eastern Europe was taking shape, although in the short term it did not translate into major territorial changes. Poland's partitions and ultimate disappearance might still be a long way off, but its future role of being the football of eastern European power politics was already earmarked. By the 1710s, Charles XII of Sweden had exhausted his country's already over-stretched resources in attempting to enforce his hegemonic designs in eastern Europe. Russia, having secured outlets on the Baltic and the Black Sea was poised for its subsequent drive westwards and southwards. And with Peter the Great taking the imperial title, Russia staked its claim to be regarded as a major European power. The final decades of the seventeenth century had seen the Austrian Habsburgs rid of the nightmare of an Ottoman assault on the hereditary lands, and undertake the gradual conquest of the Balkans.

As a result, the top table of European powers in the early eighteenth century was significantly different to what it had been a century or so earlier: apart from the winners and the losers, there were newcomers like Russia and Britain which had hardly counted at all around 1600. Sweden had figured among the latter category in 1600, and was set to rejoin it by 1720. In their different ways, the Dutch Republic and Sweden were the shooting stars of the European political firmament of the day. Above all, inter-state relations had grown far more complex as a consequence of wars and diplomacy, both of which spun ever-expanding webs of alliance and interaction. Whereas there had previously between, crudely speaking, a western Bourbon-Habsburg axis and an eastern Sweden-Poland-Muscovy axis, by 1715 the two constellations were slowly fusing into a Europe-wide state-system that, without entirely subsuming 'regional' questions, was as likely to spread conflict as to contain it. It is hardly an accident that for the first time in the wording of a peace treaty, the texts agreed at Utrecht explicitly referred to Europe's need of a 'balance of power' in order to check the hegemonic drives of individual powers. Not only was Utrecht the first serious stab at a general 'pacification' among Europe's states, but in pursuing that objective it also felt impelled to insist that states should possess 'natural frontiers', another geo-political notion with a chequered history before it. But in practice the detailed negotiations over boundaries and barriers at Utrecht, during which even cartographers and geographers were pressed into service, were driven by the need to stabilize frontiers (particularly those of France), and thereby to eliminate territorial claims that could trigger future wars, and not by a Wilsonian concern with 'national' claims to territorial sovereignty.

The notion of a balance of power in Europe which Utrecht attempted to apply was criticized at the time by writers like Defoe and Davenant who doubted it could be made to work. The French abbé de Saint Pierre went even further, noting that the power of states simply fluctuated too much for such an idea to be feasible. Instead, he precociously argued in his *Projet pour rendre la paix perpetuelle* that a special military force be created to police Europe and ensure that peace was maintained effectively. Rather more unexpectedly, it was an Englishman, John Bellers, who took the question a step further in a work whose title may surprise the modern reader— *Some Reasons for an European State proposed to the powers of Europe.*

The states that made up the map of Europe in 1715 had themselves changed in significant ways in the previous century. More than ever, dynastic monarchy was the dominant form of statehood across the continent; it had even consolidated its position during the century, the few remaining medieval-renaissance urban republics having either mutated into territorial states or sunk into obscurity. The Dutch Republic remained *sui generis*, as it wavered between loose federation and quasi-monarchy in the form of the stadtholdership exercised by the house of Orange in times of emergency. With Poland as always the main exception, elective monarchy was progressively eliminated in the course of the century in Denmark, Bohemia, Russia, Hungary, giving way in each of them to its 'hereditary' cousin. A desire to enhance monarchical power at home and to keep outside predators at bay normally lay behind this particular trend, given the well-known weaknesses of elective monarchy, as the example of Poland clearly demonstrated. But although a 'necessary' prerequisite, this shift was not a 'sufficient' cause of the growth of state power in this period. The subdivision of states which even hereditary monarchy could entail—as for example when the right to rule was still vested in the dynasty as a whole rather than in a single member of it, whether it be the eldest male or even female—also came to be seen as a source of weakness. The map of the Holy Roman Empire was eloquent testimony to its effects, where the states with the best chances of surviving the conflicts of the seventeenth century intact were those which, like Bavaria, had been among the first to declare their lands indivisible and inalienable. The Austrian Habsburgs continued to practise subdivision, yet still somehow managed to retain their hereditary lands as a single patrimony rather than permitting them to develop into autonomous states. When in the Pragmatic Sanction of 1713 the Emperor finally decided to declare the hereditary lands indivisible, he was only following the practice of other states in bringing form and practice into line, but in doing so he was also unwittingly opening the door to two of the eighteenth century's biggest conflicts—the War of Austrian Succession and the Seven Years War.

The pressures on the seventeenth-century 'composite' states were so intense that the loose structures they had inherited from the past seemed seriously deficient to an increasing number of rulers and political observers alike. The drive towards 'absolutist' forms of rule so evident across the continent was largely a response to this situation, although we should not exaggerate the 'systematic' character of such efforts. Reinforcing the hegemonic position of the 'core' political centre or territory within such states seemed the only way forward for the likes of Olivares, Richelieu, Charles I and others. Without in the least neglecting traditional dynastic right or the notion of a divine right to govern, rulers increasingly laid claim to a form of sovereign power that transcended all other forms of authority within their borders, so that in the exercise of that power they were not subject to the scrutiny of their subjects, individually or collectively. As often as not, such claims to rule 'absolutely' were made under pressure, when there was opposition to their military, financial and other demands on subjects. Revolts, as we saw, by both elites and ordinary subjects, were a common response to those demands. This in turn obliged rulers and their publicists to hedge about their claims to absolute power with all kinds of reservations to avoid the accusation of seeking to rule tyrannically: they were, they insisted, Christian rulers ruling Christian subjects, and despotism was against religious as well as secular precepts. A prince could scarcely claim divine sanction for his authority and then exercise it in ways that blatantly contradicted its ultimate source and model.

In practice, things could of course be very different. If seventeenth-century states pursued anything of an 'absolute' nature, it was arguably 'absolute' obedience from their subjects rather than 'absolute' power over them. Because of its historical origins, the ideology of absolutism was designed above all to deny subjects any basis for resistance to, or participation in, the business of government. In that particular domain, the rhetorical force of 'absolutist' language was probably greater than most historians admit. Even in France, the theatre of so many revolts—aristocratic, corporate and popular—there was scarcely any attempt by those in revolt to compete with the 'absolutist' tenets of the monarchy, let alone provide a full-blown alternative to them. All parties used essentially the same political idiom: they wanted more royal absolutism, provided it was 'better' than what prevailed at any given time. The *quid pro quo* for the acceptance of 'absolute' princely power throughout western and central Europe was that the princes in question would respect the property and privileges of their subjects—they would not cross the boundary which separated legitimate 'absolute' rule from despotism. Most forms of revolt instinctively justified their action in terms of attacks upon their rights and privileges, not as an attempt to subvert the underlying forms of government. But it was precisely because the frontiers between 'liberties and privileges' on the one hand, and the recognized sphere of unfettered princely rule on the other were less susceptible to clear definition and agreement than the frontiers between states, that political conflicts within states as undefined as those of the seventeenth century were bound to continue. Absolutist monarchies clearly sought the active and full co-operation of the societies they governed, but they were rarely interested in providing the kind of forum in which those frontiers could be renegotiated.

In political conflicts within seventeenth-century states, the role of the different nobilities was of the greatest importance, not just because of their obvious political and military clout, but also because they were often the repositories of political traditions which were at variance with moves towards the centralization of power in the hands of a sovereign prince. Their political culture often made generous provision for a 'right to revolt' in defence of the ancient constitution, whether it was the Polish or the French. These traditions could be most dangerous where they overlapped with strong 'national', provincial or local particularism, as the Spanish monarchy found to its cost in Catalonia and Portugal; it might have faced even worse problems in southern Italy had it not been prepared to allow the local nobility to increase their power in local government there. The Austrian Habsburgs' problems with the Hungarian nobility only became serious when they began making military progress against the Ottomans in the Balkans: the nobility had previously been able to thrive on the rivalry between the two powers, but by the 1680s it feared that a military occupation of Hungary by the Habsburgs would lead to the kind of punitive, 'absolutist' settlement which has occurred earlier in Bohemia. Other states faced broadly similar problems in their attempts to extend their grip on society.

That there were fewer revolts in the second half of the century was due in no small part to a growing mutual understanding between rulers and nobilities, the history of which has attracted less attention than the revolts themselves. The case for an undeclared marriage of common interests has been strongly argued for France under Louis XIV, countering the classic thesis that has often acted as a pillar for older views of royal absolutism, namely that the French nobility under Louis XIV was a cowed, domesticated one, living in splendour but also in subservience at Versailles. The ethic of service, military or otherwise, had always been a powerful one among the European nobility, and it was probably reinforced by the educational experiences of seventeenth-century nobles in the colleges and academies that they frequented in increasing numbers, as well as in the growing armies of the period. But ultimately it could only really flourish if it was grounded in substantial respect for their interests. Philip IV's declaration of 1652 that he would respect the privilege of the Catalans, the Habsburgs' compromise with the Hungarians at Pressburg in 1687, were explicit versions of the same search for a *modus vivendi*. Success in this endeavour was not instant or guaranteed, as the Hungarian revolt of the early 1700s showed, but in most of the core states of Europe, it was no longer in doubt by then. Peter the Great was alone in making it a formal obligation for all adult nobles to serve the state.

For their part, the nobility gradually learned to live with the fiscal-military state that was still taking shape in this period. Indeed, it turned out to be a state which, its irksome features notwithstanding, offered them increased opportunities to pursue careers, fortune, and family aggrandizement; in many cases, it also shored up their economic position by channelling both money and opportunity so generously in their direction, most obviously in wartime. Such an outcome, which admittedly entailed the demise of autonomous military activity by nobles in most of Europe, obviously tied them more firmly than heretofore to the prince's service. In many important respects, more continuous periods of service at court, the army, the provinces, and so on, redefined and restructured the nobilities of individual states along lines which would not change much until the traumas of the French Revolutionary period.

Without this state-nobility compact the kind of 'absolutist' rule that most states engaged in by the later seventeenth century would scarcely have been possible. We should not ignore the different routes taken by individual states towards such an outcome. There are some illuminating counter-examples to it. In the case of Denmark and Sweden, where the aristocracy controlled the crown around mid-century, it was their failure to govern effectively while at the same time cornering the economic spoils for themselves, which made absolute monarchy an alternative that was in some respects 'popular' within society in the second half of the century; here absolute monarchy was a way of forcing the nobility *out* of a dominant position at the centre of government. On the other hand, the German princes managed to emerge from the disasters of the Thirty Years War stronger than the Estates which had dominated their affairs in previous generations and, from Bavaria to Prussia, they pursued policies that would enhance their power, yet crucially retain the goodwill of the nobility while detaching them from the Estates. Nor did this particular state-nobility compact always mean that the nobility were given *carte blanche* to extend their grip on rural society. Even in Brandenburg-Prussia, the interests of the prince came before those of the Junkers in the reconstruction and subjugation of the peasantry after the Thirty Years War. The princes of the western German states were among the only ones in Europe who managed to impose a socio-economic system which was unique in its capacity to protect the tax-paying peasantry not merely from seigneurial exactions but also from normal economic forces such as debt and bankruptcy. Other states might have identical grounds for preserving their tax-paying peasantries but, like France, were too heavily involved in power politics to pursue such single-minded policies at home. In nearly every part of Europe, the eighteenth century inherited a legacy in which rulers and governing elites were clearly more united than they had been during previous generations.

But the political geography of Europe is only a part of the picture, and its evolution should not be regarded as a pattern that applies in other spheres. In terms of social change, the century seems far less dynamic than either the sixteenth or the eighteenth centuries. Through the progressive introduction of serfdom in much of Europe east of the Elbe, the social structure there became even less fluid than it had previously been. In a vast area where humans were more precious than acres of land, a thinly-spread population was tied to the land it worked on; its urban societies continued to vegetate in marginal positions, their inhabitants often subjected to the kinds of restrictions of status and activity which would have been unacceptable elsewhere in Europe. Many parts of the Holy Roman Empire, one of the most urbanized regions of Europe since the Renaissance, experienced what might be termed social regression after the Thirty Years War, in that German society was now more dominated than in the past by the landed nobility. Towns and cities, especially capital cities, did continue to grow across Europe, but in many cases, especially in the Spanish kingdoms, this was not necessarily because they were economically dynamic, but because they attracted rural immigrants fleeing misery in the countryside. Elsewhere, as Thomas Munck shows, the bonds of household and patriarchy remained as strong as ever: the *societas domestica* in which patriarchy held sway was not merely the basic building block of society, it was also the dominant metaphor for understanding society as a whole, much more widely used than any notion of a society orders or of estates. Jean Bodin's famous definition of 1576 of the commonwealth as 'the rightful government of many families and of that which they have in common' was one which the following century could instinctively cleave to.

If the legacy of the seventeenth century in the sphere of social change seems so modest, it is largely because of the century's economic record. As Robert Nash shows in this volume, the economy of seventeenth century Europe was moving along a set of diverging rather than converging paths. The shift in the centre of economic gravity to north-west Europe was a slow one that had been in progress since the early sixteenth century. The 'Atlantic economy' which emerged from this was for a long time relatively confined in its impact on the economies of the main countries concerned, being limited mostly to the port cities and their immediate hinterlands. In the seventeenth century, when the Netherlands and England began to emerge as the main beneficiaries of the shift, the connection between their inland and 'Atlantic' sectors became more intensive and routine, bringing with it a much greater prospect of commercialization, even within the rural economy. Consequently, their economies as a whole could begin to move into a different phase of development. But elsewhere in Europe the traditional constraints of the rural economy continued to operate as before. Agricultural productivity rates actually fell during the century because in many places, from Italy to northern Europe, the rural economies were unable to produce enough food to sustain what limited population growth there was. Only a small triangle containing England, the Netherlands and the Paris region managed to do better and raise their productivity rates, stimulated no doubt because of the prospect of profits to be derived from feeding the growing urban populations there. It would take a very long time before anything similar would happen elsewhere in Europe. Those of Europe's peasantry who escaped enserfment were not guaranteed a secure future on the land: the seventeenth century was one in which the dispossession and pauperization of the peasantry reached record levels in many parts of Europe. The gap separating wealthy peasant farmers from cottiers and day labourers widened imperceptibly. On the other hand, by 1700, the demographic nightmare that had hung over Europe since the original Black Death might at last be ending and the population of Europe facing a less threatening future. Yet in the light of the famines and epidemics in France in 1693–4, 1709–10 and 1720 such assurances also seem more evident with the benefit of hindsight. Overall population levels had only moved shakily upward during the century, with each advance vulnerable to unexpected setbacks from war or epidemic. The eighteenth century, beginning from a low baseline and benefiting from far better conditions, would experience the kind of population growth that its predecessor never had the chance to achieve.

The 'modernity' of the seventeenth century, like that of its predecessor, now seems much less obvious than it did a generation or two ago. This is no doubt partly because our own notions of what constitutes modernity have themselves changed considerably, but also because historians' knowledge of the century is substantially more broadly-based than it used to be. Perhaps because the legacy of the century to its successor was an uncertain, even negative one in important respects, historians understandably find it easier to argue that something more decisive occurred in the realm of ideas, broadly conceived. Isaiah Berlin once remarked that the eighteenth century was not the age of reason but of reasonableness, and that the term 'age of reason' really belongs to the seventeenth. There is some truth in the contrast, provided we do not confine our understanding of seventeenth-century intellectual life to the giants of the age—Grotius, Descartes, Newton, Leibniz, for example—who towered over their eighteenth-century counterparts. The piecemeal but irreversible shift which Laurence Brockliss has traced in his chapter here—away from the deeply-entrenched Augustinian and geocentric world-view inherited from the Middle Ages—constitutes a much more balanced view of both the immediate intellectual heritage and legacy of the seventeenth century. The small groups of scholars and searchers that he brings to light operated in conditions of both danger and uncertainty. Their departures from the pessimistic views of human nature, and all that they entailed—whether it was orthodox religion, magic, witchcraft or astrology—were tentatively and cautiously expressed, and with good cause: everyone knew perfectly well what had happened to the likes of Bruno and Galileo. Heroic reasoners who would openly challenge established first principles, in religion, cosmology, physics or elsewhere, were therefore thin on the ground. But what they may have lacked in individual boldness, the curious (as Brockliss labels them) made up for in the extensive correspondence and networks that they painstakingly put together, sometimes within, but mostly outside of the established academic structures of the day. Their vulnerability in the face of vigilant intellectual establishments which could quickly spot any challenge to orthodoxy, meant that they also had to seek safety in numbers—though, as Brockliss reminds us, the 'republic of letters' had no more than 1000 members around 1700. They came together in a variety of salons, private academies, libraries and the like, enjoying the discreet but effective patronage of princes, ministers, and aristocrats. By the end of the century, the Augustinian world-view had been irreparably holed below the water-line; its detractors had achieved just enough critical mass to ensure their own survival, which in turn meant that their work of criticizing the old world-picture and searching for the new one could continue. But this achievement could not hide the fact that the mass of the population, the churches and the established cultural institutions remained viscerally tied to the older views. It would take another generation or two before something deserving the label of the Enlightenment was to take shape, but it would not have been possible without the endeavours of the curious of an earlier age working with a different agenda. A close study of that shift provides yet another instance of how fascinating but also how elusive the continuities and the discontinuities between the centuries turn out to be.

Further Reading

Economy

Two fine surveys of European economic history in the early modern period are, Jan de Vries, *Economy of Europe in an Age of Crisis, 1600–1750* (Cambridge, 1976) and Robert S. Duplessis, *Transitions to Capitalism in Early Modern Europe* (Cambridge, 1997). For two important collections of essays on the debate about the seventeenth-century crisis see, T. H. Aston (ed.), *Crisis in Europe, 1560–1660* (London, 1965) and G. Parker and L. M. Smith (ed.), *The General Crisis of the Seventeenth Century* (London, 1978, new ed., with new chapters, London 1997). For the major debates about agrarian, economic and social change, and proto-industrialization, see T. H. Aston and C. H. E. Philpin, (ed.), *The Brenner Debate: Agrarian Class Structure and Economic Development in Pre-industrial Europe* (Cambridge, 1985); S. C. Ogilvie and M. Cerman (ed.), *European Proto-Industrialization* (Cambridge, 1996); H. Kisch, *From Domestic Manufacture to Industrial Revolution: The Case of the Rhineland* (New York, 1989) and Philip T. Hoffman, *Growth in a Traditional Society: The French Countryside. 1450–1815* (Princeton, 1996), which combines a fine survey of France's agrarian institutions with a less accessible mathematical study of productivity change in French agriculture. For a number of excellent economic histories of particular countries and regions, see C. Clay, *Economic Expansion and Social Change: England 1500–1700*, 2 vols. (Cambridge, 1984); I. A. A. Thompson and Bartolomé Yún Casalilla (ed.), *The Castilian Crisis of the Seventeenth Century* (Cambridge, 1994); Jan de Vries and Ad van der Woude, *The First Modern Economy: Success, Failure and Perseverance of the Dutch Economy 1500–1815* (Cambridge, 1997); D. Sella, *Crisis and Continuity. The Economy of Spanish Lombardy in the Seventeenth Century* (Cambridge, Mass., 1979); A. Maczak, et al., *East-Central Europe in Transition: From the Fourteenth to the Seventeenth Century* (Cambridge, 1985); S. Ogilvie (ed.), *Germany: A New Social and Economic History*, vol. 1, 1450–1630, vol. 2, 1630–1800 (London, 1996).

Society

A starting point for further reading is T. Munck, *Seventeenth-Century Europe: State, Conflict and the Social Order in Europe 1598–1700* (London, Macmillan, 1990), which provides a comparative study covering much of Europe in some detail, with references and bibliography on core material published by 1990. A useful overall guide to unrest in the period is Yves-Marie Bercé, *Revolt and Revolution in Early Modern Europe*, trans. Joseph Bergin (Manchester,

Manchester University Press, 1987). The fundamental structural elements of early modern society are covered in H. M. Scott (ed.), *The European Nobilities of the Seventeenth and Eighteenth Centuries*, 2 vols. (London, Longman, 1995) and Tom Scott (ed.), *The Peasantries of Europe from the Fourteenth to the Eighteenth Centuries* (London, Longman, 1998). A. Cowan's *Urban Europe 1500–1700* (London, Arnold, 1998) is an imaginative and thoughtful overview of a complex area, with suggestions for further reading, which might be read in conjunction with the wide-ranging and colourful study of Roy Porter, *London: a Social History* (Penguin Books, Harmondsworth, 1996). Finally, on specific aspects which this chapter has been unable to cover in any depth, good starting points are provided by Jean-Louis Flandrin, *Families in Former Times: Kinship, Household and Sexuality* (Cambridge, CUP, 1976), and more recently by Olwen Hufton, *The Prospect Before Her: a History of Women in Western Europe*, vol. 1 (London, HarperCollins, 1996).

Politics

A reliable and up-to-date general account of the period is found in T. Munck, *Seventeenth-century Europe, 1588–1700* (London, 1990), and a comprehensive survey of the key political players of the age in H. M. Scott (ed.), *The European Nobilities in the Seventeenth and Eighteenth centuries*, 2 vols. (London, 1995). The following works, chosen from a range of possibilities will give an introduction to developments in the individual countries of Europe in this period. France is covered in R. Bonney, *Political Change in France under Richelieu and Mazarin, 1624–1661* (Oxford, 1978) and J. B. Wolf, *Louis XIV* (London, 1968). A stimulating comparison of French and Spanish experience can be found in J. H. Elliott, *Richelieu and Olivares* (Cambridge, 1984), and a reliable survey of Spain in the seventeenth century in John Lynch, *Spain under the Habsburgs*, vol. 2 (London, 2nd edn., 1981). There is a very thorough survey of the history of the Dutch Republic in J. I. Israel, *The Dutch Republic* (Oxford University Press, 1995). The Baltic area is competently surveyed in D. Kirby, *Northern Europe in the Early-Modern Period: the Baltic World* (London, 1990). The most convenient English-language study of the development of Brandenburg-Prussia is still F. Schevill, *The Great Elector* (New York, 1947). The beginnings of the future Austrian Empire are studied in R. J. W. Evans, *The Making of the Habsburg Monarchy, 1550–1700* (Oxford, 1979). Finally eastern Europe can be covered through N. Davies, *God's Playground: a History of Poland*, vol. 1 (Oxford, 1981) and P. Dukes, *The Making of Russian Absolutism, 1613–1801* (London, 1982).

War and international relations

A substantial literature has been devoted to the theme of military change in early modern Europe. The resulting debates can be followed in G. Parker, *The*

Military Revolution. Military Innovation and the Rise of the West, 1500–1800
(London, 1988, 2nd edn., 1996); C. Rogers, (ed.), *The Military Revolution Debate. Readings on the Military Transformation of Early Modern Europe* (Boulder, Colorado, and Oxford, 1995), F. Tallett, *War and Society in Early Modern Europe, 1495–1715* (London, 1992). The conflicts of the early decades of the century are well treated by G. Parker, *The Thirty Years' War* (London, 1984; 2nd edn., 1997) and, more succinctly, by R. Asch, *The Thirty Years' War. The Holy Roman Empire and Europe, 1618–1648* (London, 1997). Those of the end of the century are chronicled from different perspectives in J. Lynn, *The Wars of Louis XIV, 1667–1714* (London, 1999) and J. R. Jones, *Marlborough* (Cambridge, 1993). J. Brewer, *The Sinews of Power. War, Money and the English State, 1688–1763* (London, 1989) is an authoritative analysis of how one state became a 'military-fiscal' power. Diplomacy and power politics are the subject of R. Hatton (ed.), *Louis XIV and Europe* (London, 1976) and Lucien Bély, *Espions et ambassadeurs au temps de Louis XIV* (Paris, 1990). The continuing dynasticism of most European states and its impact on their conduct can be gleaned from P. Fichtner, *Protestantism and Primogeniture in Early Modern Germany* (New Haven and London, 1989) and Herbert H. Rowen, *The King's State Proprietary Dynasticism in Early Modern France* (Rutgers N.J., 1980).

Culture and ideas

There is no good over-view of the history of European culture in the seventeenth century. The most recent account of the Scientific Revolution is Stephen Shapin, *The Scientific Revolution* (Chicago, 1996), which has a strong thematic and contextual line. For a more traditional approach, A. Rupert Hall, *From Galileo to Newton, 1630–1720* (London, 1970) is still serviceable. Useful, too, for its comparative focus is Roy Porter and Miklas Teich (eds.), *The Scientific Revolution in National Context* (Cambridge, 1992). The most detailed study of the process of validating observational knowledge is Stephen Shapin, *A Social History of Truth: Civility and Science in Seventeenth-Century England* (Chicago, 1994). The developments in philosophy across the century are most fully explored in Daniel Garber, (ed.), *The Cambridge History of Seventeenth Century Philosophy* (Cambridge, 1998). Also recommended for their insight into two of the most important philosophical currents of the period are Richard H. Popkin, *The History of Scepticism from Erasmus to Spinoza* (Berkeley, 1979) and Richard Tuck, *Natural Rights Theories: Their Origin and Development* (Cambridge, 1979). The most recent history of seventeenth-century art is José Antonio Maravall, *The Culture of the Baroque: Analysis of an Historical Structure* (Manchester, 1986). The starting-point for any study of the size and impact of the community of the curious in the final part of the century must be Paul Hazard, *The European*

Mind, 1680–1715 (London, 1953; original French edn., 1935). The organization of the Republic of Letters at the turn of the eighteenth century is carefully documented in Anne Goldgar, *Impolite Learning: Conduct and Community in the Republic of Letters, 1680–1715* (London, 1995). A good corrective to Hazard's account of a world in crisis towards the end of our period is Michael Hunter, *Science and Society in Restoration England* (Cambridge, 1981). The development of popular culture across the period can be followed in Robert Muchembled, *Popular Culture and Elite Culture in Early Modern France 1400–1750* (London, 1985), although the work exaggerates the gulf between high and low. There are many good books on witchcraft: one of the best and most recent with a French slant is Robin Briggs, *Witches and Neighbours: The Social and Cultural Context of European Witchcraft* (London 1996).

Europe and the non-European world

The background to European expansion is amply covered in G. V. Scammell, *The World Encompassed* (London and New York, 1981). John Elliott, *The Old World and the New 1492–1650* (Cambridge, 1970) is a classic brief survey which embraces cultural as well as other forms of interaction. A more recent approach to the same topic is exemplified in James Axtell, *The Invasion Within. The Contest of Cultures in Colonial North America* (New York and Oxford, 1985). K. N. Chaudhuri, *The Trading World of Asia and the English East-India Company 1660–1760* (Cambridge, 1978) and Jonathan Israel, *The Dutch Republic and the Hispanic World 1606–1661* (Oxford, 1982) both focus primarily on the commercial rivalries of the European powers, while Robin Blackburn's, *The Making of New-World Slavery* (London, 1998) is a massive and passionate analysis of one of European expansion's most enduring black spots. Some of the themes of the present essay are also to be found in James Tully, *An Approach to Political Philosophy: Locke in Contexts* (Cambridge, 1993) and Anthony Pagden, *Lords of All The World. Ideologies of Empire in Spain, Britain and France, c.1500–c.1800* (New Haven and London, 1995). Richard Koebner *Empire* (Cambridge, 1961) traces the long-term evolution of a key political concept.

Chronology:
The 'The Long Seventeenth Century', 1598–1715

1598   Edict of Nantes.
        Treaty of Vervins, peace between France and Spain.
        Death of Philip II.
        King Sigismund of Sweden deposed, replaced by Charles IX.

1600   Time of Troubles in Russia.
        Creation of English East India Company.
        Giordano Bruno burnt for heresy, Rome.

1602   Creation of Dutch East India Company.

1603   Death of Elizabeth I of England.
        Union of crowns of England and Scotland under James I.

1604   Peace between England and Spain.

1606   Settlement of the Hungarian revolt against Emperor Rudolf II.
        Paul V places Venice under Interdict.

1607   Venetian interdict removed.
        Monteverdi's *Orfeo* first performed.

1609   Death of John William of Cleves-Jülich.
        Twelve Years' Truce between the Spanish and the Dutch Republic.
        Emperor's 'Letter of Majesty' to Bohemian Protestants.
        Rival confessional alliances formed in Empire (1608–9).
        Expulsion of Moriscos from Spain.
        Kepler, *Astronomia nova*.

1610   Assassination of Henri IV of France, Marie de Medici regent for
        underage Louis XIII.

1611   Accession of Gustavus Adolphus of Sweden.

Polish garrison driven out of Moscow.

1612 Death of Rudolf II, election of Matthias as Holy Roman Emperor.
Treaty of Xanten settles disputed claims over Cleves-Jülich.

1613 Michael Romanov elected Tsar by Assembly of the Land.

1614 Aristocratic revolt followed by convocation of last French Estates General before 1789.

1616 François de Sales, *Treatise on the love of God*.

1617 Ferdinand of Styria recognized as designated Habsburg successor to kingdoms of Bohemia and Hungary.
Louis XIII seizes control of government from Marie de Medicis and her favourite, Concini.

1618 Defenestration of Prague, beginning of Bohemian revolt.
Dutch synod of Dort, victory of strict Calvinists (Gomarists) over Arminians.

1619 Ferdinand succeeds to Bohemian throne on death of Matthias, elected Holy Roman Emperor by the college of German Electors, but deposed by the Bohemian rebels who elect Frederick V, the Palatine Elector, as king of Bohemia.
Fall and execution of Oldenbarneveldt, grand pensionary of Holland.
Kepler, *Harmonices Mundi*.

1620 Austrian and allied forces crush Bohemians at White Mountain.
Spanish occupy and garrison the Valtelline.
Resumption of Huguenot wars in France.
Pilgrim Fathers found Plymouth, Massachusetts.
Francis Bacon, *Novum Organum*.

1621 Philip IV king of Spain.
War in the Netherlands resumed.

1622 Olivares become *valido* of Philip IV.

Canonization of Ignatius Loyola, Philip Neri, Francis Xavier, Teresa of Avila.

1623   Palatine Electorate transferred to Duke Maximilian of Bavaria.

1624   Richelieu enters royal council and replaces leading minister, La Vieuville.
Spanish begin successful siege of Breda.

1625   French intervene in Valtelline, launch unsuccessful attack on Genoa, Spain's ally.
Fall of Breda to Spaniards.
Accession of Charles I in Britain.
Danish invasion of Northern Germany.
Hugo Grotius, *De iure belli ac pacis.*

1626   Huguenot revolt in France.
Peace settlement with Spain at Monzon, leaving Valtelline under Spanish control.
Christian IV of Denmark defeated at Lutter.

1627   Death of duke Vincenzo II, Gonzaga of Mantua, opens succession struggle.

1628   First Spanish siege of Casale-Monferrato.
Habsburgs impose settlement on Bohemia.
Fall of La Rochelle after year-long siege.
Petition of Right in England.
Harvey, *De motu cordis.*

1629   End of Huguenot revolts in France.
French relief of Casale.
Dutch capture of Hertogenbosch.
Ferdinand II issues Edict of Restitution.
Treaty of Lübeck ends Danish involvement in Empire.
Treaty of Altmark ends Swedish-Polish wars.
Personal rule of Charles I begins.
Foundation of Massachusetts Bay Company.

1630   Gustavus Adolphus of Sweden invades Germany.
        Electors reject dynastic wishes of Ferdinand II at Diet of
        Regensburg, Wallenstein dismissed as imperial general.
        Franco-Dutch alliance.
        Day of Dupes in France, Richelieu survives challenge to position.
        La Tour paints *The Fortune Teller*.

1631   Peace of Cherasco ending Franco-Spanish war in north Italy.
        Swedish victory at Breitenfeld.
        Franco-Swedish treaty of Bärwald.
        First issue of French *Gazette*.

1632   Wallenstein checks Swedish army.
        Death of Gustavus Adolphus at Lützen.
        Dutch capture Maastricht.

1633   Swedish-led League of Heilbronn formed, subsidized by France.
        France invades duchy of Lorraine.
        Galileo's views condemned by Urban VIII as heretical.

1634   Battle of Nördlingen.
        Wallenstein, imperial commander, assassinated.
        'Form of Government' in Sweden.

1635   Peace of Prague.
        France declares war on Spain.
        Letters patent granted to French Academy.

1636   Spanish and Austrian armies invade France.

1637   Ferdinand III Emperor in succession to Ferdinand II.
        Spaniards lose Breda.
        Peasant revolts in France.
        Descartes, *Discourse on Method*.
        First performance of Corneille's *Le Cid*.

1638   Covenanter revolt against Charles I in Scotland.
        Galileo, *New Science*.

1640   Revolts of Catalonia and Portugal versus Castilian monarchy.
        Short and Long Parliaments in England.
        Frederick-William succeeds as Elector of Brandenburg.
        Posthumous publication of Cornelius Jansen's *Augustinus.*

1641   Grand remonstrance in England.
        Revolt in Ireland.

1642   Death of Richelieu.
        Civil war in Britain.
        Rembrandt, *Night Watch.*

1643   French victory over Spaniards at Rocroi.
        Death of Louis XIII, his son Louis XIV a minor. Anne of
        Austria regent, Cardinal Mazarin chief minister.
        Disgrace of Olivares.
        Swedish attack on Denmark.

1644   Peace conferences assemble in Westphalia.
        Descartes, *Principia philosophiae.*

1645   Battle of Jankow.
        Treaty of Brömsebro between Sweden and Denmark.
        Formation of New Model Army in England.
        Accession of Tsar Alexis.

1646   English parliament wins first civil war.

1647   Anti-Spanish revolt in Naples and Palermo.

1648   Spanish-Dutch peace at Münster.
        Bavarian defeat at Zumarschausen and Swedish siege of Prague.
        Conclusion of peace negotiations within the Empire.
        Fronde erupts in France.
        Army coup in England, Pride's purge of parliament.
        Rebellion in Moscow, Assembly of the Land summoned.
        Ukrainian peasants revolt against Polish landlords.
        Helmont, *Ortus Medicinae.*

1649   Execution of Charles I. Republic declared.
        Ulozhenie (law code) voted by Assembly recognizes the autocracy
        and tightens serfdom in Russia.
        Beginning of noble Fronde.

1650   Failure of William II's coup in Holland.

1651   Louis XIV comes of age, noble revolt continues.
        English Navigation Act voted.
        Hobbes's *Leviathan* published.

1652   Castilian reconquest of Barcelona.
        First Anglo-Dutch War.
        End of Ukrainian peasants' revolt.
        First use of *liberum veto* in Polish Diet.

1653   Collapse of noble Fronde, return of Mazarin from exile, prince
        of Condé serves with his troops alongside the Spanish army of
        Flanders.
        Elector of Brandenburg reaches agreement with nobility of
        the Estates.
        Swiss peasant revolt.
        Innocent X condemns Five Propositions from Jansen's *Augustinus.*
        Patriarch Nikon's church reforms in Russia lead to schism of
        Old Believers.

1654   Outbreak of Russo-Polish War.
        Anglo-Dutch peace treaty.
        Abdication of Christina of Sweden.

1655   French defeat at Valenciennes.
        Sweden attacks Poland-Lithuania.
        La Peyrère, *Prae-Adamitae.*

1656   Death of Ferdinand III.

1657   Denmark attacks Sweden, and Swedish troops overrun Jutland.
        Publication of Pascal's *Provincial Letters.*

1658   Anglo-French victory at battle of the Dunes.
       Swedish/Danish Peace of Roskilde.
       Leopold I elected Emperor.
       Death of Oliver Cromwell.
       Gassendi, *Syntagma philosophicum.*

1659   Peace of the Pyrennes.

1660   Restoration of Charles II in England.
       Treaty of Oliva between Sweden, Brandenburg and Poland.
       Frederick William of Brandenburg takes control of East Prussia.
       Regency government in Sweden for Charles XI.
       Foundation of London Royal Society.

1661   Death of Mazarin, beginning of the personal rule of Louis XIV.
       Start of major army reforms of Michel Le Tellier and Louvoi.
       Declaration of hereditary monarchy in Denmark.

1665   Carlos II king of Spain.
       Second Anglo-Dutch War.
       Royal Danish law codifying absolute monarchy.

1667   War of Devolution in the Spanish Netherlands.
       Peace of Breda.

1668   Triple Alliance between Dutch, English and Swedes.
       First Partition Treaty for the Spanish inheritance of Carlos II.
       Peace of Aix-La-Chapelle.
       Castilians concede independence to Portugal.
       Publication of La Fontaine's *Fables.*

1669   Grimmelhausen, *The Adventures of Simplicius Simplicissimus.*

1670   Secret Anglo-French treaty of Dover.
       Hungarian revolt against Habsburgs.
       First edition of Pascal's *Pensées.*
       Spinoza, *Tractatus theologico-politicus.*

1672   Franco-Dutch war (to 1678).
        William of Orange stadhouder, captain- and admiral-general
        of Dutch Republic.
        Third Anglo-Dutch war.
        Declaration of Indulgence by Charles II provokes fears of
        popery in England, leads to Test Act of 1673.

1673   Malebranche, *Recherches de la vérité*.

1675   Defeat of Swedes by Prussians at Fehrbellin.

1678   Peace of Nijmegen.
        Opening of popish plot and exclusion crisis in Britain.
        Bunyan's *Pilgrim's Progress* published.

1680   Sweden's Estates formally recognize royal absolutism, authorize
        resumption of crown lands.

1681   French take Strasbourg as part of the policy of *réunions*.
        Revolt of Hungarian magnates against Habsburgs.

1683   Ottoman siege of Vienna, defeated at battle of Kahlenberg.
        End of exclusion crisis in Britain.

1684   Pierre Bayle begins publishing *Nouvelles de la République des
        Lettres*.

1685   Revocation of the Edict of Nantes.
        Death of Charles II of England, succession of James II.

1686   Formation of League of Augsburg in the Empire to resist French
        aggression.
        Buda recaptured from Ottomans.

1687   Habsburgs and Hungarian nobility reach compromise at Diet
        of Pressburg.
        Newton, *Principia mathematica*.

1688   France intervenes in dispute over Archbishopric of Cologne.

Glorious Revolution, and establishment of William and Mary as rulers of England.

French devastation of the Palatinate.

Habsburgs take Belgrade from Turks.

1689   First campaign of Nine Years War.

Tsar Peter I ('the Great') seizes power in Russia.

1690   William of Orange defeats James II and Irish supporters.

John Locke's *An Essay Concerning Human Understanding* and *Two Treatises on Government*.

Anglo-French naval battle of Bézeviers (Beachy Head).

1692   Battle of Steenkirk.

1694   Bank of England created.

University of Halle founded.

1696   Treaty of Turin between France and duke of Savoy seeks to neutralize the Italian theatre in return for French abandonment of Pinerolo.

Peter the Great captures Azov from the Turks.

Toland, *Christianity not mysterious.*

1697   Augustus Elector of Saxony is elected King of Poland.

Austrian army commanded by Prince Eugene defeats the Turks at Zenta; reconquest of Hungary completed.

Treaty of Ryswick ends the Nine Years War.

Pierre Bayle, *Historical and critical dictionary.*

Consecration of St. Paul's Cathedral, London.

1698   Second Partition Treaty (of Spanish succession) between Louis XIV, Leopold I and William III.

1699   Death of Joseph Ferdinand, son of the Bavarian Elector and heir-designate by the Partition Treaty to the Spanish inheritance.

Peace of Karlowitz ends war between Austria and the Turks.

Fénélon's *Aventures de Télémaque* published.

Russia replaces Byzantine calendar with Julian.

1700   Death of Carlos II, who willed Spanish inheritance to Louis' grandson, the future Philip V of Spain.

Louis XIV accepts Spanish legacy.

Great Northern War against Sweden begins.

1701   Act of Settlement establishing Hanoverian succession in England.

Grand Alliance formed against Louis XIV.

War of the Spanish Succession begins.

Elector Frederick III of Brandenburg becomes King Frederick I of Prussia.

1702   Charles XI of Sweden takes Warsaw, and defeats armies of Poles and Saxons.

Death of William III.

Grand Alliance of English, Dutch and Austrians declare war on Louis XIV and Philip V.

Revolt of Protestant *Camisards* in southern France.

Revolt of Hungarian magnates.

1703   Peter the Great founds St Petersburg.

Rakoczy revolt versus Habsburgs in Hungary.

1704   Battle of Blenheim.

First national daily newspaper founded in England.

1705   Siege of Barcelona.

Death of Emperor Leopold, succeeded by Joseph I.

1706   Battle of Ramillies and relief of Turin.

1707   Union of England and Scotland.

1708   Battle of Oudenarde, siege of Lille.

Vauban publishes *Project d'une dixme royale.*

1709   Marlborough's pyrrhic victory at Malplaquet.

Peace talks open at Getruydenberg.

Defeat of Charles XII at Poltava, and collapse of Sweden's control over the Baltic states.

Louis XIV suppresses the Jansenist convent of Port-Royal.

Darby produces coke-smelted cast iron at Coalbrooke in Shropshire.

1710   Breakdown of peace negotiations between Bourbons and Allies.

Meissen porcelain manufactory established in Saxony.

Leibniz, *Theodicy*.

1711   Resumption of Anglo-French peace talks.

Emperor Joseph I dies, succeeded by Charles VI.

Compromise between Habsburgs and Hungarians at Szathmar.

Spectator appears for first time.

1712   Preliminaries of Utrecht conference.

Battle of Denain.

Abbé de Saint-Pierre's *Mémoires pour rendre la paix perpetuelle en Europe* published.

Leibniz, *Monadology*.

1713   Treaties of Utrecht (to 1715), followed in 1714 by Treaties of Rastatt and Baden.

George Elector of Hanover becomes George I.

Papal bull *Unigenitus* condemns 101 propositions tainted by Jansenism.

1715   Death of Louis XIV.

Map section

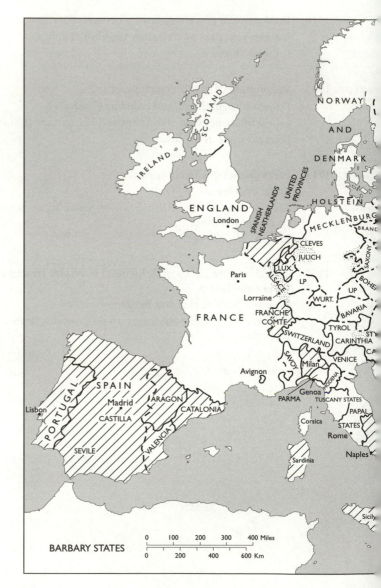

Map 1 Europe in 1600.

Stable frontiers
Uncertain frontiers and regions of conflict
Bondaries within larger political units
Regions of broken frontiers and 'islands' of teritory
Spanish possessions
LP   LOWER PALATINE
UP   UPPER PALATINE

VEDEN
(Danish)

ESTONIA
INGRIA
LIVONIA

LITHUANIA

• Moscow

KALMUKS

RUSSIA

EAST PRUSSIA

ERANIA

ESIA

POLAND

DON COSSACKS

Vienna

ZAPOROZHIAN COSSACKS

HUNGARY

JEDISAN

TRANSYLVANIA

MOLDOVIA

KHANATE
OF THE
CRIMEA

SLAVONIA

WALLACHIA

BLACK SEA

SERBIA

BOSNIA

TREBIZOND

OTTOMAN

Constantinople

IGDOM
OF
APLES

ALBANIA

EMPIRE

KURDISTAN

MOREA

ANATOLIA

Crete

Cyprus

Map 2 Europe in 1660.

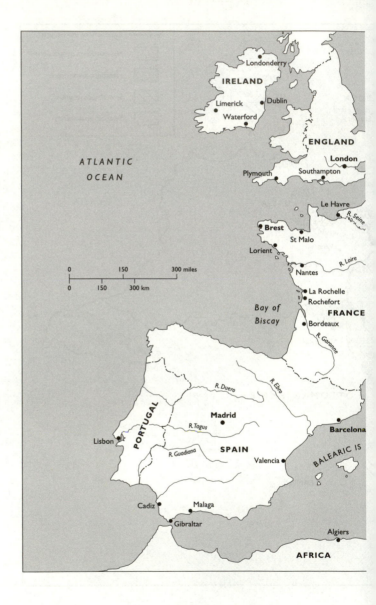

Map 3 Europe in 1715.

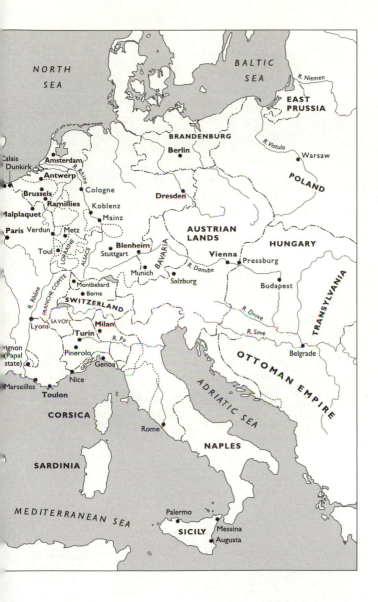

Index